Zero to 100 in a Lifetime

The Memoir of Tom Robb

by Tom Robb

iUniverse, Inc.
Bloomington

Zero to 100 in a Lifetime
The Memoir of Tom Robb

iUniverse books may be ordered through booksellers or by contacting:

iUniverse
1663 Liberty Drive
Bloomington, IN 47403
www.iuniverse.com
1-800-Authors (1-800-288-4677)

ISBN: 978-1-4620-0103-3 (pbk)
ISBN: 9781-4620-0105-7 (cloth)
ISBN: 978-1-4620-0104-0 (ebk)

Printed in the United States of America

iUniverse rev. date: 3/14/2011

Contents

Dedication

For LaVerne

A young LaVerne

Acknowledgements

First I want to thank Chelsea Robb for the valuable critiques and advice she has given me in writing my books.

I'd like to thank Richard Robb for his efforts in getting my books published.

I'd also like to thank Mercedes Robb for transporting me around and helping me with the many copies necessary to write and finish a book.

And I'd like to thank Jane Norton for her support and being a "reader" during the process.

Also, I'd like to thank any others who have contributed materials or helped in other ways for this book to come to fruition.

Sincerely,
Tom Robb

It all starts here

Glen leaning on car

Introduction

1900——In our country, at the beginning of the 20th century, there was a feeling of euphoria and satisfaction. America was the envy of the world. William McKinley was the new president, defeating famed orator William Jennings Bryan, for a second term. The stock market was up, up, up. Then on September 8, 1900, the country's deadliest hurricane ever hit the popular seaside town of Galveston, Texas, population 40,000. Six to eight thousand died. Five thousand injured. Galveston was the Pirate Kingdom of Jean Lafitte.

1901——September 6, 1901, President McKinley was assassinated. Shot twice in the abdomen by anarchist Leon Czolgose. The president died of gangrene. Vice-President Theodore Roosevelt became president. October 24, 1901, Edna Edson Taylor became the first person to go over Niagara Falls in a barrel; just shock and minor bruises.

1902——April 29, 1902, the Senate voted to extend the Chinese Exclusion Act for the second time, barring Chinese immigrants to the U. S,, to protect American workers from cheap labor. May 8, 1902, Mount Pele (Bald Mountain) on the Caribbean island of Martinique, erupted. The city of Saint-Pierre, population 30,000, was wiped out, except for two survivors – Leon Compere-Leandre, a young shoemaker; and Louis-Auguste Cyparis, a felon, who was in a dungeon. Cyparis was trapped underground for four days. He later toured with the Barnum & Bailey Circus. The eruption caused President Teddy Roosevelt to choose Panama as the location for a canal.

1903——December 10, 1903, three French people were awarded the Nobel Prize for physics: Physicist Henri Beequerel, who discovered radioactivity in 1898; and a married couple, Pierre and Marie Curie, for their discoveries with radiation.

1904——March 27, 1904, Irish born orator, writer, and penultimate union organizer, Mary Harris "Mother" Jones was ordered out of Colorado for stirring up striking coal minors. She was called by some as "The Most Dangerous Woman in America."

1905——One million immigrants came to the United States in 1905. Most came through Ellis Island. Albert Einstein introduced his theories of relativity, E=MC2.

1906——March 6, 1906, Finland was the first country to give women the vote, women twenty-four and older. April 18, 1906, at 5am, an 8.3 earthquake hit San Francisco, population 400,000. The quake and fires that raged for several days destroyed two-thirds of the city; 315 were listed as killed and 352 missing. Researchers later put the total lives lost at up to 3,000.

1907——The New York Times reported that John D. Rockefeller was the world's richest man. He was worth $300,000,000. October 21, 1907, the five Ringling brothers (Al, Alf, Charles, Otto and John) buy out their main competitor, Barnum & Bailey, making them a virtual monopoly of the circus business in the U. S.

1908——March 29, 1908, "Mutt & Jeff" comic strip was introduced in William Randolph Hearst's San Francisco Examiner by cartoonist Harry Conway. Bud Fisher, then twenty-three years old, would continue the strip until his death in 1954. May 22, 1908, Wilbur and Orville Wright register their flying machine at the U.S. Patent Office. September 16, 1908, General Motors Company was founded by William B. Durant in a holding company with other auto makers. Henry Ford didn't join, because Durant didn't believe that Ford's price of $8,000,000 was worth it. October 1, 1908 the first Ford, known as the "Tin Lizzie", rolled off the assembly line in Dearborn, Michigan. Top speed was forty miles an hour; cost, $850.50. Price dropped to $600 in 1912; $290 in1924. Another 1,000,000 immigrants came to the United States; most through Ellis Island.

1909——March 4, 1909, William Howard Taft was sworn in as President of the United States during a howling blizzard. Because of the weather, the ceremony took place in the Senate Chamber. Taft didn't really want to be President. He was a jurist. He said, "Politics makes me sick." April 6, 1909,

Robert Peary reached the Geographic North Pole on his third try. His African American assistant, Matthew Henson, planted the American flag at latitude 90 degrees north. Peary wound up with only two toes. August 9, 1909, Mark Twain's doctor advised him to cut down his cigars to four a day, because of his heart problem.

1910——April 21, 1910, Mark Twain (Samuel Langhorne Clemens), author of "The Adventures of Tom Sawyer," died in Redding Connecticut. He was seventy-four years old. July 4, 1910, race riots break out in several cities after black boxer Jack Johnson knocked out Jim Jeffries for the World's Heavyweight Title. As you can see, the first decade of the 20th Century had both disasters and successes and many odd happenings, in spite of the enthusiastic efforts of our diverse population. One notable thing happened in that first decade—Halley's Comet for at least 2,000 years had swept by our earth causing fear and apprehension. Astronomers had observed that it flew by about every 75 years. Therefore it was expected again about May 18-19 in 1910. Some believed that it's 60 to 90 mile long gaseous tail might contain deadly poison. There was much speculation as to whether it would hit or even destroy earth. People worldwide were worried. From Berlin to St. Petersburg, Paris to Mexico City, people gathered to pray. Suicides were common. Some celebrated. In New York City, crowds gathered in Central Park, Greenwich Village and on rooftops. Newspapers, coast to coast, carried the story. And then it flew by. What a relief! There were many celebrations and prayers of thanks. Our busy and resilient nation settled down to the problems of making a living and avoiding trouble, realizing that our world was both dangerous and wonderful. What a decade!

That brings me to another event that occurred six months after Hailey's Comet flew by—November 16, 1910.

Picture of Garza house

Chapter 1:   1910–1922

IT MUST HAVE BEEN a beautiful day on November 16, 1910 in the little community of Garza, Texas. In a little white bungalow on the edge of town, Doctor Taylor had just delivered a blue-eyed surprised baby boy to Gabrilla (Rillie) Robb. She hadn't really planned on having a baby so soon after her daughter, Sylvia, who was 20 months old, and her brother, Delbert, who was 5, but she was glad that it happened. (My first lucky break) After a spank and a yelp, the little one was quickly taken care of like all babies; lovingly washed, powdered and tucked into the bed prepared for him. The little tyke was me, Glen Robb, who was also glad to be there. I excitedly looked around the big room and at the funny looking people.

"Well, Mrs. Robb, I think you're in good shape. Just take it easy for a week or so. That little boy seems alright, too. He's a kicker. Lots of energy. A good fit for your fine family."

"Thank you, Dr. Taylor." Dr. Taylor left after congratulating Mr. Robb on his new son and thanking the two ladies that had assisted him.

I was later named Thomas Glenmore Robb, after my Dad and a family acquaintance, Glenmore Savage, who was the area undertaker. My mother, Gabrilla Elizabeth (Dixon) Robb and my Dad, Thomas James Robb had married in 1905. My Dad was the MK&T Railroad Agent for the little town of Garza, located between Dallas and Denton, Texas. I don't remember much about my very early years. I was only eighteen months old when the Titanic passenger ship hit an iceberg and sank. That happened on April 15, 1912. It was a huge ship on its maiden voyage to America with 2224 passengers and crew. It sank within 2 hours and 40 minutes after hitting the iceberg. It didn't have enough lifeboats for half of those on board. Only 711 out of 2224 were saved, mostly women and children. The rest perished in the cold water. (If you haven't seen the movie of this awful tragedy, you should try to see it.)

I do remember a few things that happened when I was young. We lived within a block of the center of town. We had a cousin, Bill Morgan, who lived in the area. He was a baseball player. There was a baseball park just a block from our house. One day my sister, Sylvia, and I decided that we'd like to watch a game that Bill was playing in. We could hear the cheering of the crowd. Since it was so close, we just walked over to the park, not thinking to ask permission to go. We climbed up and sat down in the bleachers and started watching the game. Dad, just coming home from work, looked around for us. Mother, who was busy preparing dinner, hadn't missed us.

"Where's the kids?" He asked. Mother looked around.

"They were in the yard just a few minutes ago. I can't imagine where they went," she said. "Delbert is in his room."

Dad, hearing the cheering from the ballpark, "I'll bet they went to see Bill play ball." Mother agreed and Dad took off for the park. He found us easily, since the crowd was thin. He called us down and directed us toward home.

It was then that we realized we should have asked for permission to go. To emphasize that point, Dad walked behind us, switching our bare legs with a little limb from a bush on the way. It didn't hurt much, but the stinging nettles we ran through, was enough to convince us that next time we had to ask permission.

Another thing happened one day that I learned a lesson from. I hadn't noticed what Mother was doing, when she handed me a quarter and asked me to go to Cromwell's General Store for a bit of cheese to go in something she was preparing for dinner. By the time I had walked the long block to the store, I had forgotten what I was supposed to get. Mr. Cromwell greeted me in the store.

"What'll you have, young man? He asked. He knew me, since we bought all our groceries from him. I was trying hard to remember. – "I forgot," I admitted, a bit embarrassed.

"Was it milk? He suggested.

"No."

"How about thread?" Mother used lots of sewing materials.

"That's it!" I agreed, relieved.

"What color? White?"

"Yes. White. That's it," I said.

When I got home with the thread instead of cheese, Mother had a good laugh at my expense. She kept the thread and sent me back for the cheese. It was a good lesson for me to pay close attention when someone is giving you directions. One of my cardinal rules since is: Don't make the same mistake twice. Now, if you send me out for a chunk of cheese, I won't bring back a spool of pink – I mean white thread.

I had typhoid fever when I was three or four, and was very sick.

When I was five years old, Dad rented a house up on a hill just on the outskirts of town. There were a few acres with it and Dad farmed a little, along with his job with the railroad. We had a few fruit trees, beehives, chickens, a couple of horses, and a few turkeys. The nests for the chickens were built two tiers high, with the top tier about shoulder high. Mother gathered the eggs each day. There were two or three hens sitting in the nests. If you didn't keep gathering the eggs regularly, the hens instinctively would try to hatch them, especially if three or four eggs accumulated. Mother hens love baby chicks. Did you ever watch them "mother" their little ones? One day, mother reached up to feel for eggs in the top nest. She immediately jerked her hand back, as she screamed in surprise.

"There's a snake in there!" Dad, who was near, immediately hurried over with a hoe, fished the snake out and killed it. It was a five foot chicken snake, named because it liked eggs. They are not poisonous and were common in the area. At a later date, Dad killed a copperhead snake in the barn that I almost stepped on. Copperheads and water moccasins are area snakes that are very poisonous. I was always barefooted, except on Sundays when we went to church. How did the snake get up into the top nest? There was a walk-up board that ran in front of the row of nests. Many snakes are climbers. Mother always looked before she reached after that. The old saying, "Look before you leap," is good to remember.

Dad kept three or four hives of honeybees about 150 feet from our house. They pollinated several fruit trees on the farm. He robbed them of their honey for our needs, but always left plenty for the bees' winter food. We had two apple trees that had the best juicy flavor I've ever tasted. There was a high wire fence between the orchard and our yard. One day I was playing in the yard and Dad was in the orchard cleaning and trimming.

"Glen, hand me that hoe, he said, I need to cut these weeds." I got the hoe, which was on my side of the fence, and started to sling it over, handle first, like a javelin. Dad always kept the hoe sharpened.

"Wait! Don't throw it! Hand it over," he urged. But, I wasn't listening to him. I was an Indian, throwing a javelin at the enemy. The javelin sailed forward. The sharp blade caught on the top wire of the fence and shot back at me. I put up my right arm to ward it off, but the blade hit my forearm, cutting an ugly gash. Dad rushed over to stop the bleeding.

"Next time—," he said.

"I know!" I answered. His look was enough. I learned a hard lesson. Keep your mind on what you're doing! I haven't thrown a hoe over a wire fence since, but if I ever start to, I'll take a look at the scar on my right arm, and hand it over.

We didn't have a storm cellar on the "hill". In case Dad thought we were in danger of a cyclone, we went to the Henry family's cellar on our road about 200 yards up toward town. I remember they had a large one with lots of canned fruit and watermelons, potatoes, etc.

Let me say a few things about the little town of Garza. It was on the MK&T railroad line that ran from Dallas to Denton. Most of the people in the area were farmers who lived outside the town, but came into town to shop. Garza featured, besides the railroad station, a Cromwell's General store, Swisher's drug store, Dr. Taylor's office, a blacksmith ship, and a school for the kids of the area. Mr. Swisher, owner of the drug store, had a daughter, Edith, a very pretty girl in her 20's. Dad's friend, Homer Carlyle, a local boy, now an officer in the army, was her boyfriend. This was in 1915. My younger brother, Homer Ray, was named after him. I remember how good looking Homer was in his officer's uniform. He would always bring a treat for my Mother and a box of cookies, fruit, etc. for us kids. I'm sure that he and Edith ended up getting married, but I don't remember it.

Dad's job at the railroad station was to sell tickets, take care of any incoming or outgoing supplies, products, mail, etc. He was also the telegraph operator. I think he had a part time helper, but I don't remember him. Dad also had to dispatch, or receive anything that the freight trains had for Garza. Not all passenger trains stopped at Garza. There was a signal tower that indicated - "stop" or "clear" for the train, and a smaller pole that had an arm out toward the track. Mail and other outgoing items from the agent were pouched and hung from the arm. A "through train" carried a hook operated by the mail or baggage clerk. If the signal showed "clear", the train snagged the hanging pouch, and sped on through without stopping; for incoming Garza mail, the train slowed and the mail pouch thrown off to a waiting agent.

Dad had learned to play cornet, and along with a half dozen other men of the area, formed a little brass band. They practiced at the depot. Mother and Dad played a few songs on the piano (mostly religious.)

Homer Ray was born at the little house in Garza on December 3, 1914. We moved to the "hill" the next year, 1915.

One day, when I was four years old, and we still lived in Garza, Dad had just come home from work. (We had electricity there because our house was near the stores and the ballpark that all had it.)

"Where's McAdoo?" he said, looking in the empty living room. (McAdoo was his nickname for me.)

"He's in there playing the reels of the (player) piano," answered Mother, as she continued preparing dinner on the kerosene stove.

"He's not in there, but the piano's playing."

"I guess he went to his room for something," suggested Mother. Just then they heard a "tap-tap-tappity-tap-shuffle-tap-tap-shuffle-tap-tap."

"What's that noise?" asked Dad.

"It must be Glen, keeping time with the music."

"Where is he? I don't see him," said Dad. Dad walked into the living room. The music was still going. Another series of "tap-tap-tappity-tap-shuffle-tap-tap" came from behind the piano, which was across a corner of the room. Dad looked behind the piano. There I was, trying to do a tap dance like the boys I'd seen at the store.

"What are you doing back there?" he asked.

"Oh, I was just practicing," I replied.

"Why don't you do it out here instead of back there?"

"I wanted to get good at it and surprise you."

"Well, I thought that was pretty good. You don't need to hide behind the piano. I'd like to watch you," he said, giving me a pat on the shoulder.

We lived on the "hill" during 1915-1916. I grew up a lot there and had many interesting and memorable experiences.

Old Mr. Peters lived in town, but had a big watermelon patch down past our house just beyond the Hickory Creek Bridge. He was in his 70's and not in very good health. He had a problem with his lower eyelids, causing his eyes to water and be red. In spite of his frailties, he grew a lot of delicious large red-meat melons, which he sold to the General Store. I felt sorry for him. Mr. Peters used to pick me up in his wagon and I would help him select about 20–25 ripe melons. He would drop me off at our house, giving me a couple for my help. We didn't have a melon patch on our farm.

The Briscoe automobile

I liked to sit out in front of our house in a spot that overlooked the road and watch the traffic that ran into town. One day, as I sat watching the buzzards lazily circling in the still summer air over the area looking for a dead rabbit or something for their next meal, I wondered how they stayed up with so little effort. Suddenly I heard the darndest racket! It wasn't a car. I'd never heard anything like it. I thought of a locomotive struggling up a hill. Whatever it was, it was approaching on the road from the bridge over the creek. I was standing up now, staring at where it would appear. And then I saw it, as it slowly came in view! It was a threshing machine, struggling along about three miles an hour and making that ungodly chugging noise as it rattled along the deep sandy road. I had never seen one before. The whole contraption was at least three times as long as a car, and much higher. It had arms and things sticking out over it, and a cab for the driver. It pulled a trailer full of pitchforks and supplies. Besides the driver, three other men were perched on the top. It slowly passed by, going toward town. I could hear it for a long time before the sound faded away. I would tell my Dad all about it when he got home. I sat back down and watched a trail of piss-ants struggling with tiny seeds almost as big as they were.

"Glen, don't you want to come in and take a nap?" called Mother from the front door.

"No, not right now," I answered. "Why are Mothers always checking on kids? I know how to watch out for snakes and stuff."

In 1916, new fast, fancy cars were sold by several manufacturers. We still used a wagon. Dr. Taylor used a horse and buggy. There lived a family down the road and over the bridge from us. They had two grown sons, early 20's, who still lived at home. They evidently were financially well off, as each boy bought a new Briscoe. One was yellow and the other was green. You could hear them coming as they came through the old wooden trestle bridge over Hickory Creek. Then the boys would roar by our house at about thirty miles an hour. The road in front of our house, in the summer, had ruts in the dry sand from the traffic of cars, buggies, wagons and horses with single riders. I was fascinated by the fancy cars, and their daredevil drivers. They had leather headgear, goggles and gloves. When I heard them coming, I always stopped and watched them zip by.

One day when I was sitting out front, tired of watching the ants with their loads of seeds and stuff, I decided to conduct an experiment. It was about time for one of the Briscoes to roar by. I wondered what would happen if I built up a bump of sand in each track? Would he see them? How high would it bounce? It depended, of course, on how fast he was going. And since they usually went at top speed, it was very intriguing! The only way to find out was to try the experiment. I ran out and built the bumps about 8 or 9 inches high, then ran back to my porch and sat down to watch. In about 4 or 5 minutes I heard one of them rattle the wooden timbers as he flew through the bridge over the creek. Then he picked up speed as he came into view, a cloud of sand dust behind him. It was the yellow Briscoe. That would be Josh. As he neared my "bumps", he was at full speed. I was holding my breath as he hit them!

It looked like the car jumped two feet high. Josh flew even higher, and his headgear flew off. There was a loud "bang" as the motor backfired and died.

"Golly Bum!" yelled Josh, as he landed back down in his seat. I was a little scared. I didn't think the bumps would be that bad. So, I just sat there and watched. Josh got out of his car, walked around inspecting it, and scratched his head. He looked around and spied the bumps. Then he kicked them down more level, got back in his car and put his headgear back on. The motor started on first try and he drove off, but not so fast this time. I decided I wouldn't tell anyone about my experiment, and didn't. until now. But I learned a valuable lesson: when you do one of your experiments, be sure it's safe for everybody. (Sorry, Josh!)

Our only mode of travel, except on horseback or walking, was our wagon. One weekend, Dad and Mother decided to visit Grandpa Robb and the girls – Dad's sisters, Lula and Minnie. They lived in the community of McCurley Prairie. It was about four miles away. Dad's older sister, Annie, was married and lived in Oklahoma. Mother and Dad rode in the spring seat at the front of the wagon, with Mother holding baby Homer Ray. Delbert, Sylvia and I were on quilts in the wagon bed behind them. "Old Bertie", one of the horses, was hitched to pull the wagon. Dad used her for light duty because of her age, and the young horses for plowing and heavy duty. The trip would take about two hours. It was about daylight on a cool October morning. Still sleepy, we three kids huddled together in the back. After about an hour of travel we came to a shallow creek with a small stream of water still running from the rain a few days before. There was no bridge over the stream. "Old Bertie" stopped and surveyed the scene. Dad shook the lines to urge her to ford the stream. She wouldn't budge. He tried several more times, but no luck. He got out and tried leading her over by the bridle. "Old Bertie" stood her ground.

"Why is she so afraid? She's forded streams before," said Dad. He opened a sack of oats from under the seat and put a couple of scoops in a bucket. He went to the front and offered it to Bertie. She eagerly ate it. Dad patted her a couple of times and climbed up in the wagon. This time, when Dad shook the lines, Bertie cautiously crossed over and we resumed our trip. Grandpa Robb (Aaron B. Robb) lived on a farm at that time in the community of McCurley Prairie. The land around there, including Grandpa's farm, was later put under water by Lake Dallas. Dad's Mother, Ella Jones-Robb, died in 1902, and a second marriage by A.B. lasted only a short time. So, Grandpa was now living in the 1 story house with two of his daughters. I don't recall the extent of his land, except that he had a large pasture and a barn adjoining the house. He had five or six cows, and when he was ready to bring them into the barn lot to feed or milk, he would just point and say to his white collie dog: "Go get 'em!" and collie would dash out to the pasture and herd the cows in, barking and nipping at their heels. Collie also liked to play catch with a rubber ball pitched to her. If thrown over the house, she would race around the house and catch it as it tumbled down, and bring it back to you. In the front yard of his house was a huge old, dead tree laying on its side. It was ideal for kids to climb or sit on, which we did. Just beyond Grandpa's farm

Sam Bass, the outlaw, hid out there for a short time, while Grandpa lived on his farm. Bass used to go into Denton for supplies and used a road very near Grandpa's place. In fact, he is said to have shot a man on that road. Stories about Sam Bass abound, some true. The one I know says he became a cattleman. When he accumulated a herd of about 700 steers, he drove them up north to sell them. After collecting his money he went to Deadwood, in Dakota Indian Territory, which was sort of the Wild West's version of modern day Las Vegas, robbing trains, stagecoaches and such. After about two years he came back to Denton County and settled down in the woods back of Grandpa's farm. He was generous with his money and had many friends in the county; he was considered a hero among the cowboys of the area.

Grandpa was well known and a respected member of the McCurley community. He served as a member of the School Board. He played the guitar for local dances at the School House. We always enjoyed the visits there. Minnie, who was about fifteen at the time, was fun to play with. I loved her. The adults listened to music on the Gram-a-phone, and looked at scenic pictures on a contraption that magnified them. We had a delicious dinner (dinner being the meal at the middle of the day) – prepared by "Aunt Lula" and "Aunt Minnie". Lula was about twenty. About four o'clock we said "Goodbye" and left for home. We stopped by Aunt Sally Carter's house on the way, just to say "Hello" to her, her daughter Nonnie, and son Newt. Milt, her other boy, was not at home this trip. We only stayed about half-an-hour. We arrived back home just as it was getting dark.

In the summer of 1916 I was playing in our yard, barefoot as usual, and the sand burned my feet. I stopped to cool my feet in the shade of a plum tree at the edge of a potato patch. (I went barefoot in the summer until I was about fourteen, except for Sundays.) Suddenly, I heard a distinct buzz that I had never heard before. It wasn't one of the Briscoes. As it grew louder, I spotted it. It was a dark spot in the sky toward Dallas. A buzzard didn't make that noise. Then, I remembered Dad talking about a new airfield at Denton. So, it was an airplane! The first I had ever seen! It had swept back wings. I was mesmerized. I couldn't imagine how that thing could fly. It didn't flap its wings; I watched it until it disappeared toward Denton. It was a thrilling thought to me that people could fly in an airplane. I would like to do that. For the first time, I thought of myself, and the future, and the world outside. I ran back across the hot sand to tell Mother what I'd seen.

Hickory Creek was only a short distance from our house on the "hill." There was a bend in the stream just a little above the bridge that had a deep flowing current. It was an ideal place to go swimming. Delbert, my older brother, and some of his friends used the spot as a swimming hole. I had splashed around in shallow water, wishing that somebody would teach me how to swim. One day as he was preparing to join a couple of his buddies for a swim, I questioned him.

"How deep is the water?" I asked. I was nearly seven years old.

"It's different in different places. Right in the middle of the bend it's about 9 feet. Why?"

"I'd like to learn to swim, too," I said. Delbert was already a good swimmer.

"Well, come on. I'll teach you. It's time you learned." I told Mother I was going with Delbert to the creek. She warned both of us to be careful. We met the other guys, both Delbert's age and good swimmers, at the creek. We all stripped and they dived in. I stayed in the water about up to my chest. I knew how to kick and propel myself, from watching others.

"Come on. Get up on the bank and dive in like we do," called Delbert.

"I'll dive in with you," he said. I knew that I had to get it over with, and agreed. We got out and stood on the bank at the deep area.

"Now, don't get excited. Hold your breath until your head is back above water. I'll be right behind you," he assured me. I looked down at the slowly flowing water. The 3three foot bank looked more like six feet. Suddenly I got a shove from the rear. I hit the water and went under. Instinct took over. I came up kicking and paddling with arms and legs. I remembered his instructions not to breathe until my head was above water. I was surprised and elated that I was moving forward and on top of the water. It was a wonderful feeling. I was swimming! I reached the bank. The three guys cheered and clapped. I jumped off two more times. By the time we decided to leave and I put on my clothes, I felt like a new person. I couldn't wait to tell my Dad and Mom.

Delbert in swim suit

It was now late summer and Dad decided that he needed to plow a small plot of level land that he called "the bottom land." It was adjacent to Hickory Creek and was covered with dry grass about five inches high. In order to prepare it for planting in the spring for something like corn, he needed to plow it with a turning plow, which turns the top 3 or 4 inches of dirt to the right, upside down, thus burying the grass, which rots, enriching the soil and helping prepare the ground spring planting. Dad loaded the wagon with the plows and tools that he needed and went down to the spot; I was riding "Old Bertie" as he drove the wagon. Right after he started plowing with the turning plow, he looked back and discovered that the grass was on fire. Evidently, the metal blade of the plow had hit a rock, causing sparks that set the grass on fire. It was spreading quickly. A gentle breeze was blowing. Dad acted quickly. The danger was that it would get to a neighboring field of corn, or burn on down to other properties along the creek. We tried stomping and beating it out, but it was beyond our control. Dad quickly replaced the turning plow blade with one called a "middle-buster". He plowed a furrow far enough ahead of the fire, and downwind, that it couldn't spread any further. Then, he plowed several times around the fire. We had to fight several "jumps", but the fire finally burned itself out, and we sighed in relief. Dad decided we'd had enough for one day, and after carefully checking the area again, we loaded up and went home.

Meanwhile, the U. S. was in the middle of World War One, in France, and more troops were being sent over there. Soon after the "fire in the bottom", mother got word from her brother, Ernest, who had been in an Army training camp nearby, that he was among the fresh recruits being sent "over." His Army unit was to leave on a troop train from Denton. Mother, of course, wanted to see him off. On the day of the troop train's departure, Dad had arranged for a friend, Cleve Turbeville, to take us to Denton for the event. Cleve had a new Overland Touring Car, with all the fancy accessories: brass rimmed headlights and radiator, side mounted rubber horn, brass around the windshield, canvas top and spare tire on the rear. It had a running board on each side, with a metal scraper to clean the mud off your shoes in wet weather. When we got near Denton, the road was a mass of cars, wagons and buggies. Cleve found out that there was no chance to get near the station because of the crowds. So, we parked along the road, as close as we could to the crossing where the train would pass. We didn't have to wait long, until the train arrived, rushing through the crossing with the engineer blowing his whistle. The crowd, including us, yelled and waved. The troops hung out the windows, yelling and waving back. All the horses hitched to wagons and buggies were stomping and rearing in excitement. It was a long train, but soon passed out of sight. There was an eerie silence, then, everyone started talking, some laughing, and some crying. Mother was quiet and worried. She wiped tears from her eyes, and Dad put his arm around her. It was over. Cleve turned the car around and we headed home.

That was in 1917. The same year Dad bid on a job as Mail/Baggage Clerk at Seymour, Texas, for the GT&W (or Gulf, Texas & Western Railroad.) We moved to Seymour. The GT&W was a short line that ran a passenger train on a round trip each day, so Dad was always at home every night. Dad let me make the trip one day. I rode in the baggage car with him, while he sorted the mail between stops. He wore a pistol because of the mail. That pistol lay in the back of his desk drawer, at home, for thirty or forty years after that job. The trip was uneventful, except, out in open country the train suddenly came to a stop. It was a fire on the track and grass alongside. Several passengers and most of the train crew (except Dad and the Engineer) poured out to fight the fire. They beat the fire with wet burlap sacks (carried for just such an event) and splashed water from the Water-Tender behind the engine. Eventually, the gang put out the grass fire, and the smoldering creosote-soaked ties of the roadbed. Those fires were usually caused by a "hot-box". The box that enclosed the axles on each car contained shredded burlap soaked in oil to lubricate the axle. Sometimes the burlap would dry out and heat from the friction would ignite the burlap. Some burning scraps would fall out onto the ties, causing the fire. Dad and the Engineer had to stay on the train. Dad had to protect the mail, which could include cash transfers between banks, bonds and other valuables. They soon had the fire out and our trip was resumed. It was an old-time trick of train robbers to stop a train with a fire on the track.

I'd like to say a few things about our history: The name Robb is derived from Robert, as are Roberts and Robinson. The name was plentiful in Scotland and England, and Richard found it so in Scotland today. The name is found on documents as early as 1196 when the names Robbe and Robe appeared. A Jok Robb lived in Monkland, Scotland in 1519. My Dad told us that our ancestors were Scotch-Irish-English and Dutch. The first Robbs that came to America were women: Ellen Robb and her daughter, Elizabeth. arrived on the SS Falcon with forty passengers from Gravesend, England, a scant fifteen years after the Mayflower landed at Plymouth Rock in 1620. Benjamin Franklin's mother was a Robb.

Henry Robb is believed to have been born in New York City about 1806, and is buried near Lake Village or Eudora Arkansas. Henry had 21 slaves which he bought in New Orleans. One story is that Henry told his slaves that Lincoln freed them, and twenty stayed with him on the farm. The twenty-first had been purchased recently for $90 in gold. He went back to New Orleans to try and return back to his home in Africa. Henry had two brothers, Jeff and Will. When the Civil War started in April, 1861, Will was only sixteen or seventeen, and too young to be drafted. But, he volunteered to be a messenger. In one long march, during cold, rainy weather, he became ill and they left him with a family, where he died of pneumonia. Henry had a second wife named Susan Ovelton Develton, who was born in Alabama. Her family was Irish. Their son, Aaron Byron Robb, was my Grandpa.

Aaron Byron Robb was born June, 9, 1851 in Vicksburg, Mississippi, and died in Oklahoma, of a stroke, December 22, 1940. He was a farmer. He is buried in McCurley Cemetery (formerly Old Hall) at Lewisville, Texas. "Aunt Sally" Carter was his sister and my Dad's aunt. Aaron married Ella Jones on December 29' 1878. She was born April 24, 1863 and died November 4, 1902, at the age of twenty-four. Their children were:

William Delbert, 1880–1881, buried in Zion Cemetery, Little Elm.
Thomas James, born Aug.22, 1882–died July 13, 1984, in Lewisville.
Annie Bell, born 1885, died June 23, 1989, Oklahoma City.
Lula Pearl, born 1886, died in Lewisville.
Minnie Marie, born 1900, died 1922 or 1923. The Grandfather and Grandmother of T.J. Robb, on his Mother's side, were:
John Adam Crane Jones, Jr. and Sara Jane (Long) Jones—Scottish. They are the Great-Grandparents to: Delbert, Sylvia, Glenmore, Homer Ray and Marie Robb; AND Gatie, Pauline, Hershel and Olivia French.

The Dixons:
Alexander Toons Dixon married Emma Loard. Their children were:
Gabrilla Elizabeth, born July 14, 1885 in Selma Alabama; died August 20, 1967 in Texas. She is buried in McCurley Cemetery, Lewisville.
Idus B Dixon, born in Alabama, buried McCurley Cemetery.
Lydia (Liddy) Jane, born in Alabama, buried McCurley Cemetery.
Ernest Henley, born in Bethel, Texas, buried McCurley Cemetery.
Claude Victoria Dixon, born Bethel, Texas, buried McCurley Cemetery.

When my Grandpa, A.B., used to visit us in the 1920's, he liked to sit in our swing in the front yard, smoke his pipe and talk. I loved to sit and listen in excitement, as he would tell about his life. His father, Henry, moved from New York City to Mississippi, Arkansas, Kentucky and Tennessee. Grandpa told me that when he was about twenty years old, he took a trip to New York City to visit relatives. One of his uncles, a successful lawyer, urged him to stay, offering to help him get established in business. One of the Robbs owned the land that the Woolworth Building is built on, and at that time held a 100 year lease for the land with the Woolworth Company. But, A.B. had already planned to go to Texas to seek his fortune and soon set off for that frontier.

It was fall, and the rainy season was beginning. He crossed the Mississippi River by ferry. When he came to the White River, it was rising; when he got to the Beth River, The Beth was flooding over its banks. He swam his horse across and stayed there to help some of others rescue their horses and cows cut off by the floodwaters. Next day he continued his trek. Arriving in Eudora, Arkansas, where he had previously lived, he settled down for a while, long enough to get re-acquainted with a girl he used to know. She became a steady girlfriend. One day, when this girlfriend was visiting out of town for a couple of weeks, A.B started dating another girl. Then he got word by the "grapevine" that girl number 1 was back in town, had learned about the dates, and was mad as a hornet. A.B. knew he was "in for it"! He decided that discretion was better than valor, saddled up very early the next morning and took off for Texas. Brave lad that he was, he settled down in McCurley Prairie, hired out, saved his money, bought a farm, and married Miss Ella Jones. Dad was born in a 2-room log house on August 22, 1882. Three sisters followed. Ella died in November 1902, when Minnie was two and Dad was nineteen.

Later, when the girls were grown and gone, Grandpa sold the farm and moved to Sulphur, Oklahoma to live with relatives there. He used to visit us in Cooper, Texas and stay several months. We kids would never know he was going to visit, until one day, getting home from school, there he was. He loved to surprise us kids. I'm sure Dad and Mother had received a letter about his plans; probably the letter had a P.S. that said, "Don't tell the kids." He would stay with us about three months. As I said, he loved to sit in the swing I had built and smoke his Prince Albert pipe tobacco, while I asked him questions to keep him talking. I loved nothing better than to hear the stories of his early life. Cooper was the county seat of Delta County, and when the County Court was in session, he liked to go to the Court House and listen to the trials. He'd listen for hours to his favorite attorney, Charley McKinney. Then one day we'd come home from school and he'd be gone. He lived out of his suitcase with us, then, do the same, visiting his daughter, Annie French and family in Oklahoma City. Then, back to his base with Arch Robb and family in Sulphur. That's where he would spend the winter. What a life! And everybody loved it. In 1938 he was in a car wreck in Oklahoma City and received a broken hand. His health began to decline, and he died up there at the age of eighty-nine.

Back to my early story: We didn't stay long in Seymour. I was seven years old. There was a large vacant lot and a big barn just a block from our rented house. I liked to play on the lot and watch the dozens of beautiful pigeons on the lot and on the barn. I was with a neighbor boy there one day. We were tossing pebbles to see which could throw one the furthest, when a man came by on a horse. Without thinking, I threw one in the direction of the horse. It came closer than I had intended and horse shied quickly to the side. It caused the man to struggle to calm it down. I realized, immediately, that I had made a stupid mistake. The man turned his horse and rode over to us. I thought he was going to ride over me. He bawled me out and threatened to call the police. He warned me never to do it again. I said I was sorry and he left. I was pretty scared and shook up. I thought of my sand bumps and the Briscoe. I didn't mean to scare the horse. Why are people so "touchy"? My friend, I think his name was Jimmy, just looked at me. He hadn't said a word during the episode. I went home, but I didn't tell my mother. I learned another lesson. I'm not sure exactly what the lesson is, but I don't throw rocks at horses anymore.

In Seymour, our house was on a major street. A lot of flat-bodied dray wagons from a saw mill came by. They didn't go very fast, being horse drawn. I used to like to run out and hang on to the back end of these wagons, ride about a block and then jump off, or until the driver yelled, "Get off, kid!" and snapped his whip at me. Hadn't HE ever been a kid? I wasn't hurting anything! Some drivers didn't care. Anyway, Mother put a stop to my fun the first time she happened to see me. During the time we were in Seymour, there was a race riot in town. We were not involved, and I don't remember anything about it except the rumors.

Dad bid on a job as a clerk with the Santa Fe Railroad in Garland, Texas and he was successful. We moved to Garland in early 1918. Dad rented a little yellow house trimmed in white. We were living there when the awful worldwide Spanish flu struck the area. In the U.S., 549,000 people died, including 18,000 military men. We all came down with the flu, except Dad who fought it off until Mother got better. Then he gave up and went to bed. Eventually, we all recovered. Soon, a larger white house across the street became vacant and we moved into it.

Not long after we made that move, Delbert came down with Smallpox. Our house was quarantined. A notice was posted on the front of the house. The only one restricted was Delbert, who had to stay in his room. He was badly broken out and was miserable. Mother passed his meals, etc., to him through a window from the front porch. She also ignored her danger and went into his room to treat his pustules and make him as comfortable as possible. Mother and the rest of us were vaccinated as soon as the disease was recognized in town, but it just wasn't soon enough for Delbert.

Henry Merrill was Delbert's best friend in Garland. His dad owned the most prosperous grocery store in Garland. Henry delivered customer orders in a small one-horse hack. Few people in town had cars. One day, while Delbert was sick with the smallpox, Henry stopped by to see Delbert after a delivery. Henry just left the rig standing in front our house with the reins looped around the whip holder. Usually, the horse would just stand there while Henry carried groceries into the customer's house. One of us kids asked Henry if we could sit in the hack while he visited Delbert. "OK. Just be quiet. Don't bother the lines," he said. Sylvia and Homer Ray climbed up onto the seat, and I stood in the back. Homer Ray, now almost four years old, evidently had heard only the "OK", he immediately spied the whip, grabbed it and gave the horse a surprising "whop" on his back! Well, the horse lurched forward, turned and ran across a ditch, then ran alongside the street. That sharp turn and the big jolt from the ditch, threw us all out of the hack. Sylvia was thrown clear; I felt a blow from something on my shoulder. Homer Ray was catapulted out and fell to the ground with his head between the spokes of a back wheel. Miraculously, he was tossed free of the wheel before any damage was done and none of us was seriously hurt. It all happened so fast that Henry, who was sitting on our front porch talking to Delbert at the window, yelled at the horse to stop, but it was no use…Horse and hack disappeared and later ended up back at the grocery store. Mother was so thankful that none of us was hurt, that Homer Ray got off with a good lecture.

Two other things happened while we live in Garland. I got an air rifle for my birthday, and I started to school in the first grade. I was a proud eight years old.

This was an era when there were a lot of small railway lines, and a lot of them were consolidating or being bought by the bigger lines. If you didn't stay with a line for a long time, you didn't have much seniority, and seniority ruled in being promoted, or even staying in the same spot. If your railway was bought by a larger one, seniority was questionable. Then there was POLITICS. If an owner or a senior executive wanted to promote a friend, or a friend's son, he did it, ignoring any seniority factor. My Dad got "burned" several times while working for the railroad in Cooper. In the smaller stations, a train might pull in and a fellow would step off and tell the agent, "You're bumped! I've got seniority over you." Your only choice was to go down the line and "bump" some other poor fellow – or seek another line of employment. While we lived at Garland, Dad toyed with the idea of bidding on a railroad job out West. He was especially interested in Portland and Cheyenne areas. He was preparing to make application for a job with the Union Pacific at Cheyenne, when Mother said,

"Why don't you write your friend, Charley Raney? He lives in that area. Ask him about the weather."

"That's a good idea," agreed Dad. "I'll do that." Dad was always pretty sure of himself, but I'm sure he had talked this move over with Mother. That's why she spoke up with her question. Dad wrote the letter and mailed it to Riley. We anxiously awaited his reply. What is it like out West? Would we be in a big town like Cheyenne, or some small town? What about the school we'd go to? I'd have to make new friends. Even so, I was excited about change. It was like we were at a fork in the road. -A different life either way. Which one would we take?

For two weeks we waited. Then a letter from Riley came. Riley expressed his pleasure for hearing from Dad. He brought him up to date on what he'd been doing, etc., etc. And then, on the last line, he answered the question about the weather. Riley said it was pretty cold in Wyoming, but he enjoyed it, because he liked to hunt and fish. He included a picture of himself squatting beside an animal that he'd just killed, in a scene of snow everywhere. Dad and Mom decided that it was too cold for our family in Wyoming. Instead, Dad bid for a job with the Texas Midland Railroad in Cooper, Texas. He was accepted. My second lucky break!

When we moved to Cooper, in 1919, we rented a house on East Waco Street. One of our next-door neighbors was the Ed Adair family. I remember they had a very pretty daughter named Cleon, and a son named Harry. A few months later, Dad bought a house at 432 West Waco St. It was next to the "cotton yard" (a vacant lot for storing bales before shipment.) When the lot wasn't filled with bales of cotton, we kids used it for a baseball playing field. Our house was just two blocks from the railroad station where Dad worked. The only elementary school, East Ward, was across town, near our first house, and the Baptist Church that we attended.

Let me say a few things about the town of Cooper. It was the County Seat of Delta County, which was the second smallest of Texas' fifty-four counties. Nearby Rockwall County was the smallest. When we moved to Cooper, the Court House stood in the middle of a red brick paved square. There were two paved streets: one went south from the square, toward the town of Commerce; the other, going west, was paved to the railroad station where Dad worked. The four sides of the square, around the Court House, were alive with prosperous businesses to serve the town and surrounding farms. There were three banks, three drug stores, a furniture store, two barber shops, two moving picture theaters, two clothing and merchandise stores, two hardware stores, a café, a men's clothing store, a variety store, plus various stores in each direction just off the square. Doctor and dentist offices were on the second floor of some of the buildings.

Black people had their own close little community just beyond the Power & Light plant, with a church and a school. They worked at various jobs around town, a few had businesses serving their neighborhood. My Dad worked with Clate Stout and a man I only remember as "Dick", double-decking cotton bales in boxcars outbound for mills and ports, etc. Cotton bales weigh 500 pounds apiece. THAT was a job for the Strong!

by Tom Robb

When old Butler Ivey, the janitor at the Railroad Station, died, "Russ" Russell took his place. I had the opportunity to know Russ, when after graduating from high school, I worked there delivering telegrams for $30 per month during the summer. Russ was also a teacher in the local black school. He was a personable, well-educated man. I had many talks with him during that summer. With his two jobs, he barely made a living for his family. I learned some lessons during this time. Can anybody help it that they were born who they were, or into what circumstances they found themselves? Of course not! I think that refutes the old saying that "we're all born equal." "The sky is the limit" applies to all of us, but how far up an individual goes is determined by the "baggage" he carries; health, family circumstances, genes, education, planning, being a friendly helpful person, then there's luck and the economy. Being at the "top" is not always the most satisfying or happiest. I think now, it's more toward the middle.

It was a mile or so from our house on W. Waco St. to East Ward elementary school. My siblings and I walked to school. I entered West Ward as a second grader, but was soon put in the third grade. I also skipped the fourth grade. I have always liked school and have been an avid reader. Mother helped me a lot in my early grades. Dad was a good reader, too, having gone through the eighth grade. The eighth was the top grade in his area. Two books of his that awed me by their depth of subject matter were "Power of Will", and "An Illustrated History of the Old Testament".

Dad was about 5 feet 8 inches tall and weighed about 180 pounds. He had short curly, light brown hair. He was muscular and very strong. He had lots of energy, a brisk walk, friendly but matter-of-fact in communication. After finishing his local school, Dad went to Telegraph School in Dallas. While he was living in a boarding house there, he met his lifelong friend, Delbert Todd, who was also going to the same school. After graduating from Telegraph School, Dad got a job as Station Agent at the little town of Garza, Texas. Dad like to learn, but didn't have the money for college. The railroads, at the time, offered good jobs and the opportunity to advance.

One story told me by my Grandpa Robb was: When Dad was courting Mother, he rode his horse on weekends to see her. The Dixon girls, Gabrilla and Lydia, were pretty and popular girls. One of Mother's other suitors was jealous and put out the word that he would kill Dad if he went to see her the next weekend. A friend of Dad's heard of the threat and advised him to go a different route to and from the Dixon's place. Dad was not intimidated, and borrowed a pistol from a friend. On Sunday he took his usual route. At the supposed to be interception spot, the guy didn't appear, so nothing happened.

Dad and "Rillie" (my Mother's nickname) were later married in a double wedding ceremony, under a huge oak tree in Waxahachie, Texas, in 1905 by a Baptist preacher. The other couple was Dad's double cousin, John Robb and his bride, Pearl. John and Pearl settled in Waxahachie; Dad and Mother rented the little house in Garza.

When I was growing up in Cooper, Dad kept a 210-gauge shotgun in the bottom of a big trunk. I never knew him to have any other weapon, or even using that one. Dad also had a bundle of Confederate money in that trunk. I just happened to see it one time when he had it open. I think he later gave it to Grandpa, who took it to Oklahoma. Dad and Mother were Christians, and they followed the "John Scopes vs. William Jennings Bryan trial about Darwin's theory of evolution, in 1925. They followed the trial coverage on the radio and in the newspapers. One of Dad's heroes was Bryan. Another was William Gibbs McAdoo (my nickname).

Mother left her political thinking up to Dad. She attended Bethel school, which I think went through the seventh grade. Mother was twenty and Dad was twenty-three when they married in 1905. She was smart and a good reader. Mother was the one who helped me when I had a problem in school. Mother was always the quiet, efficient person. She worked hard and always had a happy, well cared for family. The longer I live, the more I appreciate my Mother and Dad. I realize that their main interest was our care, and preparing each of us for our breakaway jobs.

I don't think any of us had any serious health problems, except for the normal children's diseases, and that Spanish Flu. Mother's favorite remedy for most of our minor ailments was castor oil or "black draught" for our innards, and iodine for cuts and stings. Dad's old standby for the latter was "coal oil". Mother was the house doctor; Dad took care of discipline. We avoided "treatment" as much as possible. At one time, Mother was diagnosed by her doctor as having a suspicious goiter. She went to Mineral Wells, Texas for about three weeks, taking hot baths there. The baths and the doctor's prescriptions seemed to reduce it and I never heard any more about it.

I never in my life heard either Mother or Dad angry at or say anything unkind to the other. and, I never heard either of them say "I love you" to each other, or to us. But, I know they loved each other and all of us kids. In that time, and our circle of people, it was just understood, not said. None of us gave them any serious trouble and I'm sure they were quietly proud of our outcomes, even though none of us became rich or famous. Dad (and Mother) had a hand in helping each of us getting started in our jobs, through his acquaintances or help.

I went to East Ward School for three years, through sixth grade. Mother fixed me a lunch each day; a sandwich, a boiled egg, a fried pie and a piece of fruit. John McDaniel and I used to eat our lunches, together. He didn't care for boiled eggs, and I loved them (still do.) So I usually traded and apple or orange for his boiled egg. Mr. Flowers was the principal of East Ward. On May 1st, each year, there was the Mayflower Festival at the school. Classes were knocked off at noon and the festival put on in the afternoon. There were supervised games and races, but the highlight was the large Maypole with its many colored streamers carried around the pole with girls and boys dancing to the music from a Victor Victrola phonograph set outside. The Victrola was electric and plugged in inside a classroom. The Maypole was very pretty, but, I didn't like it much, since I was conscripted to be one of the boys to carry a streamer. I figured that was more a girl's thing to do. Anyway, I was only ten years old. But, I did it, with the silly hat and all.

Going to and from school, my route went along the south side of the square. One day, when I was in the fifth grade, and I was walking home, I walked by the Stovall Hardware store on the square. A group of men was excitedly listening to a radio placed at a side door of the store. I immediately knew they were listening to the World Series baseball game, between the New York Yankees and the New York Giants. I was a fan of any kind of competition in sports, and the World Series was the current hot topic with the men there. I stopped on the sidewalk to listen. The excitement of the men there, and the roar of the crowd on the radio, quickly got my interest. I moved up closer. Babe Ruth had just stepped up to the plate for the Yankees. He pointed to where he was going to hit it. By this time I wasn't standing in the street in my little town. I was in the cheering crowd in New York City. The Babe let a couple of pitches whiff by, and then BAM! The ball soared high. Babe dropped his bat and started trotting toward 1st base. The ball soared higher. The group of men at the store and the crowd at the ballpark let out a roar as the ball sailed over the fence, just about where the Babe had pointed. It was exciting! I came back to Cooper and walked home. Later in 1927, when Ruth was being interviewed after hitting his 60th homerun, he said, "If I tried for them dinky singles, I could have batted around 600." "We boys at school, tomorrow, will talk about that game and how high that ball went!" I thought. That enormously whetted my interest in sports. I'm 100 now and am still an avid fan, especially baseball, and the Oakland "A's" are my favorite.

Back from Yankee Stadium and that exciting game—

I had a happy and busy time growing up in Cooper. I had lots of friends. Opal Preas and his mother, Nanny Preas, and his grandmother, Mrs. Taylor, and her son, Johnny Taylor, all lived just over our back fence. Johnny owned an abstract business with an office in the courthouse. He had been crippled by polio, but was one of the most cheerful people I knew. He was a dedicated golfer.

About 1921, Dad, Opal, Johnny Taylor and I, and Johnny's brother, Lewis

Taylor, took an auto trip up to Sulphur, Oklahoma, to check out the sulphur baths there. The main hotel was about eight stories high. It was managed by a relative of Mother's, Noel Singletary. We stayed at his hotel. Opal and I enjoyed the swimming pools, both hot and cold pools. But, swallowing any of the sulfur flavored water was for the birds. Opal and I enjoyed a lot of activities and games, together. We played marbles, pitched washers and horseshoes; we caught all kinds of bugs–doodle bugs, tumble bugs, ants, centipedes, flies, lightning bugs, etc. It was a nice trip. In the spring, summer and fall, we collected crawfish by lowering a piece of bacon on a string into their holes (they'll clamp their claws on anything) and just pull them out. Some are beautifully colored, and the meat of their tails is delicious when fried. Si Pagan, Opal's cousin, lived across the railroad tracks. He sometimes played with us. He was taking violin lessons. Dad used to tease him about the music leaking out of his violin case as he walked by on his way home… Si never laughed, he just grinned.

One summer, I think it was about 1923, I was about thirteen and Opal was eleven, we managed to scrape together enough money to buy a dozen bottles of soda pop and iced them in a large bucket.

Looking back at the making of a bale of cotton: the farmers and their hired pickers would pick a wagon full of cotton. Pickers were paid one cent per pound to pick it. Pickers drag a special-made sack, six to nine feet long that holds 25 to 60 pounds of cotton. The sacked cotton is then weighed at the wagon and dumped into it. When full, the wagon holds enough to make a bale of ginned cotton, weighing 480 to 550 pounds. The farmer keeps a record of how much each picker has picked and pays him accordingly (or her). The farmer then takes his wagon full of cotton to a gin, where the seed is ginned out. The cotton is then compressed into a burlap wrapped bale, weighing approximately 500 pounds. The gin owner takes the seed for his pay, which he sells, usually to a cotton oil mill. The oil mill breaks the seed into cottonseed hulls, cottonseed cake and cottonseed oil. Some seed is saved for planting. From there, the farmer next takes his bale of cotton up to a vacant lot near the square where cotton buyers slash a spot of the burlap, dig out a handful of cotton to estimate its quality (dirty, clean, etc.) and length of staple. He will bid what his company will pay per pound (.20, .27, etc.). Other buyers will sample and bid. The farmer will sell his bale to one of them and the bale is tagged for the buyer (e.g., Japan Cotton Co., etc.) Next, the farmer takes his bale to the cotton yard platform again where it is officially weighed and stored on a long platform. The platform is adjacent to a sidetrack of the railroad line. If the platform is full, it's stored on the vacant lot that we kids play baseball on. Bales to be shipped right away go to the platform where Dad and the two husky Negro workers, Clate and Dick will double-deck them into boxcars, using sharp hooks to roll and hoist the bales into position inside the boxcar. Finally, the farmer takes his receipt to the bank and the money is paid to him, or deposited to his account. By the end of summer the cotton yard is covered with hundreds of bales of cotton, awaiting orders of where they are to be shipped—some to Galveston or New Orleans for boats, or out by train.

Opal and I still had that bucket of pop to sell. As the farmers lined up at the cotton yard platform to be weighed, or deposited for shipment, it was usually a twenty or thirty minute wait in the hot sun. That's when Opal and I would walk along the line of hot thirsty drivers, yelling, and "Ice cold sodas! Coca cola, orange or lime! Cream sodas, lemon-lime, root beer! Like a cold soda, Mister?" We sold all but two in a half-hour at a nickel profit on each one; we drank the last two bottles. We did the same thing the next day. The glut of drivers would only last an hour and a half. The reason I didn't do it anymore was, I got a job picking cotton myself, which was more profitable to me.

Delbert, Sylvia and I got jobs chopping and picking cotton on nearby farms for several summers. We did well. Chopping earned us $1.00 per day. It was sunup 'till sundown—until I rebelled and quit. The next day the farmer asked Dad to tell me that an eight hour day was OK. I went back to chopping. The reason I quit was, other farmers were using choppers for only eight hours for the $1.00 pay.

In the summer a tent show usually came to town for a week's shows. I managed to go a couple of times during that week. Their tent was always pitched on a vacant lot near the square. When their week was over and they left town, I tried to be the first to go and search for coins in the grass where the bleachers had been. Before the show started, and during the intermissions between acts, show employees wrangled the crowd to buy popcorn, cold drinks, trinkets and stuff. People standing up on the plank seats to make change quite often dropped coins, which fell down into the darkened grass underneath. If I got there early enough, I'd find up to a dollar or two in coins. One time I found a dollar bill! That was gravy!

Delbert learned that we could get a penny each for scraping old mortar off the bricks from the old High School building. The contractor was using them for the new High School building. Delbert, Sylvia and I all volunteered for the job, as did a few other kids. Homer Ray went along, but he was too small to earn much. There was a mountain of old bricks. We used chisels, putty knives, etc. It was hot work in the sun. The pile of bricks lasted a couple of days. We had sore hands, but we made 2 or 3 dollars each. Every bit helped in those days and I liked to make money.

There was a little natural competition between Sylvia and myself, there being only 21 months difference in our ages. Things like whose turn is it to dry the dishes? Who helps Mother in washing the clothes? (Maybe both) Which one of us has to churn the milk for butter? I loved my sister, but sometimes she could be SO aggravating, like slipping some okra (which I hated) into the pinto beans (which I loved.) Sylvia had lots of girlfriends. She was a pretty girl, but being her brother I never noticed it. Besides, there was Lola Mae Stockton and Kathleen Hooten, girls from school, her basketball team. — And then there was Tootsie Wallace, the best player on the team. One of her friends was Gladys Williamson, who was older, but they had piano in common. Sylvia was taking lessons from Mrs. Berry, a teacher who lived up the street from us. One day Gladys was at our house visiting. I was in the yard. I had never heard Gladys play the piano. Suddenly, I heard someone playing a real jazzy song. I knew it wasn't Sylvia. Mrs. Berry didn't teach anything like that. I eased into the room to listen.

"What was that? I didn't know you could play like that. Play something else." I pleaded. Gladys played another popular song that I had heard on the radio.

"That's great! I wish I could play like that," I said.

"Dad offered to pay for you to take lessons from Mrs. Berry and you said you didn't want to," put in Sylvia.

"Mrs. Berry doesn't teach anything but classical stuff," I said.

"Everybody starts out on the classical. After you advance, you can play both kinds," explained Gladys.

"Play that first song again," I pleaded.

"Gladys didn't come here to play a concert for you, Glen," said my sis.

"I'll play the first one again, then, I have to go home." She did. I thanked her and she left. Sylvia walked part way home with her.

I was really impressed with Gladys' playing. She was a pretty girl, which I had never noticed before. I was inspired to give the piano a try. When Dad came home later, I mentioned to him that I would like lessons on the piano. Dad was happy to have me start. He sent Mrs. Berry a note with Sylvia's next lesson, that if she could take him on, Glen would like to start lessons. Sylvia brought back a schedule for me to start the following week. So began my musical education.

Mrs. Berry started me from "scratch"; the scales, sharps, flats, etc. I was twelve years old and was anxious to learn. After about six months, I worked up to "The Minuet in G" by Ignace Jan Paderewski.

One day as I went to my lesson (a little early,) Mrs. Berry was just finishing a lesson with a girl about ten years old. As the girl was gathering up her music and preparing to leave, Mrs. Berry said: "Glen, this is LaVerne Dawson. She lives out in Amy community. - - LaVerne, this is Glenmore Robb. He lives down the street from me."

LaVerne turned and looked at me and for the time I saw her face. "I'm glad to meet you," she said, as she smiled and looked me squarely in the eyes.

"Hi," I answered, noting her friendly tone of voice and how nice she looked. She shot me another glance as she said "Goodbye" to Mrs. Berry and left.

The last glance was different. It kinda shook me up. She was really pretty, I thought.

**********DEFINITELY TO BE CONTINUED LATER**********

Chapter 2: 1923–1927

I HAD LEARNED ALL about girls from the other guys, who were as ignorant as I. I thought that girls generally were dumb, obnoxious and unimportant until I walked into Mrs. Berry's and met LaVerne, who was definitely an exception.

I was still wondering about Miss Dawson when I took my next lesson. A different girl was finishing a lesson when I arrived.

"Where's the girl from Amy," I asked as I sat down for my lesson.

"She has changed her lessons to Saturdays," said Mrs. Berry.

"Why does she come all the way into town to take a lesson?" I asked. "Aren't there teachers in Amy?"

"No, there aren't," said Mrs. Berry. "She's been taking classical lessons by mail from a St. Louis conservatory and is pretty advanced for her age."

"She's different," I observed.

I didn't see her again at my piano lessons. Besides my music, I was getting very interested in reading books, especially "boy's" books. Some of my friends did, too. We'd exchange stories of the "Rover Boys", "Tom Sawyer", etc. I also discovered that the school library had a lot of interesting books in it.

I wasn't a complete nerd. Sylvia and the Hooten girls, Kathleen and Geraldine, liked to get together and practice their dance steps at the Hooten's house across the street.

I could hear the music and wished that I could learn to dance, but I was too timid and wouldn't ask them I remember that Sylvia used to tease me about a girl just a year older than I, who lived on our street. I would walk on the opposite side of the street by her house, just in case she came out and started walking and talking to me.

I took piano for two years. I stopped after Dad bought me a beautiful silver Conn trumpet. It cost $100. I started lessons from Mr. K.D. King, the leader of the Cooper Band. As I got better, Dad sent me to Paris to take lessons from the director there who had the reputation of being a very good teacher.

Other interests occupied my time and I soon forgot the cute girl from Amy. From the time when I was twelve, I had been a Boy Scout. Brother Kidd, the preacher of the Baptist Church was the scoutmaster. I spent time working on passing merit badges, camping, etc. My main scout buddy was a boy named Howard Nolan. Our troop went to a two weeks camping trip on a river at Iron Springs, Okla. Howard was my tent mate.

As I have mentioned, I was an avid reader of "Boy's" books and ever since I had spotted that first airplane on the "hill", I was also an enthusiastic aviation fan. In one of the aviation story magazines, I found a section labeled "Pen Pals", with the names and addresses of several boys. I picked out a name, Harry Weir of Duluth, Minn., and wrote to him. He wrote back and for a couple of years we corresponded regularly.

I was beginning also to take more notice of other girls. Those former snaggle-toothed, snotty nosed, tousled haired, knobby-kneed, uppity, "think you're smart" girls were changing. Like a rattlesnake shedding its skin—No, forget that—more like a larva turning into a butterfly. I began to view girls differently, especially when my girl cousins began to be 14 or older: Pauline from Okla. City, Nadine from Waxahachie, Ottie Lee from Lewisville, Rosa Lee from Bartonville, Lorene from Shreveport and our cute cousin from Cumby. It started me to wonder when these girls all began to look better, even attractive, and then to cap it all off; there was that girl, LaVerne, that I had met at the music lesson at Mrs. Berry's.

It's like when you realize that music can be beautiful. Thanks to our Creator for a wonderful job!

The following song "GIRLS" kind of sums it all up:

GIRLS
(Music and lyrics by Tom Robb)

Now I learned in kindergarten class
That girls, they sometimes bite.
And though" that hasn't happened since,
They still give me a fright.
Each time I was alone with them-
This awful thing occurred:
I got goose bumps, itchy goose bumps,
Sometimes worse.

And just between the two of us,
I find as I survey;
The girls I met when I was young, are-
Not the same today.
They've grown up into something new.
I can't quite make it out.
They may not bite you any more,
But they've got plenty clout.

Now passing time and lonely nights-
Have made a change in little me.
I found out girls are pretty neat-
And sometimes they are pretty sweet.

A funny thing that strikes me now-
Is, what became of me.
I finally married one of them.
We're living happily.
And now when I am close to her,
And she looks up at me;
I get goose bumps, thrilling goose bumps. Happy Me!

When we first moved to 432 W. Waco St. it was not paved. In the rainy season the street was pretty muddy. Dad had to pull our car over a side ditch to get it into our yard using rocks and gravel, etc.

Cooper house

In the spring of 1920, Dad had the house wired for electricity and we stored or got rid of our lamps and Mother's oil stove. At the same time Dad hired a Mr. Murray and his son to build another bedroom and bath on to our house. They also built us a separate single garage. The Murrays were paid $1.00 each per day. I built a bridge over the ditch with lumber left over from the additions. The bridge lasted until our street was paved.

I don't remember the sleeping arrangements before the new rooms but we 3 boys took over the new bedroom. It held a double and a single bed. It had a small closet.

Before the new additions were built, we were pretty crowded. We all had to take our baths in a washtub in the kitchen. Both the little breakfast area and the kitchen had linoleum floors. We ate our dinners (the middle meal) and our suppers in the large dining room, which also featured a coal (or wood) stove. Mother used coal oil for the lamps and the cook stove.

Blankets and sheets could be bought at the stores but quilts had to be made by Mother or be a gift from a relative. Aunt Ney was good at making quilts and helped Mother make them when she visited. They hired me (no pay) to help with the tying and carding of the cotton that is the inside of the quilt. Aunt Ney sometimes gave me a tip for an ice cream cone.

We still had our ice chest for such things as milk, meat, etc. The ice wagon came by every day. Delbert worked on the ice wagon one summer. The fresh meat wagon occasionally came by and the "Hot Tamale" man came by regularly.

Then there was the man who served the outhouses of the area (ours before we built our bathroom). I hate to mention it. He came by very early in the morning. Ours was a two-holer. You knew when he was in the neighborhood. Poor guy! His morale must have been the lowest of the low.

While construction was going on was a good time to visit our relatives in Shreveport, La. Delbert, 14, stayed home with Dad, while Mother, Sylvia, Homer Ray and I took the train for Shreveport.

Cordie and Ray Hooper (Cordie was Mother's cousin) had 3 children: Lorraine and Lorice (ages ten and seven) and a son who was about four. Cordie, I believe, was the daughter of Mr. and Mrs. Loard of Lewisville, Tex. Mrs. Loard was my grandmother Dixon's sister. Ottie Lee Loard (my age) was the daughter of a son of the Loards of Lewisville.

Ray Hooper worked for the railroad. He was a brakeman. Several years earlier he had the misfortune to lose an arm in an accident while connecting two boxcars. He still worked for the railroad in some capacity.

I don't remember much that we did in Shreveport. Mother and Cordie reviewed the good times they had growing up in the Lewisville area. Sylvia and the girls found a lot to do including games, telling about school, etc. I was kind of on my own. I did join in some of the games: hop-scotch, pick-up-sticks, jacks, etc. Homer Ray and their son enjoyed the time playing with balls and toys. Time passed. We said "Goodbye" and caught the train home.

We found the construction of the addition to our house in the finishing stage. It was soon finished and with great relief we adjusted to the larger house.

The lot already had a barn, a chicken coop and a pigpen. The barn lot was fenced as well as our back yard. In the next 6 months, Dad bought two cows, two pigs and about a dozen chickens, so we were set up comfortably to operate as a normal family in the little city of Cooper, Texas.

During the time of 1921–1922, Mr. Williamson, Gladys' dad, was building his house using concrete blocks on the lot next to the Depot Grocery, which was on a corner near the railroad station. He had built the grocery building, which he owned, out of concrete blocks also. He needed a little help making the blocks and I was handy. I lived near and Dad worked at the Depot so I got the job (another instance of Dad promoting his kids). It was hard work. The blocks weighed about thirty pounds each. I didn't work a full day and I think I got about twenty cents an hour. He took his time building the house. It was one story with a small basement. I'm sure that his two sons, Weldon and Otis, helped him a lot, also. His older son, Walter, was a doctor in St. Louis. Weldon also became a doctor. In the course of that work, I got acquainted with Otis, who was about twenty years old and was building a radio in the attic of a garage that he rented for his car (this was about 1923). He was building it from "scratch" in and on an empty Quaker Oatmeal box.

My family didn't have a radio yet. Otis finally got it working and I think that what we first heard was some music from WGN in Chicago. Even though it came in pretty weak and through earphones, it was very exciting. So the first time I ever heard anything on a radio was on one that had been constructed with a Quaker Oatmeal box. Otis soon got the agency selling radio receiving sets and Dad bought one. I don't remember the brand, but the music came in clear if you had the two dials exactly on the station. It came with earphones and was powered by two heavy batteries that sat on the floor. I loved it. I could get Chicago, Cleveland, New York City and a weather station in Godhaven, Greenland.

Otis also experimented with connecting a Ford Chassis and motor with an airplane propeller at the back; pusher type. You could hear it coming for blocks. It was noisy and windy. He soon gave it up and concentrated on selling the radios.

It was hard for me to find time to listen to our radio except after I had done my lesson assignments and Mother and Dad had gone to bed. About 11:30 PM, I'd hear his voice from the bedroom:

"McAdoo, what are you doing? Turn that light off and get to bed."

"In just a little bit," I promised. "I'm listening to the radio."

Then about 12:30 am:

"Glen, are you still up? Turn that dang thing off and get to bed!"

Dad never gave the third warning. I knew better than to risk it. Click. "It's off. Goodnight." I went to bed.

Dad loved music and loved and was proud of his kids. I just couldn't get enough of the wonderful music from Rudy Vallee, Guy Lombardo, Ted Weems, Russ Columbo, etc. Paul Whiteman, in the early days of the 20s - 40s, helped many singers and musicians starting out. He was the most popular band leader before the Big Band Era.

About Dad's warnings and our duties: I remember one time that my job was to get a scuttle full of coal and kindling from the coal pile in our yard. This was for him to start a fire in our dining room when he got back from meeting a 6:00 am freight train. It was winter and the early mornings were frigid. I had forgotten my job. When Dad came home after meeting the train, there was no coal or kindling by the stove. He took a look at a sleeping ME. Suddenly, there was a shower of ice cold water on me. Dad didn't say a word. I jumped up. I knew what it was about. Dad just went into the kitchen where Mother was lighting her oil stove. I ran outside in my bare feet and quickly gathered the coal and kindling.

"I'm sorry," I said. I didn't forget it anymore.

Let me say something about the 20s, called by some the "roaring" 20s. That's the time of MY life from 10 years old until I was thru high school and was working in the post office in Dallas. All of that time, except the last four months of 1929, I spent in Cooper, Texas.

World War One had been over about a year and a half when the economy started picking up. The soldier boys were home from France and were itching to reenter the fight for a happy and prosperous life. Some of the things that are interesting now that were current and happening are:

Prices: Average annual wage $ 1402.00
Overland touring car 1035.00
Piano 50.00
Girl's bicycle 10.00
98 lb. sack of flour 7.33
Men's felt hat 3.85
5 cans condensed milk 1.00
Flannel dress 3.00
Petticoat 1.19
Pkg. Wrigley's gum .05

Many people had a garden, as we did, and raised and canned some of their fruit and vegetables in glass jars.

Dad bought a new blue Chevrolet sedan in 1921 that I learned to drive as soon as I was sixteen (1926). Dad made just a medium salary with the railroad, but it was enough that we kids never lacked good food and other things that we needed. We kids all helped in the summer, chopping and picking cotton and other jobs that helped us earn our spending money and new clothes. None of us were ever given an allowance. Mother didn't work outside our home.

Cooper Review masthead

Cooper, being a town of about 2300 and the county seat of Delta County had its own newspaper, the Cooper Review. The Dallas News and the Dallas Times Herald were brought in and dropped off daily at the Hooten Drug Store corner by "Bussey" Good in his Red Ball bus that ran from Dallas to Paris. I carried a paper route for a while as did Delbert and Homer Ray. Cooper had two auto sales companies, Ford and Chevrolet. If you wanted any other kind, you had to go to Dallas, Paris or Greenville.

In the 20s Dallas was the largest city in Texas with a population of about 240,000. Houston was 2nd in size. Dallas was the financial center and had the Texas State Fair. Houston was the center of the oil industry and eventually passed Dallas in population.

Ft. Worth, only thirty-three miles west of Dallas was about a quarter as big as Dallas. It was a very different kind of city. It had a large stockyard and was the center of the marketing and shipping of cattle, hence its nickname, "Cow town" and "Where the West Begins". There was a natural competition between the cities, as well as their two excellent universities, TCU in Ft. Worth and SMU in Dallas.

An example of that competition happened much later when the cities were planning a new enlarged airport between Ft. Worth (Tarrant Co.) and Dallas (Dallas Co.). After much talk and disagreement the two Chambers of Commerce met to try to agree on the details. They had not agreed on what to call the airport but had finally decided to put it on the county line, ½ in Tarrant County and ½ in Dallas County But they couldn't agree on where to put the entrance and how to split the taxes, police and fire protection, etc. They met one day for dinner at a Dallas hotel. Amon Carter, Mayor of Ft. Worth and head of the Ft. Worth delegation, brought his own dinner in a paper sack. He said he didn't trust that Dallas crowd. Reading about it in the newspaper, I gave him a double plus for a good joke on Dallas. They decided to put the entrance in Tarrant County. I don't remember what Dallas got, but I suspect they got "slickered" by that bunch of cowhands from Ft. Worth.

One thing that happened during the early part of the 20s that had a huge effect on our country:

On Jan. 16, 1918, the 18th Amendment to our constitution had been passed and took effect. It banned the sale, possession, consumption and commercial production of beer, wine and hard liquor in the U.S. 3.2 beer was okay at the option of each state. The taps serving liquor closed down and the "speakeasies" opened underground. Alphonse Capone, "Bugs" Moran and others in Chicago and the "Mafia", Jack "Legs" Diamond and others in New York City soon had their clandestine operations going full blast to serve the thirsty customers. Their battles for "territory" were headlines throughout the U.S. I was enthralled at their gory conflicts. With lots of money at stake, the clubs and backrooms of some hotels presented PRIVATE and lavish places "members" and their "liberated" flapper lady guests could rendezvous for entertainment and drinks. Many singers, musicians and dancers got their start in those places. Our FBI is still fighting a remnant of the Mafia family even today. J. Edgar Hoover and his fledgling FBI fought these gangs for years, before getting most of them killed or in prison. The repeal of the 18th amendment in 1933 helped.

The styles of both men and women were influenced by the well-dressed men and the elegant costumes and dresses of the women at the better entertainment establishments of the day.

Ballroom dancing was popular. Jazz music was at the top of its popularity.

Clothing styles in New York City and Paris gradually trickled down to the smaller cities. Dallas, during my life in Texas, was the style center for the bigger towns. Sears, Roebuck and Montgomery Ward Catalog Service greatly influenced the people in small towns like Cooper.

Most men in downtown Dallas businesses wore a suit and tie. Suits had vests and shirt collars and cuffs were usually starched. The men wore hats such as a wide brim Stetson or a smaller brim Dobbs. I wore a Dobbs because my friend, Bill Harper, worked for the Willard Hat Co. and they featured the snappy Dobbs. In the winter most men wore overcoats outside in really cold weather, gloves and maybe spats to keep their feet warm if they were outside like a mail carrier, etc. I sometimes wore a pair of spats.

Women wore a winter coat, often with a fur collar that varied in cost; rabbit and possum, moderately expensive, ermine and fox still more expensive. The ladies, bless their hearts, gradually raised their dresses, I mean the hem lines of their dresses, until they were just below the knees. Young girls wore them just above their knees.

It was a time when there was general respect between the sexes. It was mostly a man's world, in that businesses and the police were run by men and the women didn't have to work. Most men and women chose to marry and have a family. Not everyone did, of course, and some jobs were popular for females, whether married or single such as nurses, school teachers, clerks in stores, typists, assistants, etc. However, change was on the horizon. Henry Ford was hiring women in his factory, paying the same as men, $3.00 per day.

Almost all men respected and protected women, evidenced by such things as greeting them when passing on the street with a "hello" or a "hi" if they know them or tipping their hat to them if they were strangers. Even men didn't pass another man on a street (but not on a crowded street) without some sign or word of greeting. If you were sitting while riding a streetcar and a lady was standing near you, you didn't duck your head, as if you didn't notice her, and sit there 'til your ears turned red from embarrassment. You would immediately get up and offer her your seat. I learned that in the Boy Scouts.

Earrings, rouge, lipstick and perfume were in vogue for ladies of the 20s. Bobbed hair became popular, especially with the teen girls and younger women. I can remember when my dear Mother had her hair cut down just above her shoulders. She left enough hair to "put up" and to pin down some of the "dinky" or larger hats. It was windy some days and it wasn't unusual to see a hat, man's or woman's, scooting down the street with a man running after it. Norman Rockwell illustrated that in The Saturday Evening Post. Many other items of the 20s are part of the rest of my story.

It used to be that Halloween was very different in Cooper in the early 20s. There was no "trick or treating" on that day. It was just an ordinary day. The younger kids at school drew goblins, hollowed out pumpkins, made masks, etc. Teachers told about the early history of Halloween, etc. Some went home to afternoon parties, but home by dark. After dark, the older kids had costume parties. Young girls had slumber parties. Both maybe tried the latest waltz, fox-trot steps by music from the radio or victrola.

After it was really dark, the more adventurous of the boys, usually high school or a bit older, did their "thing". Anything not nailed down, was likely to be found moved across town or some unusual place.

I remember one Halloween, some of the bigger boys took the wheels off a car (I think it was a Ford roadster), made it as light as possible, and muscled it up the wide stairs of the courthouse all the way up to the belfry, which was above the second floor, and put it back together. It must have taken at least a half dozen husky boys to accomplish that trick. No one admitted doing it, but some were under suspicion. After about three or four days, these same guys volunteered to bring it down, which they did. Everyone thought it was a great "trick".

Also, the signs that hung from the overhang in front of most of the businesses around the square were switched, so that the variety store the next morning had a sign that read "Turner's Barber Shop" and "Stovall's Hardware" became "Poe's Ladies Wear". Imagine trying to buy a buggy whip at Poe's!

Souvenir flight ticket

One summer Dad took Delbert and me out to a large meadow on the outskirts of town where a barnstorming pilot was taking people up in his plane for a $5.00 fee. Dad bought us a ride together. It was a two-seater biplane. We both rode in the front seat. It was a thrilling ride. The pilot took us up to about 2500 feet, banked left and right, circled the town and made a long glide, engine barely turning the propeller, to a perfect landing. It was a memorable ride for me.

At Christmas time, I think in 1922, I got a beautiful baby blue bicycle. But it was a "girl's" bicycle. When Dad saw the confusion on my face, he explained.

"Glen, it's yours. We couldn't afford to buy both you and Sylvia one, so we bought one that both of you can ride. The only difference is the bar. Although I was disappointed, who's to argue with their parents on Christmas morning about a bar on a bicycle? I was happy to finally get one. Sylvia didn't object either. We worked out a schedule on sharing it. As it turned out, neither of us needed it very badly. I was used to walking. I used it on a paper route and she used it delivering milk and eggs to two or three customers. I think what Dad and Mother had in mind, was that Delbert was graduating from high school soon and was now driving the car a lot. I could inherit his bigger bike later.

That was what happened when Delbert left to go to work at Brown Cracker & Candy Co. in Dallas I used the bigger bike on my job at Western Union after graduating from high school and while waiting to hear from my application for a job at the Dallas Post Office.

Dad's job at the Texas Midland Depot was a busy and very responsible one. The depot was on the east side of the tracks and the freight office, general office and telegraph business was in a building on the west side. The depot or passenger station was an attractive one story, red tile roofed structure. It had two waiting rooms (white and black), two sets of rest rooms (white and black), a ticket office and a storage room for baggage and a dolly or two (trucks). The early 20s was the peak of business for the railroad in Cooper. Dad was in charge of selling tickets and the dispatch and receiving products including the U.S. mail. There were two coal burning passenger trains each way per day. Oil burning engines didn't supplant the coal burning ones until the 1950s. The Texas Midland ran from Paris to Ennis, stopping at towns in between. Tickets could be bought over other lines to anywhere in the U.S. For instance, a ticket from Cooper to Buffalo, NY might be over several lines and be four or five feet long. Dad usually had help selling tickets in the busiest seasons. This was before truck and bus lines came to Cooper. Minnie Robb was the ticket clerk for Dad one summer.

Here is an example of the scene of a train coming
into Cooper station in the early 1920s:

There were a lot of people at the station. The concrete area between the stationhouse and the track was crowded with many dollies piled high with crates, packages, produce, etc. to be loaded for destinations down the line and to other parts of Texas and beyond.

A whistle was heard and around a curve in the tracks came Engine #27. With its bell ringing, it eased to a stop in front of the waiting crowd, with a hiss and a gush of steam to adjust the pressure in the brake lines. The conductor stepped off the train. The loading was ready to begin. Butler Ivey, the janitor and handyman had the loaded dollies arranged in line, according to which was to be loaded first.

Just at that moment, a truck arrived with the outgoing mail from the post office. In the truck were Herb Stewart, Paul Webb and their mascot, Duncan Parsons. One of the men carried a pistol. They quickly loaded the mail onto the baggage/mail car of the train and received the mail for Cooper, which they carried back to the post office.

The train was five cars long behind the engine and a coal/water tender car. Two cars for baggage and mail and three cars for passengers followed.

The engineer leaned out of his cab and waved to the kids. The brakeman stepped out with his red lantern to supervise the unloading and loading. A fireman kept the fire in the engine stoked and the steam regulated. Dad hurried out to the baggage man with waybills that described the merchandise to be loaded and their destinations.

Two porters in their tailored black uniforms, white shirts and fancy caps stepped out of the passenger cars. They put down their little step-ups and started checking the tickets of the boarding passengers.

Porter, addressing the first passenger, a lady, to board:

"What's your destination, Ma'am?"

"I'm going to Dallas," answered the lady, presenting her ticket.

Porter, checking her ticket: "You're okay. Go ahead." She went aboard. The porter continued checking tickets.

Meanwhile, activity up and down the length of the train was brisk. The unloading came first. Not much of it, since Paris was the starting point of the run, mostly a few supplies for the station. Next, the merchandise is loaded, the farthest destination first. The train mailman, after securing the mail, helped the baggage man. Then at the last moment a black touring car came rushing up to the station. A man jumped out and rushed into the station, while Sterling "Si" Rattan unloaded two large suitcases for the man. The man was a drummer (salesman), who had been calling on wholesale customers up on the square. The ticket clerk quickly sold him a ticket and ticketed his bags. Butler Ivey loaded them onto an outgoing dolly and the drummer boarded the train.

Si Rattan then parked his "jitney" and waited to see if there would be a customer from the train. Si operated jitney (taxi) service for Cooper and for any community nearby that a customer wanted to go. It was a valuable service for people coming to Cooper. He was also available for emergencies that sometimes happened. His car, when not in use, could usually be found parked on the street close to Hooten's Drug Store at the square. His very pretty young daughter, Bonnie had a beautiful voice and was a very popular young lady.

When everything was loaded, the conductor waved his lantern to signal "all aboard". The engineer rang his bell and gave a toot on his whistle and the train pulled out. By the time it was out of sight, the crowd was about gone, too. Dad and his crew began sorting the incoming items for their delivery.

Across the tracks on the west side was the main office, a large room that included the Agent's desk, Dad's desk, and the telegrapher and his instruments for sending and receiving telegrams. Enclosing this area was a long counter for customers and a long passageway leading to a huge room for incoming and outgoing freight.

The janitor stayed in the large freight area where all freight was received for shipment or dispatched on the freight trains, which usually ran one each day, each way.

There were spur tracks off the main line to park boxcars, coal cars, flat cars that brought in or carried out various things such as coal, lumber, gravel, new cars, etc. Items going out were cotton bales, scrap iron, empty boxcars, etc. Perishable items like fresh meat, fresh vegetables, fresh fish and oysters were brought in on special refrigerator boxcars, kept cold by huge blocks of ice put in from the top of the car. All boxcars containing products were sealed and their locations and routes carefully recorded.

During the summer of 1921, Dad managed to get his young twenty year old sister, Minnie Marie Robb, the temporary job of selling tickets. She was a beautiful girl, dressed elegantly and smelled SO good. I was ten years old and I adored her.

Minnie was a bit shy and the men at the Depot Grocery liked to tease her. It was hot summer time and Minnie usually stopped by the grocery both before and after her work. She bought a cold drink and drank it in the cool store. One day, as Clint Mosley got the coke from the cooler for her he asked,

"Minnie, you drink a lot of these. They're pretty strong. Don't you think you ought to cut down a little?"

"Why? I like these the most. I don't think they're bad for me," she argued.

"Well, you're young and healthy now, but it may cause you stomach problems later on. I just thought you ought to try something else," said Clint.

"You're just trying to scare me. If this drink was damaging, they wouldn't be allowed to make them," she said as she finished the bottle.

Minnie Robb

"I'll see you later," she said and left.

"I hate to see her have stomach problems," said Clint. "She's Tom's sister."

"She's not convinced. I could tell she thinks you're just jokin'," said the other clerk.

"Well, I'll just carry it on a bit farther. Get me a little slice of bacon. I've got an idea." Clint took the bacon, popped the cap off a bottle of coke, poured out just a little and inserted the bacon.

"What's that goin' to prove?" asked the clerk.

When Minnie came by on her way home that day, Clint greeted her,

"Hi. What are you goin' to have this time, Minnie?"

"I'll take a coke," said Minnie with a broad smile on her face. Clint got a coke, popped the cap and gave it to her. When she had finished it and was about to leave, he stopped her.

"Wait, Minnie. I want to show you something," said Clint

He got out the bottle with the bacon in it.

"You may be right about cokes not being damaging to your stomach, but I just want to test it to see. You can see that this piece of bacon is fresh. I just put it in there," explained Clint. Minnie examined it carefully.

"Looks alright to me," she said.

Clint put the cap back on the bottle.

"What's that supposed to do?" asked Minnie.

"I don't know," said Clint. "I'll set it up here on the shelf and when you come in Monday morning, we'll take a look." He set it up on a high shelf. Minnie smiled at Clint, still sure that it was some kind of joke.

"Okay, we'll see," she said as she left.

After she left, Clint took the bottle down, took the piece of bacon out of it and gave it a good chewing, then put it back on the shelf. The store was closed on Sunday. When Minnie came in Monday morning for her usual drink, Clint said,

"Wait, let's look at that bacon."

He got the bottle down, popped the cap, fished out the bacon and put it on a piece of paper. It was pretty mutilated. Minnie's smile faded. She looked really concerned.

"Did that coke do all of that?" she asked.

"You saw it Saturday. You saw how it looked then. It's been up on that shelf all weekend," said Clint soberly.

"Hmm! I can't believe it. I haven't had any trouble with my stomach. I guess I'd better cut down on cokes. Give me a crème soda." She looked at the piece of bacon again. "I still can't believe it," she sighed.

The next time she came in, Clint owned up to the ruse. They had a good laugh. But Minnie did switch to other drinks often after that.

"This one's on the house," said Clint. "You're a good sport, Minnie!"

Aunt Minnie went back to Dallas after that summer. The next summer, she and her girlfriend, Gladys Galloway, went to a World's Fair in Detroit, Michigan. Then she married Johnny Parnell and settled down in Dallas, but her young life was ended when she died in a Dallas Hospital from a ruptured appendix. She was buried in a cemetery in Dallas at Peak St. (or Haskell) and Ross Ave. I visited her grave once. An awful tragedy to a beautiful Lady! She was only 23.

The summer after Aunt Minnie was the ticket clerk, Dad helped Uncle Ernest to get the job. He, as Aunt Minnie had, stayed briefly at our house. After that summer, he went to work as a cashier at the 1st National Bank in Cooper. Then he got married to Miss Rosalie Brumley of Lewisville, Texas. And moved to Lewisville where he worked at the Lewisville State Bank.

Back to Dad's job:

Besides Dad's duties at the passenger station, he had other duties as well.

He had charge of most of the ins and outs of the freight business, along with the Agent, who supervised the "overall" of both stations and had the primary responsibility.

Since the Agent's job was a political job, usually someone was transferred in to be in charge. Seniority was a big factor, but not always. Not knowing specific operations of the local office, he would leave those details to the current clerk, (who was Dad) and concentrate on getting acquainted with the local merchants and drumming up business.

The tariff rates for products shipped were even more complicated than the passenger rates. But Dad was an expert at it since he had studied the 3 inch, finely printed tariff book of rates, categories, different routes, etc. which changed constantly because of the seasons and the competition between different railroads. Usually a new agent was not up on these tariffs and was glad to have Dad continue doing the job. Dad could save the maker of say, wicker chairs, thirty per cent of the transportation costs by routing a shipment by way of Kansas City on "X" railroad instead of by way of St. Louis, the chairs ending up in Chicago by both routes. If the sender was a regular supplier of wicker chairs for a furniture store in Chicago, it would be a good savings over a year's time. Because of the competition, railroads often changed the rates, if the U.S. Railroad Commission allowed it. Dad kept up with the changes that affected his customers. The merchants of Cooper appreciated his expertise and depended on him for it. Dad sometimes had a shipment that was refused by a merchant (scratched piece of furniture, a barrel of iced fish, etc.). Usually, the sender would refuse to pay for the item's return and would instruct the Agent (Dad's job) to sell it for the best offer or just dump it. Dad would try to get as much for it as he could for the sender. With things like iced fish, he would have to act fast. He would sell as many as he could to the restaurants, bring some home and dump the rest.

I remember Dad bringing home a small barrel of iced oysters that a restaurant refused (they still had plenty on hand). Dad gave away some and brought the rest home. We ate oysters until they were coming out our ears. Since Dad bought catsup by the gallon we finally got the rest of them eaten. Dad once brought home a little black and white dog. I think it was a terrier. The consignee (the person to receive it) had moved out of our area. For some reason, it couldn't be returned. We kids fell in love with it. We kept it about a month, until Dad located someone to take it.

As I mentioned, we usually had two cows, two pigs and about a dozen chickens. One of our cows, "Old Jersey", should be listed in the "Cow Hall of Fame". She was a real wizard for finding ways to cause trouble and outwitting us humans. To her credit, she gave us about 1½ gallons of rich milk each day. Jersey cream content is high and we always had plenty of butter from churning her milk. Boy! I hated that churning job. She was milked early in the morning and later in the afternoon, depending on whether she was about to or had just had a calf. Delbert being older than I usually milked the younger cow that was nervous and unpredictable. I milked "Old Jersey". She was gentle but because of the ever-present flies and during wet weather, she could almost knock me off my stool by flinging her wet, cockle-burred tail in my face or around my neck.

Cow Court is still in session. Prosecution talking:

Sometimes, when she was thinking about something that excited her, she would suddenly run forward, knocking the bucket of milk out of my hands, or step in the bucket and ruin the morning's milk.

She was always pulling some new event.

(A) With her horns, about eight inches long, she learned how to open the sliding wooden bolt on the door in the barn where we kept a sack of cottonseed meal. It was very rich and we only gave her a small scoopful, like a dessert, with her main meal of cottonseed hulls.

One morning when I went to feed her, I discovered not only the door of the bin open, but the sack of cottonseed meal was almost chewed to pieces. Luckily, the sack was almost empty or she would have been a sick cow. Penalty: No dessert for two days.

(B) Another day, Mother washed a blanket and a few other things and hung them on the clothesline in our back yard. The next morning when she went out to gather them in, they were still on the line, but were badly chewed by something. They were ruined. The lot gate was open and "Old Jersey" was in the lot where she was supposed to be but she looked awfully guilty. She had managed to open the lot gate (same kind as the bin) with her horns, according to the circumstantial evidence.

(C) Mother made soap in a huge iron pot in our back yard, using the fat stripped from a pig that Dad and Clate Stout had killed a few days before. All day the fire burned under the fat mixed with a certain amount of lye. Late in the afternoon, when the fat was reduced to the proper consistency, she let the fire die and stirred the mixture. The next morning the soap would have come to the top and would be cold and hard. Mother could then cut it into sections (bars) and store it for washing our clothes. After breakfast she went out to finish the soap job. To her surprise, there was "Old Jersey" eating the newly made soap. Evidently she hadn't had time to eat very much for she didn't show any ill effects. The lye in the soap could have ruined her stomach.

(D) Then one day, she decided that she wanted to see what the world outside looked like, OR maybe she could smell the fresh aroma of cottonseed cake being cooked at the Cooper Cotton Oil Mill a few blocks away. At any rate, she manipulated the lot gate and also for the first time, the gate to the front yard. She was FREE! She looked around quickly, sniffed the air and headed across the street and up the nearest cross street. As it happened, Mother was in her bedroom, which was near the outside gate and heard the noise as "Old Jersey" barged through the gate and disappeared from view.

"Glen," she yelled at me. "Old Jersey's out!" I was in the kitchen, helping myself to a left over fried egg sandwich.

"Where?" I asked, taking a bite, stuffing the rest in my jacket pocket and hurrying to her room.

"She just went through the gate and across the street. She's headed up the side street by the Anderson's house!" I immediately grabbed a halter and took off up the same street. I saw her. She was about 1½ blocks away and was grazing on the green grass along the side. When she saw me, she took off running further up the street. She looked back at me and started grazing again. But as soon as I got within about a half block of her, she would take off running again.

"I've got to outsmart her someway," I thought. After she had toyed with me a couple of times I decided to go over to a parallel street, run until I was sure I was ahead of her, then double back and cut her off. So I did that. I went over to the parallel street, ran as hard as I could for two blocks and started back up to her street.

Would you believe it? There in the middle of the intersection of the street, stood "Old Jersey" watching me! If cows can laugh, I'm sure "Old Jersey" was laughing with glee at having outwitted me. I was tired. She was tired, too, I figured since cows aren't use to much exercise.

I called to her and walked slowly toward her. When I got about twenty feet from her, I took the egg sandwich out of my jacket pocket and held it out to her. She eyed it for a second as I moved up so she could smell it as I slipped the halter around her neck. She rejected the egg sandwich, but with the halter around her neck, I had no trouble leading her back home. She got an extra helping of cottonseed meal as a reward for not embarrassing me any further.

Moral of this story: Always carry an egg sandwich in your jacket pocket, especially if you're chasing a cow.

When Delbert was in high school, one of his friends, Audrey Wright, lived about a block away. He and Delbert constructed a trolley that ran from about twelve feet up on a telephone pole, down to a grassy patch about sixty feet away. The down end was to a post set in the ground. They found a rope that long in the Wright's barn. They stretched it tight and with a pulley wheel fitted over the rope they had an elevated streetcar for 60 feet. Delbert was a good brother. He never shushed me away because he was older and he let me hang around when he and Audrey were working on some project.

All of that trouble to set this thing up and it didn't turn out too well. By the time he climbed up that telephone pole half a dozen times and skinned his rear when he hit the stop, he was worn out. But it worked fine for several hours until the stop anchor came out of the ground.

Audrey and Delbert tried their hand at brewing root beer (non-alcoholic). With a recipe and the necessary ingredients in hand, they mixed them in a small ex-pickle barrel and set it on a side porch at Audrey's house. It was supposed to ferment in a certain number of days. Between the flies, ants and our constant sampling it never came out just right. Besides, it had a kind of pickle taste.

Delbert was a good athlete in high school. He ran some of the races in the county track meet. He was on the basketball team that went to the state finals for the class "B" schools. They lost only to the Gober, Tex. Ploughboys. Other members of Cooper High Schools' team besides Delbert were Elmer Sloan, Goble Templeton and I think Chester Gaston and Manton Pound.

One day Delbert, Elmer Sloan and another friend rented a Model T Ford for a one day trip up to Hugo, Okla., which was just across the Red River, a distance of only about forty miles. They planned to bring the car back the next morning. Texas was "dry" and Oklahoma was "wet." They allowed 3.2 beer, which was not supposed to be intoxicating. Hugo was out of state. But the unexpected happened. It started raining on Friday. They boys decided to go anyway, since they had already paid for the car. So they took off for Hugo. It was still raining when they reached the Red River and the approaches to the bridge were open, although there was lots of water around. That didn't bother the boys and they drove on into Hugo. In the late afternoon, they decided that they had seen and done enough and they headed back to Texas. When they got to the river, they found it blocked. The approach to the bridge was under water. With more rain threatening; they were told that it likely would be several days before the bridge would be open. The boys didn't know what else to do, so they put up in a hotel.

Early on Monday the owner of the car called Dad.

"Where's my car?" he demanded. Dad told him that his car was stranded in Oklahoma. The owner hit the ceiling. He envisioned losing several days' rent on his car and threatened to charge the boys with auto theft. We (the kids) were worried. I was afraid that my brother was going to be sent to the penitentiary. When Delbert called later that day and explained what happened, Dad called the car owner and worked out an agreement on the cost to the boys. The bridge was opened again on the second day and the boys came home. It was a close call, I thought. It really worried me. I loved my brother. He just got caught up in a bad situation.

In 1924, when a vacant spot for an appointment to the U.S. Naval

Academy became available from our district of Texas, Delbert and Herman McBride were both recommended for the appointment. Delbert had just graduated from high school and was supported by many of his and Dad's friends. However, the local wholesale grocer's son, Herman McBride was appointed. He went to Annapolis for about a year and then resigned. Delbert by then was working in the office of Brown Cracker & Candy Company in Dallas, helped by Dad's acquaintance with the office manager. Delbert, who had been next in line after Herman, decided to stay with the B.C. & C. Co., where he worked for many years. The infamous Clyde Barrow worked at Brown for a short period.

On the fourth of July in the year before Delbert's graduation, we had shot up most of our firecrackers when Delbert and Audrey Wright decided to build a baby cannon. They fashioned a 1½ inch water pipe securely onto a 1½ foot long two by four, capped the back end of the pipe and drilled a hole in the top for a fuse. They managed to find a couple of shotgun shells, extracted the powder and poured it into the cannon. Next they pushed in some wadding and a few small pebbles. Last, they inserted the fuse from a "baby giant" firecracker into the hole in the top and it was ready to fire. They placed the butt of their cannon against the base of a tree and aimed the barrel toward the vacant cotton yard. They argued over who was going to light the fuse. They flipped a coin and Delbert won (or lost). Mother and Dad were not present. Delbert prepared to light the fuse. The rest of us: me, Audrey, Sylvia and Homer Ray retreated behind the tree.

"You want to light it?" He held out the match to Audrey.

"No. Light it!" we all yelled.

"Okay. Here goes." He struck the match, lit the fuse and scampered back with the rest of us.   BOOM!!!

An acrid cloud of smoke and dirt flew in all directions. When the smoke cleared, we rushed to see what happened to the cannon. It was nowhere to be seen; just a bare spot in the grass where the cannon had been.

"What was that?" Mother asked, as she stuck her head out the door.

"We just fired our cannon," said Delbert. "We're all okay." Mother went back to her work. We found the cannon in the ditch about fifteen feet away. The next day, Mr. Boyd, who lived on the corner and across from the cotton yard, said that he heard the "boom" and then several rocks hitting the side of his house. No one had to tell Delbert and Audrey that what they did was a dangerous mistake, but I'm sure Mother and Dad did. However, all kinds of powerful fourth of July fireworks were sold and a few hands badly mangled in those days.

I really worked hard learning to play my trumpet, taking lessons from Mr. H.W. King, our Cooper bandleader. Later, when Mr. King left, Dad sent me to Paris to take lessons from the bandleader there. I'd catch the Saturday morning train to Paris, then, come back on the afternoon train. Mother would fix me a lunch to take along. My first time to play with the Cooper Band, besides practice, was at the Ford Motor Co.'s showing of the newest ford model. We played outside in front of the building. Besides the popular Sousa marches, we played a jazzy "Tokio Blues"; my second taste of popular music. I decided, then, that it was the kind of music I wanted to play.

Later, when Jewel Walls, wife of dentist, Dr. Walls, organized the Cooper Orchestra, I was invited to join. She was a local piano teacher and a very good pianist. We had 12 or 13 members and met at her house once a week for practice. The Whittle Music Co. of Dallas would send her about two dozen copies of the sheet music of the newest popular songs. She would pick out four or five of the best. We would practice them and send the rest back. Soon we were invited, sometimes paid, to play at various events: a Ladies' Club Tea (where we played behind a fern screen and played appropriate softer music), a box supper, a theater production, a Merchants Fair, etc. There was not another orchestra like ours anywhere around. We were unique. Radio Station WFAA in Dallas invited us to play a one-hour concert over their radio in 1928, which we did.

COOPER ORCHESTRA
LEADER/Piano – Jewel Walls
Saxophone – Ray McClain
Trombone – Sam Leemon
Trombone – Wilbur Hart
Alto Horn – Cruz Mora
Bass Horn – T. P. Berry
Trumpet – Glen Robb
Trumpet – R. J. Brock
Bass Drum – unknown
Snare Drum – Mr. Bachelor
Clarinet – Buddy Kinard
Violin – Mildred Kinard
Violin – Mr. Andrews

We had a great time playing together.

At the same time I was playing with the Cooper Town Band every Saturday night in a concert on the lawn of the courthouse. Several other members of our orchestra also played in the Cooper Band.

I also was recruited by the director of the Honey Grove Band to fill in for a couple of weeks as a temporary first trumpet in their Friday night concerts.

Their main trumpet player was on vacation. Darrel Tait, who lived at Pecan Gap I believe, and played trumpet for Honey Grove, picked me up and took me to Honey Grove. After the concert, I spent the night at the director's house and they paid my bus fare to Cooper the next day.

One thing that impressed me the most about that trip was a bar of soap. When I took a bath after the concert, before going to bed, the soap for the bath was a fresh bar of Lifebuoy. I wasn't used to scented soap. I loved it. I still like it. It leaves a fresh feeling and the scent doesn't linger.

Darrel Tait, who took me to Honey Grove that day, had a misfortune in WW2. He was in the Navy and was washed overboard from the fantail of a Destroyer Escort during a storm in the Pacific. He was a good trumpet player and a very fine person.

We only lived about five blocks from Cooper High School. When I got to the seventh grade, our class was in a separate building than the eighth through eleventh grades. I usually walked home for lunch every day. One day Mother had fixed our lunches for school. I didn't think much about it. She sometimes did that when she planned not to be home at our lunchtime. When I got back from school about 4:15 pm (our school hours were from 8 am until 4 pm with thirty minutes out for lunch), there were a couple of cars parked in front of our house. Sylvia opened the door for me, having beaten me home.

"Mother wants to see you," she said.

"What for?" I asked, as I shed my book satchel. "Where is she?"

"She's in her room."

"Is she sick?" I asked. I could tell from Sylvia's eyes and actions that something was up. I hoped that I hadn't done something I shouldn't.

"Just go on in," she said. I went in to Mother and Dad's bedroom. Mother was in bed. Lying next to her was a tiny ruddy faced baby.

"Glen, this is your new little sister," she said, as she stroked the little one's fine, dark hair.

"Sister! Where did you get her?" I asked in surprise.

"You're not that dumb," exclaimed Sylvia, who had followed me in. "She borned her while we were at school." I really hadn't noticed that Mother was pregnant. I just thought that she was getting a little fat.

"Well, what are you going to do with her?" I asked, not knowing what else to say.

"I'm going to keep her. Aren't you glad to see her?"

"Oh, sure," I said. Where you gonna put her?"

"Right here in my room. Dad's going to get her a little bed. That's where he is now," she answered.

"She sure is little," I said, bending over to take a closer look. "What's her name?"

"We'll name her later," she said. She was a cute baby and I soon learned to accept and be proud of my new little sister. The two ladies whose cars were out front were in the kitchen cleaning and starting preparation for our supper. I went to my room to think about what had just happened. The baby was soon named Dorothy Marie Robb.

Another thing that Dad did after Marie was born, was to buy Mother a new-fangled washing machine. Dad fixed a spot in the back yard on the west side of the house. He ran a line from the kitchen for electricity. The machine was constructed of a wooden tub on a frame of four legs. A motor was underneath. A gear connected a rotating device in the tub of hot water (heated in the iron wash pot in the yard or on the stove in the kitchen). The back and forth agitation of the hot water got the dirt out. Then the clothes were run through a wringer (part of the machine) into a tub of clean water to get the last of the soapsuds out. From there, it was back through the wringer into a tub of bluing water. Then back through the wringer to get the bluing water out. The clothes were then hung on the clothesline in our back yard. You had to be careful not to let your fingers, or whatever, get caught in the wringer, as it really hurt.

"Did Dad ever fix the lock on the lot gate, so 'Old Jersey' can't get to the clothes on the line?" I asked.

"I don't know but I hope so," answered Mother. I was often selected to help Mother with the washing.

On the corner of our house, next to the washing machine, I put up a basketball goal post. I think I used a small barrel hoop for the goal. Delbert was playing basketball at high school and I liked to practice. About ten feet from the goal was our storm cellar. Mother used it to store her canned fruit and vegetables. I can remember several times we all huddled in it until the danger of a cyclone was past. One did hit Cooper once and wrecked several houses in the east part of town and a Mr. Jones was killed.

I was shooting goals one day. Grandpa Robb was visiting us and was in the back yard smoking his pipe. In my mind I was playing an opposing team and we were tied at 9 and 9. Ten was to be the end of the game.

"Dinner's ready. Y'all come in," announced Mother, at the back door. Grandpa knocked the tobacco out of his pipe and started inside.

"Just a minute," I called. "I've got to put my side out." I dribbled the ball, looked back over my shoulder and shot the ball. I hadn't noticed that the door of the cellar was open. Instead of running over a closed door of the cellar, I plunged down the cellar steps. Grandpa rushed over to help me. Lucky for me, I only got a few scratches, but I did come out feeling stupid. I knew the door was open, but in my mind I was playing a close game at the high school gym.

"Instead of putting one side out, you put both sides in," laughed Grandpa. He teased me about that the rest of his life.

One day, I think it was spring, when I was about thirteen, Mr. Barker, a neighbor who lived across the street, hired me to help him with a steam bath. He believed it would be helpful with his arthritis. Going to a Hot Springs Resort was expensive. Mrs. Barker was out of town for about three weeks. For the bath: Mr. Barker, in his bathtub in his pajamas and a blanket over him, would have me place a layer of hot, boiled corn on the cob over the blanket. Since the room was hot, I would sit in the kitchen or on the front porch until he called, about twenty-five or thirty minutes. I'd come in and take enough corn off him to climb out and I would leave. He always paid me fifty cents before he started. Mrs. Barker soon came back and took over the hot job. I wonder what they did with all that corn on the cob? They didn't have chickens. Do you think they buttered and ate it?

Ever since I can remember Dad and Mother have taken us kids to a Baptist Sunday school and church. So when we moved to Cooper we did the same. Brother Kidd was the pastor. He also was my scoutmaster. A ritual of the Baptist church was to publically confess that Christ is our Savior and then to be baptized into membership of the local church. In Sunday school and hundreds of sermons, I had learned all the stories of the Bible: Adam & Eve, Noah, Abraham, Moses, Jesus, the disciples, etc. Cooper had about six or seven denominations of churches: Baptist, two Methodists, First Christian, Presbyterian and what some called the Holy Rollers. There were two families that were Catholic who had a priest come from Paris to hold services in their little church. When we first moved to Cooper in 1919 there was practically no cooperation between the different denominations. In fact, I think they preached against each other. Each had its own "Gospel" meetings. But with time and changes of preachers, they came to respect each other and finally built a "Union" tabernacle where they held cooperative meetings to bigger crowds and more well-known "outside" preachers.

The new tabernacle was open on three sides. Even so, on hot summer nights with no breeze, the crowds produced plenty of body heat. Most of the ladies had fancy hand fans imported from Japan (a nice Christmas present), or cheaper paper fans donated by the local funeral company. Gnats love sweaty people. As time passed, some of the churches had strategically placed electric fans in their auditoriums, which helped. (Later Wendell "Squatty" Darwin went into business in Cooper of providing water cooled window fan units that were a great improvement for homes, churches and businesses.) Our family went to a lot of these meetings, which lasted ten days to three weeks. Mother and Dad loved them. Besides the Bible preaching, it was an opportunity to see friends and the other people of the town. The singing was inspiring. Several men's quartets sometimes were featured. I remember two that were very good: The Echols Quartet and The Stamps Quartet. They drew overflow crowds when they appeared. At the end of each sermon, an invitation was extended for confessions or to place membership. My Sunday school teacher, a dear little older lady, had mentioned to me several times that I should choose to be a member of the church and be baptized. I thought that I should, but I didn't want to be the spectacle of 400 or 500 people. It would be embarrassing to me. I have never wanted to be in the "spotlight". I was fourteen years old and had resisted the urge to respond so far.

Then one night, after an eloquent sermon, the preacher offered the invitation and several responded. Then another song and a young couple went down to place their membership in one of the sponsoring churches. Then another song and this little old lady that was my Sunday school teacher, got up from her seat and went and talked briefly to a young girl a few years older than I. The young lady left her seat, went down to the front and gave her hand to the preacher. My "little lady" resumed her seat.

"One more time," announced the song leader. Another song was started. I knew that I ought to go down, but I decided, "Not tonight; some other time!" The song ended and I breathed a sigh of relief.

"Now we can go home," I thought, as I sat up straight in my seat.

"One more time," intoned the song leader.

"When's he gonna' stop?" I thought. Suddenly, my "dear little old lady" got up from her seat and headed my way.

"Oh Lord, here she comes!" I said to myself.

For once, I made a quick decision. I passed my "little old lady", went down and gave the preacher my hand. I was baptized the following Sunday at our Baptist Church. My "little old lady" smiled broadly when she saw me on Sunday.

"I was going to talk to you Wednesday night," she said.

"I know," I said. Sometimes, people need help in making decisions. Later she was my seventh grade teacher (still my "Sweet Little Old Lady").

In September of 1924, I had entered high school in the freshman class. I was just out of the seventh grade in "The Little Orphan Annie" building. We were the first freshman class in the new high school building. I was elected President of our class.

I remember that Miss Mary Fling was the new Latin teacher. She was the daughter of Dr. Fling, President of ETSTC. I thought she was beautiful. I think she was the reason why I took two years of Latin in high school. Latin has helped me with other languages. The third year I switched to Spanish. Miss Valine Hobbs was the teacher. Later when I was attending classes at "ET" I resumed taking Spanish (second year). The lapse in time was tough but after about three weeks, I remembered, saving me from taking 1st year over. Miss Valine Hobbs was also the teacher there.

As soon as I was sixteen on Nov. 16, 1926, I began urging Dad to let me learn to drive. Dad agreed that it was time. Delbert had been driving since he was sixteen. So one day Dad drove the car out to the edge of town where there likely would be no traffic. He turned the motor off and switched seats with me. I had watched him and others drive so much I thought I already knew how to drive. But Dad explained the whole operation to me just to be sure. In cars those days, you had a hand brake and a foot pedal brake. The latter and the clutch pedal were connected. To stop the car with the foot pedal with your right foot, you first had to depress the clutch pedal with your left foot, or the motor would die. At the same time you lowered the motor speed with the gas lever on the steering wheel. The emergency brake was just that. If the foot brake didn't work, like because of worn brake linings, then you grabbed and pulled back the emergency brake.

"Do you understand all that?" asked Dad.

"Yes, I think so," I replied.

"Okay. Start your motor and let's see. Take it slow. Gear shift in "low". Let your foot brake off as you let your clutch out, as you advance the gas lever just enough to move forward." Our car did have a self-starter, so I didn't have to get out and crank it. The first time I tried, the motor died. On the second try, I gave it too much gas and it backfired. The third time the motor wouldn't fire.

"It's flooded," said Dad. "Let the carburetor drain just a bit and try again. On the fourth try, everything worked perfectly and I drove on down to the end of the pavement, turned around and headed back toward the square. Everything was going well.

Suddenly, I noticed a man driving a wagon pulled by two mules, just starting to cross my street. I had the right of way, so he should hold up and let me pass. But he didn't. I don't think he saw me. Now, he was in the middle of the street. I was closing the distance between us fast. Dad, sitting beside me suddenly yelled:

"Put your brake on!"

"Which one?" I screamed.

"The foot brake!" he yelled. I couldn't believe the man in the wagon still didn't see us. I had cut the engine speed down, but we were still going about five miles an hour. I stomped on the foot pedal and my foot slipped off the brake and hit the floor.

"Pull your emergency brake on!" screamed Dad.

"Where is it?' I yelled as I felt for it with my right hand, while I froze my wide eyes on the wagon just inches away. Then: BAMM! Our car hit the back wheel of the wagon and pushed it about two feet and my motor died. I found the emergency brake and put it on.

We got out and checked for damage. There seemed to be none to either vehicle. The wagon driver, who was hard of hearing, didn't see us until he was already in the intersection. He figured we would slow down to let him get on through. We all apologized and Dad let me drive on home, slowly. I got a couple of more supervised practice drives with Dad and was let loose on my own.

In the spring of 1927, when the Delta County schools held their annual athletic and other competitions, I was involved in the spelling part of it. I was a junior in Cooper High School and George Stephens and I had just tied to win the written spelling contest. In the afternoon there was a parade of all the schools. The route was from our high school up to and around the square, then back to the high school grounds. It was late May and was a hot day. My class had finished the trip and been dismissed. So I started to go home and get ready for the oral spelling that night in the auditorium. I was entered to represent Cooper High School. As I was leaving the school ground, I passed along a long line of students, slowly moving to the finish spot. I, from force of habit, scanned the faces in line as I passed.

Suddenly, my eyes locked on those of a girl. She was looking, in surprise, at me. It was her! Her who? The girl I had met at a music lesson at Mrs. Berry's about four years earlier

"Hi!" I said, not knowing what else to say.

"Hello," she said, as she smiled and I slowed down. But my feet kept walking and I looked back. She turned and watched as I went on.

"Golly!" I thought. "She's really pretty." I could have kicked myself for not stopping and talking to her. How many times, Dear Reader, have you felt like kicking yourself for letting an opportunity pass by? But I went on home to get ready for the oral spelling that night.

At the oral spelling that night, the auditorium was full. This was a popular event. Every school in the county, with grades through tenth, had students in the competition. As the school names were called out, the students competing went up on the stage and took their seats. When Cooper High was called, I went up and took a seat. Was I surprised! when a couple of names later they called out "Amy School" and the piano student I knew as Miss Dawson, arose from the audience, came up and took her seat, the second seat from me.

After the last of about fifteen schools was seated and the rules were explained by the caller, the spelling began. One after another of the contestants missed a word and left the stage. Then a boy between us missed a word and LaVerne (I remembered her name now), being next, spelled it correctly. A few misses later and Miss Dawson and I were the only ones left.

"Wow! It's she and I or me and her, whatever." I was excited! We went on spelling for a few minutes until I got the word "alright". I suddenly couldn't remember whether it was spelled with one or two 'L's". The audience was deathly quiet. I hesitated. The caller repeated the word.

I looked at the ceiling. I looked at LaVerne. She was looking at me, holding her breath. I took a stab at it.

"A-L-L-R-I-G-H-T," I said.

The caller repeated the word to LaVerne.

"A-L-R-I-G-H-T," she quickly said.

"That's correct," said the caller. "Miss Dawson, you are the 1927 oral spelling champion." Loud audience applause broke out.

I retreated off the stage, while LaVerne was given a plaque indicating her championship. The audience applauded again. I didn't see LaVerne again that night. That ended the county competition and she went back to Amy. I went back to being busy at the band and orchestra practice, but I couldn't get the girl off my mind. I didn't have a girlfriend. Miss Dawson seemed to be so different. I'd like to know more about her. I knew that Sylvia's friend Zebuline Ferguson had relatives in Amy and I asked Sylvia if one of them was the Dawson family.

"I don't know. Why do you want to know?"

"Oh, I was just curious. The girl that beat me in spelling lives out there." Sylvia wasn't fooled. She figured out right away that I was interested in Miss Dawson. Sylvia was smart. She was the most independent one of us five kids. She was her own person. She would have been as successful in a business, as she showed as a school teacher and Home Demonstration Agent.

"I'll find out for you," she said.

"That's alright. I was just curious." I didn't want to hire a detective. A girl as pretty as Miss Dawson probably already had a boyfriend. But bulldog, matchmaker Sis had the information for me within a week.

"LaVerne is Zebuline's cousin. She's fifteen and has had a few dates at school affairs with a couple of local boys. Her Dad is very strict with her. She has three younger sisters at home," she reported.

"She's fifteen? I'm sixteen, hmm. Well, thanks. As I said, I was just curious," I explained. But what could I do about it? I'd very much like to see her again. I worked as a soda skeet at Miller's Pharmacy while a regular clerk was on vacation. On Saturdays young people twelve to 16 or 17 years old liked to come to the square and just linger around or circulate around. They would maybe do a little shopping, stop in a drug store for an ice cream cone, a soda, etc. But one of the main reasons was to meet a boy or girlfriend.

The two or three Saturdays that I worked at the drug store soda fountain, I thought that Miss Dawson might stop in, but she didn't, nor did I see her circling the square. I was disappointed. There were four more weeks of school until vacation. I thought that I might never see Miss Dawson again.

One day I was talking to Curtis Robinson, a classmate of mine who lived out the Amy way.

"Curtis, you live out Amy way, don't you?" I asked.

"Yes," he said. "I live just beyond."

"Do you happen to know where the Dawson family lives?"

"Sure. I go right by their house on my way home," he said.

"Do you know LaVerne?" I asked.

"Yes. She's the oldest of the Dawson's four girls. Her parents have just recently let her start dating with the boys out there. I see her at school functions in Amy. She's pretty popular there. Do you know her?"

"Yes. I had met her before we were in the spelling thing together. I'd like to get in touch with her, but I don't know her address. "Would you drop a letter for LaVerne in their mailbox for me?" I asked.

"Sure. It won't be a problem. Glad to." I gave Curtis a letter next day to LaVerne, congratulating her on the spelling championship and asking if we might get together sometime soon. I included my address. Curtis put it in their mailbox and my wait began. Would she answer? I admitted it was a long shot.

1-2-3—4—5 weeks went by. I was beginning to feel rejected.

TGR outside Dallas Post Office

Chapter 3: 1927–1932

In Monday's mail I received a reply. She thanks me for my letter and said it would be nice to see me again, then added, "I'm pretty busy right now," and signed it LaVerne. That seemed like a rejection to me. My excitement took a dive. Then my eyes dropped to a postscript.

"As soon as I find a little more time I'll write and answer your questions and tell you more about myself—I'm at school right now practicing a play we're putting on a week from Friday." She initialed the P.S. "L.D."

Wow! Now I understood the indecision of the first part of the letter .The next weekend was the County Fair. Our Cooper band was playing for it. On opening day, Saturday, there was a big crowd. Many of the merchants had booths displaying their products: furniture, refrigerators, radios, new cars (Ford and Chevrolet), etc. During a break in our music, Sylvia came by and whispered to me: "Glen, LaVerne's here. If you want to see her, you'd better find her before she leaves." I found her. It was kind of awkward, but I think we both wanted to meet again. We hadn't seen each other since the spelling bee. She was with two girls and I had to get back to the band.

"Hi," I said. "I'm surprised to see you. How're things with you?"

"Oh. Hello! I'm surprised to see you, too. I'm sorry I haven't written you again, but I'll get around to it," she said.

"That's OK," I replied.

"What are you doing in your school? Are you a senior?" I asked.

"No. I'm a junior. I'll graduate from Amy next year."

"You're coming to Cooper High then?"

""Yes," she said—(a little lull, then)—"I mentioned in my letter we're putting on a play in two weeks. I'm in it. We're also having a box supper after the play. It's free. You're invited to come, if you like."

"Really? That would be nice. I'll try to come, especially if you're in the play. There's no 'spelling bee' is there?"

"No," she laughed. "I'm sorry about that."

"That's OK. Are you going to have any music for your affair?"

"No. It would be nice, but we can't have the expense."

"I also play in an orchestra. We play for things like that. I don't think we'd charge anything," I said. "You talk to your principal and I'll talk to our leader. Maybe we can work something out," I suggested.

"That would be wonderful," she said. Just at that moment I heard the bass drum go BOOM! BOOM! - A signal for the band to assemble to play again.

"I've got to run," I said. "I'm really glad to see you again."

"I'm glad to see you again," she said. I ran back to rejoin the band

Money for their school?—One of the aims for forming our Cooper Orchestra, was to play for things like that. I immediately contacted Mrs. Walls. She agreed and called the Amy school Principal. The result was that our orchestra was scheduled to play for the Amy school play and box supper. On the Friday night of the play and box supper at the Amy school, Dad let me have the car and I picked up R.J. Brock and another member of our orchestra. There was a good crowd when we got there. After we got ourselves together and were introduced, we played a concert of appropriate songs. Then the play was announced. I don't remember what the play was about, except that LaVerne was the heroine of it. Her name in the play was "Joy", and it lasted about 40 minutes. Then our orchestra played a couple of popular tunes while they got the box supper ready.

The way a box supper is carried out is as follows:

Most of the Mothers and/or their daughters prepared boxes of goodies (sandwiches, cookies, cakes, pies, fruit, etc.) or whatever would be a good snack for 3 or 4 people. LaVerne made a box. The Mothers had prepared plenty for everyone.

"Daddy, you be sure to buy my box. I want to invite Glen Robb. I want you to meet him," coaxed LaVerne.

"Alright, if it doesn't cost too much," he assured her. The auctioneer took the stage and held up the first box.

"Remember folks, the money goes to help our school. Who'll bid on this beautifully decorated box?" He sniffed it. "Boy! Does this smell good."

And so it went. When LaVerne's box was held up, her Dad started the bidding off at $20.00. Some boy kept raising the bid. LaVerne was worried. Finally the boy dropped out and Mr. Dawson bought her box for $40.00. Then LaVerne came over and took me over to meet her Dad and share the box of food she'd prepared. Mr. Dawson seemed a very nice man. He asked me how I was doing in school, what my family was like, what I planned to do after I graduated from high school, etc. I found him easy to talk to. He not only was a farmer, but was a contractor who had built several houses in Cooper. Mr. Dawson excused himself after about 15 minutes and LaVerne and I learned a lot about each other. All too soon the affair broke up and everyone began to leave. Since neither of us had telephones, she promised to write again and I promised to do the same.

I wrote her a letter the following week and soon received a letter in reply. Then school was out and I made a date to come to her house on a Saturday afternoon. Dad had promised to let me have the car. On Saturday, when I went to see her, I parked the car on the road in front of her house. As I walked the 100 feet or so up to the house, I heard someone say:

"Here he comes."

LaVerne met me at the door and we took our seats in their living room. In just a few minutes, she took me into the other part of the house and introduced me to her Mother and her three younger sisters. Her Dad, she said, had gone to Cooper for some reason. Back in the living room, Sue, who was about five, kept coming into the living room to show me her new white boots and how she would jump out of them or to ask LaVerne a question (anything to look me over). Since it was a warm day, LaVerne suggested that we go and sit in the swing on the front porch where it was more private. We learned a lot more about each other, our families, friends, hobbies, etc. We had music in common. I learned about her cutting the neighbor kids' hair on the front porch regularly, helping her Dad a lot on the farm, picking cotton, etc. She also was teaching a couple of neighbor kids piano lessons. I had promised Dad I'd be home early, so in about two hours I said goodbye to LaVerne and her Mother and left I felt really thrilled driving home. I really liked LaVerne. She was my kind of girl!

A couple of weeks later, LaVerne wrote me of an afternoon party that she was invited to at the Sansing's house. They lived in the country near LaVerne. She asked if I would like to go with her. I gladly accepted and promised to pick her up in our car. It had rained for two or three days earlier but the roads were not too bad, I thought. I picked LaVerne up at her house in Amy and we set out. I didn't know the area but Laverne had the instructions on how to get there. We came to a turn-off of the main road (according to the instructions). The new road was narrow and muddy, but the car was alright as long as the wheels kept in the ruts in the middle of the road. We drove along for about 300 yards and here came a car meeting us. The only way to pass was for both cars to give up a rut and then both get back in the middle after the pass. The other car accomplished the maneuver and drove on. When I tried the same thing, my back wheel slid into the shallow ditch. When I tried revving up the motor and pulling it out, it just dug the wheel deeper in the sticky, black mud. I got out of the car to study the situation. I needed to give the wheel some traction. I gathered dead branches and rocks that I found and shoved them under the front of the wheel. I got back in the car and gunned the motor. It just threw all of it out behind and dug deeper.

"Your motor is getting hot, I think," said LaVerne. "Can I help in some way?"

"No. Don't get out in this mud. Let me see what's in the trunk," I said. I opened the trunk and peered inside; some old newspapers, an old pair or work pants, a jack and some tools. I stuffed the pants and the newspapers along with more rocks and wood under the sunken wheel.

"That better be enough," I said as I got back in the car.

"Should I get out to make the car lighter?" asked LaVerne.

"No. Let me try this once more," I answered. I started the motor, put it in low, said a prayer and revved up the motor to a high pitch. The car shuddered, slipped a little sideways and suddenly lurched forward back into the middle of the road, just as the hot motor blew the radiator cap off and steam and hot water gushed out of the radiator. The clattering motor died.

"Oh, Lord!" I moaned. "What's gonna happen next? I'm sorry this is happening to you, LaVerne."

"I've been with my Dad when a motor gets hot. The motor will be alright when it cools down a little but I think most of the water boiled out. You'll have to put more water in the radiator before you start it again," she advised.

"You're right. I can't run the risk of ruining the motor." I looked around and spotted a house that we had passed.

"You just sit here. I'm going to see if they will loan me a bucket and some water. I'll be right back." I went up to the house. They gladly supplied the bucket and water. When the motor has cooled enough and the radiator filled, I stepped on the starter and it fired right off. I returned the bucket and thanked the lady and we drove on to the party. We were late, and after I cleaned my shoes, we had a good time; sang songs, ate ice cream and sodas, etc. The party lasted until 6:30 and I took LaVerne home. We were lucky that we didn't meet a car going out. I really enjoyed being with LaVerne. She was liked by everyone and was a lot of fun.

1927 was a busy year for me. Delbert had graduated in 1924 and was working at Brown Cracker and Candy Co. in Dallas. Sylvia graduated from Cooper High School in May of 1927. Homer Ray was thirteen and soon to be in high school Marie was almost three and fast bringing up the rear. I continued having dates with LaVerne every two weeks and she had a few dates with others. I was still playing in the Cooper band and with Jewel Wall's Cooper Orchestra. In the summer of 1927, our Cooper band leader, Irl Rrons, left to take a job in a larger town. Eddie Black, an actor and musician from New York, was in Cooper. He was married to the daughter of Mr. and Mrs. Culp who lived west of town. The city hired him to conduct the summer concerts on the courthouse square. Being an actor as well as a good musician, he was doing a very good job (an exciting style), until in the middle of the Summer he received a telegram from New York City to report for an acting job. I was asked to direct the band for the remaining summer concerts (four or five weeks), which I did, apparently satisfactorily. As a result of the experience, I was offered the job as band director of the Detroit, Texas band at a salary of $60.00 per month. Since I had already planned to finish school and go to college, I thanked them and declined. I was also very busy in the latter part of 1927. September began my senior year in high school. I was president of my senior class. I had also been president of our freshman class. We put on a class play and had a couple of social functions. Our senior class of about sixty students was a great bunch. We all graduated together in May, 1928. J. H. Newton was our Superintendent, R.L. Stevenson was our Principal and Miss Gertrude Perkins was our teacher class sponsor. I am proud to have graduated from Cooper High School.

As 1928 rolled on, I was even busier. After graduating in May, my friend R.J. Brock, and I were recruited to play our trumpets in the 144th Infantry Band from Greenville, Texas in their summer encampment at Palacios, Texas down on the coast of the Gulf of Mexico. Since I was only seventeen, they had to get special permission from the National Guard and my Dad's signature, which they did; the same with R.J. In the encampment, the band didn't have to do all the maneuvers, gun drills, etc. that the regular infantry did, but we did plenty of marching with them and had to learn the marching while playing during drills. The camp lasted two weeks. R.J. and I were housed in a tent with two other guys. Marc Williams, the "Crooning Cowboy" of Dallas radio station KRLD was in the tent next to ours. He had his ukulele with him. He was a real friendly guy.

This event happened about two days after our arrival in camp: I came back from dinner at the chow hall to find my cot ruined; split down the middle. Someone had switched cots with me. The Supply Dept. was closed for the day. I had to sleep on the floor that night. Next morning I was able to get it exchanged for a good one. One of the other guys in our tent said that a big guy in a nearby tent had been complaining of a rip in his cot. Since I had a replacement, I didn't check into it, but when I saw him he looked awfully guilty. I learned later his name was Denby.

SKIP FORWARD: About three years later, I boarded a street car in Oak Cliff, a suburb of Dallas. (I was working in the Post Office, and didn't have a car.) There, operating the streetcar was Mr. Denby. I think he recognized me for he took a second glance. When he stopped for a red light, I moved up to the seat just behind him. He noticed, looked at me and smiled.

"Hi," I said. "Aren't you Denby? Weren't you at the 144ᵗʰ Army encampment at Palacios, three years ago?" His smile faded.

"Yes, I was, and I remember you. I took your cot, didn't I? Someone had taken mine and left the ripped one. The supply office was closed. I apologize for that. I felt bad when I learned it wasn't a vacant one. But I'm glad to see you and apologize," he said. He seemed sincere.

"Well, that's alright. I accept your apology. Do you live in Oak Cliff," I asked.

"Yes, I live out in Trinity Heights, farther out. How about you?"

"I live on Ewing St, here. I work at the Young Street Post Office," I said.

The light changed to green. He rang his bell and prepared to go. "I'm glad to see you, Robb. I'll probably see you again."

"Sure," I said. "Take care." I moved back to my former seat. I did occasionally ride his car. I learned that he is married now and has a little girl.

In Dec. of 1927, the one regular letter carrier for the Cooper post office, Howard Barrett, got sick with the flu at the beginning of Christmas mail rush. The mail was heavy. The office didn't have a substitute. Their regular substitute had just recently transferred to Washington State. T.P. Berry, my former piano teacher's husband and the tuba player in our Cooper Orchestra, was the Asst. Postmaster. They needed a carrier real fast. T.P. recommended me and I was hired. Since I was only seventeen, they had to get a quick OK from the Post Master General in Washington D.C., which Mr. Rattan, the Postmaster did (paper OK followed). It was a Republican Administration in Washington and Mr. Rattan, and family, were Republicans. One clerk split his time in the office and also carried mail to the business district. The rural carriers delivered mail close-in on their way out of town. Some customers got their mail in the lobby boxes. Mr. Barrett, when well, delivered to the rest of town. So I started my first day in the postal service at 8 am (I think it was Dec. 22, 1927)—with a full pouch of Christmas cards and letters. I knew the town well, but I had never paid much attention to the street numbers of the outer streets. Some streets didn't have street signs. Some houses didn't have numbers displayed and some that did were hard to find. Mail that came just addressed to "Cooper, Texas", and mail addressed to people who had moved was a problem. Howard Barrett had been delivering mail in Cooper for many years and knew all of this perfectly. Then there were DOGS! A new mail carrier was an invasion of their territory. It wasn't this day, but I was later bitten by a little dog on that route and later in Dallas by a big dog that pinned me up behind a screen door. I'm leery of strange dogs. Size doesn't matter. At lunch time, I was behind on my route, but not by very much. Then, as the afternoon wore on, I could see that I wasn't going to finish in eight hours. By quitting time I had just delivered my first pouch full. The rest of the mail was in a relay box I had a key to. I felt that delivering all the days mail was a must. There would probably be even more tomorrow. I trudged on with the mail from the relay box. Darkness comes early in late Dec. At 6 pm, when I still had half a pouch full of mail to deliver, I went back to the Post Office and found a flashlight. T.P. Berry was still in the office. "Glen, I can see you're tired. Don't worry if you can't deliver all of it today. Knock it off at 8 o'clock. That'll be four hours overtime. We'll just put it with tomorrow's mail." That's what I did. With the flashlight I delivered mail until 7:50, then, headed for the post office. I checked my time out at 8 pm. Only the janitor was there then. I did better the next day and the next, etc. Mr. Barrett came back to work in about ten days. Mr. Rattan kept me on the payroll at 65 cents per hour through 1928, subbing for vacations and illnesses.

Sylvia and two other girls from Cooper were driving to Commerce, Texas, a distance of about eighteen miles, to attend East Texas State Teachers College. I joined them for the fall term of 1928 and the spring term of 1929. At long last I was a college freshman. One day, I just happened to be passing the college auditorium. I faintly heard music coming from inside. Out of curiosity I peeked inside the darkened auditorium. It was empty, except for a girl, down in front, playing a pipe organ. A single light highlighted the scene around her. It was the most beautiful sound I have ever heard. I was enthralled. I slipped in and sat on the back row of seats until she shut down the organ, turned off the light and left. I can still feel the thrill of that moment when I think of it again.

In February of 1929, I drove our car to Dallas to take the Post Office Civil Services exam for clerk in the Dallas office. It was on a Thursday. Delbert met me at White Rock Lake, since I didn't know the Dallas streets. I took the Post Office exam the next day at the main post office in downtown Dallas. I received my grade of 92.6 in the mail in about two weeks. Not bad out of about sixty who took the exam. I was third on the new list. I set about waiting for a call to Dallas.

In March of 1929, while waiting to hear from the P.O. in Dallas, I took a job as the Western Union boy at the railroad station in Cooper. The pay was $30.00 per month. Later that month I received notice to report to the main post office in Dallas. I took a Red Ball bus (I think it was a Thursday) and Delbert picked me up at the White Rock bus stop. I spent the night with him and his roommate, Clay Davis, who also worked at the Brown Cracker & Candy Co. The next morning Delbert went with me to check in at the main

P.O. building at Main and Ervay Streets. Bruce Luna was the postmaster. I was assigned to work at the Young Street Station. Delbert left me after making sure that I knew how to find his apartment when I got off work. I then went to Young Street Station. After checking in, I didn't have to wait long in the swing room before I was called. Since I was new, they put me on the "pickup" table, where I stood with five or six others placing letters onto a moving belt that carried them to a machine that cancelled the stamp and lined them up. We on the "pickup" separated the long and short letters. From the cancelling machine, the letters were carried to be worked to their proper destinations. It was Friday, the busiest mail day of the week. Businesses mail a lot of mail to be received early the next week. They kept me on the pickup table all day. I did get a lunch break (off the clock), and two rest breaks (on the clock).I worked 10 hours that first day, all on the pickup table.

I was numb and groggy when I finally rang off the clock and headed to Oak Cliff on the street car to where Delbert and Clay lived. The street car operator let me off at the right street and I started walking down looking for Delbert's apartment. It was about 9:30 and already dark. I remembered that they lived in the first block and on the left side. As I walked along I couldn't read the house number it was so dark. A streetlight on the corner was no help. I didn't have a flashlight. Most of the houses had a light somewhere but that didn't help, either. Not even a porch light was visible. I was getting worried. I'd have to knock on doors until I found the right one. I walked almost the entire block (a long block, too) of one story houses. As I doubled back, a light came on in one of the houses that I had just passed. I quickly retraced my steps. The curtain on the window was just half closed. A man was sitting in a chair reading a paper. I couldn't see his face for the newspaper. Then, as he lowered the paper, apparently to say something to someone else in the room, I saw his face. It was Clay. What a relief. I quickly went up and rang the doorbell.

"Where've you been?" demanded Delbert, as I entered.

"I've been workin'," I answered as I dropped into a chair. "I just got off. I worked ten hours. Boy, am I tired!"

"We've been worried about you. We've been lookin' for you since 6 o'clock. Have you had dinner yet?"

"No. I came here as soon as I got off."

"Well, we haven't either. Let's go get something to eat and plan what you want to do next," suggested Delbert. So we did. We went to a little café on Jefferson Ave.

In Aug 1929, Delbert and I decided to go with Kohlstrom, a friend of his from B.C. & C. Co., to visit his folks in Kansas City. We would share travel expenses. Clay had other plans. It was a holiday weekend and I wouldn't lose much time at the P.O. Kohlstrom and Delbert took a few days of vacation. We went in Delbert's car. We stopped in Oklahoma City to see our Uncle Butler, Aunt Annie French and family. It just happened that Uncle Buster had an interest in an oil well that was being brought "in" early the next morning. It was likely to be a "gusher", 20,000 gallons or so a day. We put off our departure to Kansas City to witness this spectacular even. Not much sleep that night. We got up and were at the well location by 5 am. It was supposed to be "brought in" around 7 am. but when seven arrived, it was cloudy and threatening light rain and possible lightening. The possibility of it being set afire if it was a gusher was too high. They decided to wait until it had cleared more. We sat around all morning, along with 40 or 50 people, waiting for the sky to clear. Finally the clouds drifted away enough and the crew decided to risk it. They had set the cap about four feet above the deck. There was a total silence from the crowd as the crew removed the plug. A hiss, a rumble and a shower of mud and dirty water shot from the well into a slag pool. Then the rich, black oil followed. Quickly the crew shut the well down. The cap held. It didn't BLOW! There was another sigh of relief from Uncle Butler and the other owners and a half sigh of disappointment from the newspaper photographers and others, who were hoping for a gusher. To accumulate the plot of land to drill the well on, there was one landowner who refused to sign. It would be red-headed Butler French who saved the day. Butler had been in the oil business for years and was a great salesman. The other owners offered Butler 15% royalties if he could sign the old fellow up. Uncle Butler agreed to try. He went out to see the old fellow. I don't know how he did it, but the man liked Butler from the start, as nearly everyone else did. Butler came back with a signed lease. I wasn't surprised when I heard the story. I know all of the kids loved him. He used to get all of us kids in his big 1928 Cole touring car and take us for ice cream or soda pop. We visited the French Family (kids: Gadie, Herschel, Pauline, and Olivia) several times in the early days. Aunt Annie was our Dad's sister. She lived to be 103 years old.

BACK TO OUR TRIP TO KANSAS CITY: We left Oklahoma City about two pm. and headed for Kansas City. We planned to stay at Kolstrom's parent's house that night. However, with our late start we spent the night in Tulsa, Oklahoma We drove to Kansas City the next day. Kohlstrom's parents were happy to see us. They lived as caretakers of the big three-story residence of the Loose family who owned Brown Cracker & Candy Co. They no longer used it as their principle residence. It was still ornately furnished. There was even a large pipe organ on the first floor whose pipes went up to a high ceiling. Kohlstrom's Dad gave us a grand tour of the huge house the next day and I got the chance to play on a pipe organ for the first time. It was a delightful experience. Kohlstrom's parents lived in a separate house on the large lot. We stayed two days in Kansas City. Kohlstrom took us around to see the city the next day and his mother fed us sumptuously with her delicious Swedish meals. I remember one dish called "col darmer" (my spelling), that I loved. It consisted of boiled cabbage, meat and fresh vegetables. Since we were all getting short of money and needed to get back to work, we left early on the third day for Dallas. We choose to go back a different route. We went back through the piney woods of Western Arkansas and Eastern Texas. It was already dark as we were going through Arkansas, northeast of Texarkana, when we suddenly felt a bump, bump, bump of a flat tire. Delbert was driving. He pulled over to the side of the road and stopped.

"Damn!" he exclaimed. "I must have picked up a nail."

"I hope you have a spare," remarked Kohlstrom.

"No, I don't, but I've got the patching." It was black dark! We hadn't seen another car for a long time.

"How're you gonna see to fix it? It feels like it's on the left back wheel. The headlights don't shine back there," I said. We were outside, standing there looking at the barely visible flat tire.

"Have you got a flare or flashlight?" asked Kohlstrom.

"Yes. In the trunk," said Delbert. He opened the trunk and felt around inside. "Tough luck! There's nothing in here but the jack and a pump. I must have left the flare out when I cleaned the car," he moaned as he slammed the trunk cover down.

"If we could build a little fire from dry branches or something, we could have enough light," suggested Kohlstrom.

"Who can see dry branches in these woods, as dark as it is?" asked Delbert.

"Well, if you've got a match, you can burn this old straw hat of mine. Summer's about over anyway," I volunteered.

"I have matches," said Delbert. "The only time I can think of that I'm glad I smoke." They both agreed to burn their straw hats. So with Delbert striking a match to my straw hat, we started a small fire that made enough light to take the tire off and patch the inner tube by the light of the headlights. We finished by putting the tire back on and pumping it up by the light of the other burning hats. When it was all done, we put out the embers of the fire and left. We got into Dallas about two am, tired and having a good trip.

I stayed with Delbert and Clay for a week. I didn't see much of them since our working hours were different. I decided to rent my own room somewhere. I felt that I was crowding them. I learned at work that Mrs. Simmons, a widow whose former husband was a postal employee, had a room for rent. I contacted her and she rented me the room. It was in Oak Cliff and on a street car line that would take me straight to work. So I moved there in April, 1929. She had a piano in the living room that I enjoyed trying to play by ear. On Sept.1, 1929 I enrolled at SMU, since my work at the Post Office was only four to six hours, at best, and all in the late afternoon and evenings. I took a full course of 4 subjects in pre-architecture. All of my classes were in the morning. So at the end of the month, I moved across town to rent a room in a two-story house on University Ave. My roommate was Wamba Stell, a boy from Cooper, who had graduated in Sylvia's High School class. In February of 1930 there was a record cold spell with ice and snow. One day it was 3° below zero. As I came out to attend a class, I slipped and fell, striking the back of my head on the sidewalk. I blame all of my later mistakes on that.

In Oct. 1929, the stock market "crashed" in New York. It didn't affect my job, school or other activities right away, but at the end of my first term Wamba and I both found cheaper lodging. I rented a room from a couple at the corner of University Avenue and Snider Plaza. I shared the room with another student named Charles. I can't remember much about him. He wasn't in any of my classes and at different hours. So, we didn't see much of each other except that we both slept in the double bed in the room. Wamba Stell later died of a stroke while walking down the street. He was still in SMU at the time. Carter Henson, one of my high school classmates, was visiting his sister, Erma, that summer. She was married to a fellow who ran a filling station across the street from where I was living. Carter was working at the station that summer. We enjoyed being friends again and exploring things around Dallas in our spare time. He had a car and I rode back and forth to Cooper with him a few times. While at SMU I played in the Mustang band for the football games, etc. We also made a recording of our playing. Cy Barcus was our director. Louie Long was our most noted football player that year. It was a very busy grind for me. My Post Office bosses were very understanding to allow me to be a bit late as they had plenty of subs, a result of the "depression" getting worse. The stock market "crash" was a shock to me, but it didn't affect my hours at the post office until much later, when the Post Office Department started economizing. My hours were cut in half or worse. Carl Bacon, one of our substitutes, thought that it was just the time to get into the stock market. He bought a van and equipped it with a wireless radio and set about speculating in the commodities market. He spent most of his time, after the P.O. hours, in the van parked nearby working the market all the summer of 1930 and part of the next year. Most of us were pulling for him to make it big. He finally gave it up after a year of win/lose, win/lose and sold his van. It was just too much of a hassle. I don't think he made much or lost much either. Fortunes were made and still are in times like that, but rare for amateurs.

One day in the spring of 1930, when I was attending SMU, I was on a street car on my way to downtown. The car line went close by Brown Cracker & Candy Co. The car was crowded and I was standing holding onto a strap. A very pretty young lady boarded and took up a space next to me. After a few minutes, she spoke.

"You are Delbert's brother, aren't you?" she asked me.

"Yes, I am," I replied, very much surprised.

"I'm Beatrice Brewer. I work with Delbert at Brown's. He mentioned that you were in Dallas now," she said.

Yes, I am. I'm going to SMU and working at the post office. I'm glad to meet you," I answered. Before we could say more, the street car conductor called out a stop and the car began to slow down.

"I've got to get off here," she said. "I'm glad to meet you."

"Thank you," I replied. "I hope to see you again." She got off, along with several others. I was very impressed. Delbert had often mentioned a girl named "Bea" as his girlfriend. Well, Delbert was a handsome young man. It made sense. On December 23rd of that year (1930), Delbert and Beatrice were married. I gave them a radio console as a wedding present.

I had never seen a movie until we moved to Cooper. There, Henry Sparks and his family, Earl and Bryan (Dub) Sparks, and later Bryan's wife, Lucille, operated two theaters (picture shows). The "Lyric" was on the west side of the square, and the "Grand" on the north side. I saw many picture shows there as I grew up, starring Tom Mix, Art Accord, Hoot Gibson in Westerns and Charlie Chaplin, Harrold Lloyd in comedies, for 10 or 15 cents. Later in 1929, when I went to live in Dallas, there were three elegant theaters on Upper Elm Street; the Melba, the Majestic, and the Palace. Darrold Deason, one of my high school friends, and a member of my class, was the assistant manager of the Melba. He would wave me on in free when he saw me. Even in high school, I had admired Darrold for his serious and gentlemanly character. I was not surprised that he was succeeding in the theater business. The Majestic and the Palace both had good stage shows. The best, I thought, was the Palace. Besides the gorgeous interior with a big stage and orchestra pit, there was a beautiful, gleaming white Wurlitzer pipe organ that would arise in the spotlight from the darkened orchestra pit. Sitting at the organ dressed in a white suit, would be the organist playing a short introductory chorus. After standing and greeting the cheering audience, he would sit down and play a program of about thirty minutes. He would then reverse his entrance as the spotlight, he and the organ disappeared back into the darkness, and the picture for the evening would appear on the screen. All this for about 40 cents. I couldn't get enough of it. How I would love to play like that!!

At the end of my second term at SMU the economic situation continued to decline and our sub time at the Post Office kept shrinking. I decided I couldn't afford SMU for the present, so I moved back across town to rent a space in Mrs. Murphy's boarding house on Ewing Street. Ray Moore and George Deal, two of my post office buddies, both subs, lived in Oak Cliff. It was just off Jefferson Ave. A street car line ran a block away that crossed the viaduct and passed within a block of Young Street Station where I worked. George and Ray had recommended it as a good economical place. The rent included breakfast and dinner. There was a good cafeteria on the second floor of Young Street Station that we used when working. There was a drug store on the corner near our residence that served ready-made sandwiches (egg salad, pimento cheese, etc.), milkshakes and sodas. We (Ray, George and I) had charge accounts there and paid them at the end of each month. At the Murphy's, my "space" was a long enclosed back porch on the second floor. Three other guys also slept on the porch. Ray and George occupied a room adjacent. On the first floor was a large living room for all and a dining room where we were served meals. I was still making enough at the P.O. to pay my rent and have a clothing account downtown at E.M. Kahn's. It was full dress on Sundays at church or on dates. Work was casual, but if your work required window work like selling stamps, postal savings, etc. you had to wear a tie. Slacks were OK; Jeans hadn't been invented. And then the Post Office Department in Washington DC issued a directive: Cut costs! We subs were cut to 2 to 4 hours a day. Regulars were required to work overtime, if necessary. Only one person was cut off: Henry Parsons and his wife had been single and both working at the P.O. When they got married one of them had to resign. She resigned. Things for me and the rest of the subs quickly went bad. Our monthly checks didn't cover our expenses. During the worst part of 1931, I found myself one morning without any money or car tokens. I was too embarrassed to hit anyone up for a loan. Ray and George had already left for work. So I just struck out and walked across the two mile long viaduct over the Trinity River to work. I was a little late but only a few minutes. There was only a short time of work in the mornings anyway. I borrowed return tokens from Ray. It was still a week until payday (once a month) and I still had credit so I bought a new pair of shoes for Sunday and found a quarter for a shine on my other pair that needed it after that two mile walk. There was a "swing" room on the second floor where we waited until needed, usually a little time in the morning and again in the late afternoon when the businesses poured mail into the P.O. to be sent out. That was when we got most of our time on the clock, especially around the first of the month. Most of us just waited in the swing room when not called to work. To pass the time, there were newspapers and old magazines to read, games like checkers and bridge. Some of us organized a bridge tournament that lasted about two weeks.

There was no work on Sundays. Saturday and Mondays were light and we did other things. Ray, George and I took hikes into the country. We went to Lancaster, Tex (about six miles) to visit Ray's family. His Dad, Gene, was a retired baseball pitcher from the Pittsburg Pirates. His brother, Gene, Jr., was a very good outfielder currently with the Boston Braves. Ray had tried out as a catcher with the Dallas Steers. He was good, but decided to stay with the Post Office.

Ray Moore

We went swimming, played tennis and golf. We were joined in our activities by others including Cole Nance and George Deal's girlfriend, Opal, (they later married). We went to a baseball game in which Grover Cleveland Alexander pitched for Dallas. It turned out to be a bad day for him. Dallas lost. Sam Cook was a sub-clerk like me. He and his wife, Doris, had two little girls. They decided to rent out a room of their house to help on expenses. He offered to rent it to me. Sam had a car and I could ride back and forth to work with him. So, I moved to his house from Mrs. Murphy's boarding house. I liked living at the Cook's. They treated me like a member of their family. I stayed there until I married and moved, with LaVerne, into Mabel and Aubrey Martin's on Elgin Street out near Love Field Dallas in July, 1933.

More history about LaVerne and her parents: LaVerne's mother was named Lula Viola Acton before her marriage to Jim Dawson. It was Jim Dawson's second marriage and Lula's first. The Acton family came from Alabama. They owned a large area in the mountains outside of Montgomery where later huge deposits of coal were discovered. The mountains are named the Acton Mountains. It was shortly after the Actons sold the land that the coal was discovered. I believe there was a lawsuit to recover it for the Actons but the suit was unsuccessful. Mrs. Dawson and the girls went back to Montgomery in 1935 to visit their relatives for a three week visit. Bill Jones (a cousin) from Montgomery came and visited LaVerne and I in late 1935. Gladys LaVerne (Dawson) Robb was born on Sept. 1, 1912 on a farm in the community of Amy, about three miles north of Cooper, Tex. Her father, James Thomas Dawson, was a farmer and a contractor in the area of Cooper. LaVerne had three sisters; Shirley, Blanche and Sue. Blanche died of TB in 1941. LaVerne had half-brothers, Curtis and Noble Dawson, and a half-sister, Mable (Dawson) Martin. They were from Jim Dawson's first marriage. Their mother had died. LaVerne's Aunt Evelyn Cross (one of Lula's four sisters) and her large family lived in the Amy community. LaVerne grew up with lots of cousins to visit in her early days, which she did.

George Deal one summer took time off to go on a "Hobo" trip. He dressed in old clothes, put some supplies in a backpack and went down to the railroad switching area. Just as a freight train pulled out, he and a couple of others jumped into an open box car. He didn't know where he would end up. He just wanted the experience. He immediately got acquainted with the other hobos and they exchanged experiences. George said that he changed railroads several times and saw a lot of the country around the Midwest. He even rode the "rails" once. Since it was "bad" times, a lot of the railroads didn't try to put them off. He got as far as Des Moines, Iowa. He then headed back towards Dallas. It had been a ten day memorable trip for him. At that time the "Hobo's" of America held an annual get together in Iowa. They elected an annual "King" and "Queen". I don't know if they still do.

Another item about the Depression: Carol Byrd, one of my special delivery co-workers, got himself caught behind on paying his debts, like a lot of the rest of us. Carol was so frustrated with so many "duns" for payment that he sent them all a letter saying that on his greatly reduced income, he was going to pay them all off. Instead of paying each of them a small sum each month, he was going to pay all he could to one until it was all paid off. He would then pay the next one in line. If they didn't agree to his plan and kept threatening him he would cross them off his list. I never heard how his list came out but knowing Carol. I'm sure he finally paid them all off, as I finally did, also. Finally the postmaster allowed the clerk subs to join the day shift of special delivery messengers. But we had to have a car. George, Ray and I and several subs scrambled to buy one. I bought a used, black Oldsmobile. We carried the special delivery letters and packages that came in for the delivery in the early morning on routes to all sections of the city including businesses downtown. We also carried routes going out at 11 am and 1 pm. The night crew took out the rest of the day and early night. The best routes (We earned 9 cents per letter, more for packages) were in the mornings and I had to get up early. That would be tough since I have always been a night owl. I used to hide my alarm clock under my bed to help me get awake while I hunted for it to shut it off. Sam also shot specials and had his own schedule, so I couldn't depend on him to wake me up. The extra money was a god-send to me as now I could start paying off my behind bills: rent, store, drugstore, restaurant, etc. and it was easier to go to Cooper and Commerce to see LaVerne. I went almost every weekend. Gas was cheap, 12–15¢ per gallon.

I had continued writing to LaVerne every week and Delbert and I had gone home in his car about every two weeks. LaVerne graduated from high school in 1930 and immediately entered ETSTC. Her parents moved to Commerce so she could still live at home. LaVerne joined a student girls club, the Las Choisites. She was active in club affairs. She had a lot of friends, both girls and boys. She was popular. In her senior year she was promoted as a beauty queen, only to come in second to Mary Lowery, a girl from Cooper, who was sponsored by a rival club. But LaVerne was the most beautiful! I knew that LaVerne was popular in college and had boyfriends there. One of her friends, Dale Drake, was a popular singer and sang for the local band. I was jealous, but what could I do? I went to see her every time I was in Cooper. Dad would always let me have his car to go see her. She always canceled any date, etc., when I came down. She was still #1 with me. One Sunday night, after having been to see LaVerne earlier, I went back to Cooper to say goodbye to my parents and pick up a friend, Piggy Knowles, who was also a P.O. sub. He had come down with me to see a girlfriend of his who lived in Cooper. By the time we got started back to Dallas, it was 11 pm. The highway from Cooper to Greenville was only two lanes wide through gently rolling country, one hill after another. Just before we got to the outskirts of Greenville, I ran out of gas. We were in my Olds. And it wasn't lightweight. I knew there was a gas station at the edge of Greenville. We could see the lights of Greenville but couldn't tell just how far away it was.

"What do you think?" I asked, as I had just tried for the third time to get the motor started again.

"I donno." He said. "We're out of gas, for sure."

"I think there's a gas station just ahead. If it wasn't for this hill in front, we would see the light at it."

"Well, this hill's not much. We can just push the car up to the top and let it coast downhill into the station," suggested Piggy.

"Sure," I agreed. "It's lucky we got this close." We got out and while I guided the car and pushed, and Piggy put his shoulder (he weighed about 190 pounds) to the back and pushed. We wrestled the car up the hill. As we got to the top of the hill, there was no light ahead. There was another hill, about as high as the first.

"Darn!" I said. "That was a workout!"

"Yeah!" he said, wiping his brow. "If you've got a gas can, it would be easier to just walk over this hill and bring a can full back. Do you have a can?"

"I should have," I said. I opened the trunk and looked. There was no can there. This was my first car. I hadn't thought to check for things like that when I bought the car.

"Well, I don't see any other way than to push this baby to the top of that next hill, so let's get going," opined Pig. We had rested a bit, so we put our muscles to the job and finally got to the top of the second hill. But there was no light!

"Dang! There's no light! Are we on the wrong road?" I was "give out," wet with sweat and disgusted. "I've been over this road a thousand times. I was sure that gas station was right there!" I pointed at the blackness in front. Piggy was in better shape than I was, having been a football player in high school. For some reason, he began to see the humor of the situation.

"I don't know this road like you do. I don't expect a gas station over each hill. At least it can't be much further. I'm getting a good workout, like football practice," said Pig.

"I'm glad you're enjoying it. Would you like to push it up the hill by yourself?" I answered.

"Under other circumstances I might try it."

"Well, let's try this once more. If there's no station I'm for just sleepin' in the car 'till daybreak. This time, when we roll down this hill we're on, we'll let the car roll as far up the next—there better not be another hill. There has to be a gas station," I said.

"OK. Let's get crackin'," agreed Piggy. We gave the car a hefty shove, jumped in and it coasted down the hill and about a third of the way up the next one with us pushing until it stopped. But the third hill was not quite as high as the first two and we struggled until we got to the top. Still no light!!

"I'll be a #*@+%#*," I yelled. "I give up! We might as well sleep in the car," I moaned. Piggy thought it was all so funny. He was doubled over laughing.

"Look on the bright side, Tige," he said, "It'll be a good thing to tell our grandkids."

"It'll be daylight in about 3½ hours. Don't you think we should wait 'til then so we can see where we are?" I suggested.

"I agree. It won't be the first time I've slept in a car."

"Well, this hill is awfully windy and cold. Let's roll back down to the bottom of this hill before we settle down to sleep," I suggested.

"I agree," said Piggy. We started the car rolling down the hill, jumped in and it rolled to a stop at the bottom, just in front of a Gulf filling station, closed up for the night. We weren't surprised. We were astonished! We both jumped out and I banged on the door of the station until a light came on above the station. In a couple of minutes the owner sleepily appeared, not very pleased at his interrupted sleep.

"What do you want," he demanded.

"Please, Sir, can you sell us some gas. We've pushed this car over three hills. We're exhausted," I pleaded.

"I can see you don't look too good. But I'm tired of you night owls waking me up in the middle of the night. I took my bell off, now you are ruinin' my door bangin' on it. How much do you want?"

"Give me ten gallons. I'll pay you 20¢ a gallon," I said.

"I guess that's fair," he said, "but you kids should go straight home." And we did. We went straight home to Dallas.

Gusher coming in

BLACK GOLD: On Aug. 28, 1859, oil was struck at 70 feet down in Oil Creek, Pa (near Titusville) in a well being drilled for water. "What's that?" asked Edwin Drake, the surprised driller. It was the world's first commercial oil well. Drake didn't profit from it. He was cut out. (From PPs 131-132 "Strange Stories" by Reader's Digest.) In 1859-1866 "Tol" Tolbert brought in the first Texas oil well in Melrose, Texas. The Civil War intervened to prevent his drilling in 1859. He couldn't get the materials to drill. He did bring in his first well in 1866 at a depth of 106 feet. (See "Strange Stories" in R.D.). On Jan 10, 1901 at Beaumont, Texas, Anthony Lucas, engineer, and Andrew Mellon, a banker, hired Al, Jim and Curt Hamill, experienced drillers. They drilled through sand until they hit rock. They drilled around rock but stopped for Christmas break. After Christmas, in Jan. they resumed drilling. At 1020 feet, the drill stuck. They pulled it out to replace the bit. As they began to lower it again, suddenly mud and water started rising, pushing the drill pipe with it. Then with an explosive roar, mud, air and debris shot into the air followed by a geyser of oil twice the height of the derrick, drenching all those near. People heard the explosion a mile away. It was an 80,000 barrel a day gusher. No one knew how to stop it. It roared and gushed for 9 days spewing nearly a million gallons of oil. Finally the Hamill brothers devised a way to cap it and did. Visiting Spindletop, for that's what the field was called, a Standard Oil official remarked: "Too big. Too Big! More oil here than needed to supply the world for the next century. Not for us." But he was wrong. A forest of oil derricks soon covered the area. A shantytown soon sprang up, and the oil boom was on.

That was 1901. In 1931, soon after I had bought my Oldsmobile and started shooting specials, there was a new oil field discovery near Jacksonville, in east Texas, with a rush of followers to develop it. Carol Byrd, who started work at the post office the same day that I did, was a friend. His sister was married to an oil worker who was working there. Carol decided to go down to Jacksonville and visit them and view the scene. He invited me to go along. We left after our first delivery of specials on a Saturday in his Ford. It was about eighty miles to Jacksonville. While driving, we had been discussing our cars and what we liked and disliked about them. He liked his Ford. I still had my Olds, but wasn't too fond of it.

"Why don't you try this Ford? I think you'll like it," he offered.

"OK," I agreed. We switched seats and I drove down the road. Soon I slowed down to give the driving back to him.

"Drive on awhile. I'll take a little nap," he said. "I didn't get much sleep last night."

"Sure," I agreed. "I like the feel of this car. It's so easy to handle." He settled down and I drove on. After a while, I looked over and he was sound asleep. In those days, there was no speed limit out between cities. I had been cruising along at about fifty miles an hour. Byrd had bragged that he had got his Ford up to 80 miles an hour. I had driven my Olds about 60 to 65 miles an hour and it had begun to vibrate. "I wonder if Byrd really got this baby up to 80," I mused. I pushed it up to 65. I took a quick look at Byrd. He was sound asleep. The little Ford was running smoothly. There appeared to be no cars up ahead in sight. I nudged the accelerator up to 68-72-75. Should I go up to 80, as Carol had said that he had? The motor was still purring faithfully. The telephone poles were zipping by back down the road. A little fearfully, I gave it more gas. 76-77-78. Should I do it? Suddenly I felt a slight vibration. I quickly let up on the gas. I slowed back down to 65, then 55. The little vibration had aroused Carol. He sat up and rubbed his eyes.

"Is it running OK?" he asked.

"Perfectly," I said. "You want to take over?" I asked.

"OK," he said. "I had a nice little nap." We switched seats and he drove on into Jacksonville. On the way, I told him of my getting his little Ford up to 78. It didn't seem to bother him. It bothered me later. I realized I shouldn't have endangered him and his car to an accident without his permission, even though, knowing Byrd. He most likely would have urged me onto 80. To date, seventy-eight is the fastest I've ever driven a car.

When we arrived in Jacksonville, we found a very busy scene. Lots of people were in the business district. We were directed to the oil field outside of town. It was the middle of the afternoon. It had recently rained and was a hot, muggy day. At the oil field, we found a large crowd of workers and other people. In an area close by there were a lot of tents of various sizes. Byrd knew that his Sister and her husband were living in a tent. They were routine campers. We soon found it. It was a good size. It was open and his Sister was sitting, reading a newspaper. She was surprised, but pleased to see us. We spent a couple of hours listening to her telling of the "strike" and their involvement in it. Soon her husband, Bud, arrived. He was dirty from the work and after greeting us, he rushed off to take a shower at the bath house built for the workers. When Bud came back, he suggested getting hamburgers and cokes for dinner. We agreed. With the crowds, it would be a long wait at a restaurant in town. Even the four or five "short order" places would be crowded, so Bud and I went for the "burgers" and left Byrd and Caroline to catch up on the family news. There were two lines at the order counter at the burger place as we entered. All the tables were full. We got in line with about five ahead of us. The noise was awful. We had to yell to be heard. The first guy in line ahead of us was an older bushy headed person. It seemed that he was ordering for several people. He had ordered cheese instead of the tomatoes and was protesting.

"We're out of cheese," explained the clerk.

"I'll take 'em," yelled #4 in front of me. He rushed down, paid for them and rushed out.

"I'll go someplace else," said the old guy. "My wife and I won't take those. She loves cheese." He left. We finally got our orders filled and rejoined Carol and Caroline. We really enjoyed the meal—two burgers, fried apple pie and a coke for each. After the meal, Bud took us on a tour of the well site. The crew that had replaced Bud's crew was busy with the drilling. It was a three crew, 24 hour operation. After the tour, we went back to the tent. Since Bud was on the early day crew, we all went to bed by 10 o'clock. Bud and Caroline had cots. Carol and I slept on the ground on throw rugs. We just slept in our clothes. In the morning, we got an early start for Dallas after a breakfast with Caroline at a different place, where we could get a table. It was a very interesting trip. We got back in time to take a 1 pm special route on Sunday. Since I wasn't scheduled for an early route, I didn't miss much revenue.

H. L. Hunt made it big in the Jacksonville boom and a very good friend of mine, Bill Beeman, became his accountant.

It seems I have always been a sports fan; Babe Ruth, and the Yankees, Jack Dempsey and Sully Montgomery in Boxing, Farmer Burns in wrestling, Knute and the "Flying wedge" in football, the Indianapolis 500, the storied Army-Navy football games, etc. It was all very exciting to me. I have been lucky to see in person two of our champions. In Dallas, during the late 1920s and early 30's, there was a lot of enthusiasm created by a professional girls' basketball team sponsored by the Employers Casualty Insurance Company. It was a member of a league along with teams from the Phillips Petroleum Company of Tulsa, Oklahoma, the Sun Oil Company, and a team from Mesquite, Texas. I followed the Employers Casualty teams mainly because of Babe Didrickson, She was already famous for her successes in golf, the Olympics, and any other physical thing that she tried to do. That was before she met and married the wrestler Zaharias. Babe worked for Employers Casualty somewhere in Dallas, but I wasn't sure where. The games were broadcast by a local station and I always listened, when I could, as well as reading the newspaper reports. It happened that I was on an early special delivery route one morning, when I stopped to deliver specials to Employers Casualty. I crowded into the elevator along with four or five others. A girl just ahead of me turned around to face me (and the door). It was "The Babe!" I was SO surprised! I recognized her from the pictures in the newspapers and I had read and listened to her exploits on the radio—and HERE SHE WAS! I could have touched her! She and a couple of others got off on the third floor.

I came back to earth. I had missed my stop on the second floor and rode on up to the top.

"Wasn't that Babe Didrickson who got off on the third floor?" I asked the elevator operator.

"Yes," he said. She works here. The mail room is on the second floor."

"Yes, I know," I said, still trying to take it all in.

A week or so later, I was on a special delivery route in Dallas. I was in a hurry to finish, so I could take off for Commerce to see LaVerne. It was about 4 pm and traffic was picking up. I was behind a new Chevrolet. At that point, there was a curve in the street. The Chevy suddenly slowed down. I put my foot on the brake to slow down, but my foot went straight to the floor. I grabbed for my emergency brake as I cut to the left to avoid him. I still hit and bent his left rear bumper as my car's front bumper tore into the back wheel of a gravel truck speeding around the curve from the opposite direction and crushed the front of my car. Traffic was backing up in both directions. A policeman appeared and took all of our statements, driver's license number, etc. I apologized to both the other drivers. The driver of the new Chevrolet was an older man. I felt sorry for him. It shook him up quite a bit. His young son, about fifteen, was with him. Later I got a bill from both of them and started paying them off, some each payday. My Olds was disabled and the car company that held my loan on it agreed to take it back, forgetting what I still owed on it. I had to get another car. My special delivery income was more than my clerk check. I found and bought a 1930 beige Ford sport roadster with a rumble seat. It was about eighteen months old.

One day in the fall of 1932, I was on my way to visit my parents in Cooper and LaVerne in Commerce. Homer Ray was with me. He had just graduated from high school and was working for the Brown Cracker & Candy Co. in Dallas. We were in my 1930 Ford roadster with the top down. We had just passed through Garland and were picking up speed again, when I looked up and saw a car slowing down at a crossing street that I was approaching. As he slowed down, I speeded up to get on through. But he has not seen me and instead of stopping (I had the right of way), he started on through. When I saw what he was doing, (I was too close to stop) I speeded up and tried to zip in front of him. I didn't quite make it, He hit my rear right wheel. It sent my car out of control, swerving to the right across the road, then back across the road into about a three foot ditch. My car turned a flip and landed back up on its wheels and against a telephone pole. The windshield was cleanly broken off. Quickly I jumped out on the right side and almost landed on top of Homer Ray, who was lying in the ditch. I helped him up and we dusted ourselves off. My new straw hat was found in the mud. Luckily, we both seemed to have escaped injury. The guy in the other car claimed that he didn't see me, and was sorry. We exchanged names and addresses. His car only got a bent bumper. He left and Homer Ray and I walked back into town. On the way, Homer Ray's back begun to hurt.

When we got into town we were directed to a doctor's office over a store. The doctor was out but was expected back any minute. Also waiting for him was a young boy and his dad. The boy, about eight, had a broken arm and was in a lot of pain. He didn't cry. I admired him for his grit. Finally, the doctor came and set the boy's arm. The doctor then examined Homer Ray's back. He didn't find anything wrong, except a possible sprain that he said would go away in a few days. We then went to a garage and arranged for my car to be picked up and repaired. That done, we caught the next bus back to Dallas

One night, I think it was late November and about 12:30 am, I was on my way home to Dallas. I had just left LaVerne in Commerce. The dull hum of my motor was lulling me to sleep. It was a cool night. I rolled up my left sleeve and put my arm down on the cold metal of the door frame. It didn't help much. I turned up the radio. It was irritating. I turned it back down and drove on. I was doing a steady 50—WHAM!! I woke up. I didn't realize I had been asleep. I was thrown violently against the steering wheel, as the car flew sideways and landed on its wheels in a four foot ditch. The motor died. I got out of the car. I didn't appear to be hurt. It was black dark, but I could see a white concrete culvert, about fourteen inches high that ran under the highway. That was what I had hit and landed in the ditch. I got back in and tried starting my motor. No dice! I'd have to get help in the morning. I started walking toward Royce City. I was wide awake now! It took me about 40 minutes to reach the city. As I walked into the business district, I was accosted by a policeman on a horse, and a growling dog. When I showed him my driver's license and told him my story, he escorted me to a small hotel, woke up the owner and I was given a room for the rest of the night. Next morning, I remembered that Dr. Constant, a veterinarian, formerly of Cooper and his family lived there. I knew Durward, their son, who was about my age, since we had been members of the Baptist church at the same time in Cooper. I wondered if Durward was still in Royce City. The doctor was listed in the phone book, so I called the house number. His Mother answered, and Durward was there. He came and picked me up and took me out to check on my car. It appeared that, when I hit the culvert, it had broken the housing to my transmission. A lot of oil had escaped. Everything else seemed to be OK. He then took me to a garage, who agreed to pick up and repair my car. I then called the Post Office in Dallas to advise them of my absence. It took the garage about five days to fix the car. In the meantime I spent a very enjoyable visit with Durward and the Constant family. I attended church with them, to a picnic and a movie. When my car was ready, I gave the garage a check for about $180. And I went back to Dallas to work. To cover the amount, I got an advance on my next post office check. I'd have to economize next month.

I was very interested in ballroom dancing. LaVerne was a good dancer and loved it. I wanted to learn how to dance well, too. Later, in 1932, I took some ballroom dance lessons. I answered the ad of a Dallas Dance Studio, three lessons for $50 I liked the teacher, a young, pretty girl. I hoped to be a better dance partner with LaVerne. I learned a few basic steps to the waltz and the fox-trot. The main thing that I learned was a good dancer knows a lot of different steps, at least six to eight for each dance. The fun is knowing how to change from one step to another smoothly. Each dance: waltz, fox-trot, cha-cha, rumba, tango, quick-step, etc. have their own unique steps. Until you learn a few steps for each, about all you can do is shuffle from one foot to the other. That's fun but like a milk-shake without the ice cream and strawberry flavor.

That same year, I helped Roy Cox, who was a post office employee at Young Street Station and a friend of mine, to promote ballroom dances for profit. He rented a large conference room on the twelfth floor of the second unit of the Santa Fe building on Commerce Street. Cleared of chairs it was an ideal place for dances. It had a stage and a balcony. Roy had been promoting dances for some time and had a large customer list to work from. He used small popular groups for the music. I sometimes operated the colored lights from the balcony. I had played trumpet for several dances with a group of post office guys headed by Bennet Almon. The band got $60 each night, which was about $10 apiece. Besides the enjoyment of playing, $10 extra in those days was very welcome.

When I first went to Dallas, Carnes Nance, a friend of Delbert's who worked at B.C. & C. Company, also played in a ballroom dance band. Ballroom dancing was very popular everywhere at that time. Carnes offered to introduce me to his orchestra director, with the intent of getting me into a good local band. On thinking it over, I decided against it. I was hoping to take some subjects from SMU and I didn't want to tie myself up with the band's hours. Above all else, I didn't want to interfere with seeing LaVerne often. I hadn't thought a lot about the future past my job at the post office, but any thoughts I did have, LaVerne was part of it.

Back to LaVerne and my love story. When she was a sophomore at ETSTC, her father died from a heart attack. Mrs. Dawson moved the family to another home on Bois D'arc St. and began to take in boarders. Dorothy Lawson was one of them. In late 1932, LaVerne began to worry a little about what she should do after graduation in May the following year. Everyone expected her to be a teacher somewhere. I was still a substitute clerk barely making expenses. She was the only one since high school I had ever considered. I think that we both expected to be married to each other, but how and when could we do it? If I was promoted to a "regular" position in the post office, my salary would be sufficient. Until the economy picked up, that was in the uncertain future. President Roosevelt was doing his best to get things solved, and I was an optimist. I had started my studies to be an architect and I still hoped to get back to SMU sometime. How could I, in good conscience, ask her to marry me while I was waiting and waiting, as if on a treadmill until I could improve our situation? One night when I took her to her house in Commerce (we had been out for a treat at a drive-in), we sat in the car outside her house and talked about it. The result was that we decided to have a trial separation. Trial separation? I reluctantly and she seriously decided that we would date others for an indefinite period of time. I didn't have anyone else that I dated, but I know that she has a couple of boys at college that she liked who kept urging her for dates. I didn't feel very happy going home. That really shook me up. I realized that LaVerne was at a crossroads in her life, which made it one in my own life. I realized I had to get very serious about the future! It would be awful to lose LaVerne!

LaVerne Dawson And Glenmore Robb Announce Marriage

Miss LaVerne Dawson and Glenmore Robb of Dallas have announced their marriage to their friends, the ceremony taking place on June 18th at Ardmore, Okla., by Elder E. M. Shirley, pastor of the Church of Christ of that city. Mrs. Robb was working in Dallas at the time and she returned to her position.

Mrs. Robb is the eldest daughter of the late J. T. Dawson and Mrs. Dawson. She graduated from Cooper schools in 1930 and attended East Texas State Teachers College, receiving her B. A. degree from that institution last May. At present she is teaching in the school at Hickory Grove. She is a young woman of unusual traits of character and is loved and admired by a large circle of friends.

Glenmore Robb was reared in Cooper, the son of Mr. and Mrs. T. J. Robb, of Enloe, formerly of this city. He received his education here, graduating from Cooper High in 1928. He also attended East Texas State Teachers College, also S. M. U. of Dallas. For the past five years he has held a position as postal clerk at Young Street station, Dallas. He is a fine young business man and is very efficient in his line of work.

At the close of her school Mrs. Robb will join her husband in Dallas and they will be at home at 2615 Elgin Street.

Chapter 4: 1932–1944

THE WEEKS OF SEPARATION were a "dud" for me. I couldn't think of another girl that I wanted to date. Greta Garbo, or Sally Rand, maybe? Not interested, even if possible.

I did know a few local girls I'd see at church, and a couple I'd say "Hi" to at the drug store. One cute girl was friendly, but she had a steady boyfriend that I also knew.

Another girl that I saw regularly at the drug store lived near Mrs. Murphy. I walked with her from the store several times. She invited me up to meet her parents (they lived upstairs). She said they believed in free love. I wasn't sure what she meant by that. I decided not to find out.

There was another girl that I met at the drug store that I liked OK. Her name was Penelope. She was the daughter of the local Baptist preacher. Tall, long dark hair, and pretty blue eyes. She was friendly and about eighteen. I asked her for a date to go to a movie. She agreed. The movie was only a block from her house, so we walked. But, her little 10 year old brother went with us, and sat near us. I suspicioned that it was "Daddy" who wanted junior to see the movie. It was a good movie, but we didn't enjoy it too much. I didn't ask her out again.

About the fourth week of the "separation", I received a letter from LaVerne; I couldn't wait to get it open. I think I tore it open:

"Glen, I love you. I don't want to go another day with this. I didn't do it to hurt you, dear, but for justifiable reasons I thought. I thought it would be better for both of us at the present, but now I know how much you mean to me and nothing else matters. If you love me, you will forgive me and we'll be back together again. If not, I shall be glad that I found it out.
Yours in love,
LaVerne

I quickly sent her a special delivery letter:

"I love you! I'll see you Saturday afternoon.
Glen"

I did go down Saturday. It was a happy reunion. The next Saturday I went down and we went to a co-op dance at the East Texas State gymnasium. Red Button's band played the music. We had a great time and afterwards I met some of her girl club members and other friends. LaVerne was a good dancer and in demand. I'm not so good, but I tried.

As soon as LaVerne graduated, she started looking for a job to teach school. She was qualified to teach the fifth through seventh grade kids. I took her around one Sunday to apply with the trustees of several county schools. The trustees at Hickory Grove liked her and the next week hired her as the Principal of their two teacher school. She would begin with the fall term of 1933.

LaVerne felt now that she was out of school she needed to start paying her own way. Mrs. Dawson barely made expenses taking in boarders. So, since her job of teaching was assured for the fall, LaVerne went to Dallas to live with her sister, Mabel Martin and husband, Aubrey, for the summer. She immediately found a job as a clerk at the F. W. Woolworth in downtown Dallas. Since we loved each other and wanted to be together we decided we could plan our future better when we were married, so we set a date, June 18, to elope to Oklahoma for the ceremony. That was two weeks away.

The day we got married: I was staying in Oak Cliff at Sam and Doris Cook's house. On the 18th I started playing baseball in a park in Oak Cliff. I played the outfield on our Special Delivery team against the Station "A" Carrier's team. I struck out twice against a pitcher whose special pitch was a wide curve. I could never get a hit off him. It looked like the ball was going to hit me, then as I stepped back, it sailed over the middle of the plate. "@ JK&RX#!" Finally, it was getting late. I'd promised LaVerne I'd pick her up at 3 pm, so I left about 2:30 and went to get her at the Martin's house near Love Field. She was ready and we headed for Ardmore, Oklahoma, where we planned to get married. There was a constant stream of young couples from Texas to be married in Oklahoma, since there was no physical inspection or waiting period. There was nothing wrong with us, except that we planned to keep it secret until LaVerne's school job in Hickory Grove was settled. That was the situation as we sped toward Oklahoma on June 18, 1933 to get married.

It soon dawned on me that we couldn't reach Ardmore before well past midnight. The county clerk's office would be closed and everybody asleep. So we changed our destination to Durant, which was a bit closer, where we knew that the offices for the marriage licenses stayed open very late.

As we drove into Durant, we stopped at a filling station to get gas and to ask directions. A young man, just loitering there came over and asked me if we had come to get married. We quickly said "Yes," and mentioned that we would like to get married before 12 o'clock. The following day, June "teenth", was a big holiday in the area for the black folks. We were not anti-black, but we just wanted our own holiday. Jeff (that was his name) got in our rumble seat and guided us to the courthouse. The county clerk was still open. Jeff had called them to alert them not to close, as we were on our way. The clerk called Bro. S.M. Shirley, a Church of Christ preacher. LaVerne had requested a preacher of that church, if one could be found that time of night. Bro. Shirley and his wife had already gone to bed; but, they said for us to come on over. Jeff directed us how to get there and we were married. Mrs. Shirley acted as witness. After it was over, I noted that my watch said 11:57 pm.

I had tipped Jeff $2.00 and I think it was $5.00 or $10.00 for the county clerk's marriage fee. I paid Bro. Shirley $25.00 and thanked them for interrupting their sleep to marry us. I tucked our marriage license into the canvas top of our car, and we headed to Sherman to spend the rest of the night. After going about ten miles the road split. I realized we were on the wrong road. We back tracked and finally got to Sherman. There we were given what they "said" was their "bridal" suite. It was nice, but I wasn't a judge of hotel rooms. It was about 1:30 am.

1931 Ford convertible

We both were scheduled to work the next day. I think we both did, although a bit late. We were planning to keep it a secret for a while. We told Mabel and Aubrey at a 4th of July picnic at White Rock Lake that we were married. I was still staying at the Cook's in Oak Cliff and LaVerne was still at the Martin's. It was awful not being able to get together privately for those sixteen days and nights since our marriage, except that we did sneak out one night to the bushes at the side of the house. Finally the Martin's decided to rent us a room at their house on Elgin Street and we got to live together.

About the second week after LaVerne and I were married, (I was still living at the Cook's) I went out to get in my car which was parked on the street in front of their house. To my surprise, my car top was gone. Someone had stolen it. What a shock! I was thankful that is was covered by insurance. But then it hit me. Our marriage license was still tucked in that top! We were still keeping our marriage secret. How could we prove to people that we were married? Mabel and Aubrey thought we were joking at first, but soon believed us. I reported it to the police, but it was never recovered. In time we got a new top from Ford and a duplicate license from the county clerk of Durant.

The next week when I took LaVerne by Mrs. Dawson's house in Cooper, (she had moved back there after LaVerne graduated from college) Mrs. Dawson asked me point blank if LaVerne and I were married. Of course, I had to say "Yes." From then on, it was no secret except for the school trustees at Hickory Grove. We were afraid that, if the trustees knew LaVerne had married, she would be fired, and Blanche also. Blanche had been hired as the second teacher. It was still the "depression," and many teachers couldn't find jobs. So, in September LaVerne and Blanche opened the school and taught until the Christmas vacation when LaVerne came to Dallas to be with me at the Martin's. LaVerne decided, with my 100% approval, that she just couldn't go back to Hickory Grove. So we immediately went back and told the trustees the situation. They said they understood. They hired Mrs. Dawson, who was a certified teacher, to finish out the term.

LaVerne and I moved around to several locations in Dallas for the next several years. It was no problem since we had no furniture. From Mabel and Aubrey's we moved to a house that was vacant and owned by the Ledbetter family, friends of the Martin's. Mr. Ledbetter was in Puerto Rico on a government construction job and had left his house vacant. We rented their house for about six months and when he was finished in Puerto Rico and wanted his house back, we moved to a new apartment complex at 4247 Maple Avenue which was still being finished. No sidewalks yet, just boards over the muddy yard from the street. But it was nice and furnished with low-cost furniture. Low rents, too. We thought it was a bargain until we discovered that two of the other tenants were having problems with each other and the two men had a fight just outside our door. And it kept raining. We moved out after two months.

In March 1934 we moved across town to a four-plex at 916 North Zangs in Oak Cliff, a suburb of Dallas, across the Trinity River. It was a nice older two-story building situated on a bend on Zangs Blvd. One of the tenants from Maple Avenue had become friends with LaVerne and followed us. Her name was Lucille and she had a young daughter about six years old and a boyfriend, Wheeler, who was a traveling salesman, and got to see her on week-ends. She was very nice, but didn't seem to have any other friends. The apartment building being on a corner and the street having a downhill slope caused a lot of cars squealing brakes and wrecks, especially at night. But it was a straight shot over the viaduct to my work at the Young Street P.O. and we liked the area.

The same month that we moved to Zangs, LaVerne went on a vacation trip with her mother and sisters to Alabama in Mrs. Dawson's car. It was the first time that we had been separated since we had been married in June, 1933. LaVerne had been gone about ten days and was expected back sometime in the next week—I hoped.

I had scarcely seen Lucille or her daughter since LaVerne left. Their apartment was next to ours. I was lonesome, tired of peanut butter and jelly sandwiches and couldn't get used to sleeping by myself. Then one day; I had run a special delivery route that morning and was waiting in the apartment until time to go to work at Young Street to help work the late outgoing mail from about 5:30 until 9 pm, when businesses dropped off. I had just popped a Dr. Pepper and sat down on the sofa to look over the Dallas News, when there was a knock on my door. "I wonder who that is." I said, as I set my Dr. Pepper down on the end table. I got up and opened the door. It was Lucille.

"Glen, do you have an aspirin? I'm out and have an awful headache," she asked.

"I think so," I said. I found a bottle in the bathroom and handed it to her.

"What do you hear from LaVerne?" she asked, as she shook out a couple of aspirin tablets and popped them in her mouth,

"I got a letter yesterday. She's having a great time she said."

"I miss her," she said, "I'm sure you do, too"

"It's like a morgue here when she's gone. She's still got a week before they head back. When's Wheeler due back in?"

"He's due back this weekend. Thanks for the aspirin," she said. She left.

I sat back down, picked up my paper and took a swig of Dr. Pepper. About ten minutes passed and there was a knock on my door.

"Come in," I called, thinking it was Lucille again.

"I guess the two aspirin wasn't enough," I thought.

She didn't come in, instead there was another knock on my door. I quickly got up and opened the door. Standing there was a well-dressed, attractive young lady, about twenty years old, wearing a perky little hat, and carrying a small travel case.

"Hello," I said, surprised.

"Hi," she said. "You must be Glen. Is LaVerne here?"

"No, she's not," I said trying to think who she was.

"I'm Dorothy Lawson, one of LaVerne's friends from college. I'm from Commerce, "E.T." I promised LaVerne I'd come for a visit this summer. Is she out shopping?"

"Well, come in, Dorothy. I remember who you are now. We can't stand here talkin' at the door lettin' the flies buzz in," I said. She stepped in and we settled down on the sofa.

"Dorothy, LaVerne's not shopping. She's in Alabama," I said.

"OH! Are you still together? I didn't know."

"Yes, we are still together. It's just that she, her mother and sisters are on a vacation trip visiting relatives in Birmingham and won't be back for another week," I told her.

"Golly!" she exclaimed. "I didn't know that. That presents a problem"

"Yes, it does," I agreed. "Are you staying at a hotel downtown?"

"No. I just got into town, I took a street car to here from the bus station," she said. "I'm not at a hotel."

"Well," I assured her. "That's no problem. The Cliff Hotel is a good one here in Oak Cliff, or the Jefferson just over the viaduct. It'll be no problem to drop you off as I go to work at 6 pm. I work nearby."

"Oh, Glen, I can't do that. The problem is I discovered when I was at the bus station that I had left my billfold on my dresser in Commerce. I can't even prove who I am."

"You HAVE got a problem," I agreed. "Do you have anybody else in Dallas that you could 'visit' until LaVerne gets back?" I asked.

"Let me think," (She searched her memory.)

"I can't think of anyone." She admitted. "I need to go to the bathroom, Glen. Do you mind?"

"Of course not." (I showed her the bathroom.)

When she came out she said, "I just thought of a girl, a good friend from college. Her parents live here. Their name is Wilson. Do you have a phone, Glen?"

"No. We don't have a phone, but there's a pay phone in the hall. I'll get the phone book for you." I went and got her the phone book. In about five minutes she signaled success.

"Oh, great! They're listed; Joel T. Wilson. That takes care of that problem. I'll give them a call."

"Good," I said, "Here's a couple of dimes for the phone." She went out to call. In a few minutes she was back. I could tell by the look on her face that she had another problem.

"What now?" I asked.

"No answer. I let it ring a long time," she said.

"Let's have a cup of coffee. Do you drink coffee, Dorothy?"

"Yes. That sounds good." I put the coffee on to perk.

"I've got to go to work at 6 pm. I'll be back about 8:45. You stay here and try that number every thirty minutes or so. Don't worry. It they don't answer, you should stay here tonight and we'll tackle the problem tomorrow."

"Oh, thank you, Glen. You don't know how that relieves my mind. You're a Dear. No wonder LaVerne loves you." She served me a cup of coffee. We chatted. She tried the phone again. No luck. I got ready to leave.

"Well, goodbye, Dorothy. I'll see you about 8:45. Make yourself at home. Make yourself a sandwich, if you're hungry. All I've got tho' is peanut butter and jelly. Milk and ice cream are in the fridge. I'll knock and tell Lucille you're here." (I left to go to work.) When I got off work at 8:30 I thought of just spending the night in the swing room. I worried about LaVerne's reaction when she learned Dorothy spent the night with me. But how would Dorothy feel? I decided to do the right thing and I knew LaVerne would agree when I told her about it. When I went back to the apartment at 9 pm, Dorothy greeted me with a big smile.

"Oh, Glen, I finally got hold of the Wilson's. They gave me the phone number of Frances. She's married now. In fact, her husband is a post office employee, named Herman Wright. I called her and they're on their way to pick me up. Herman knows you."

"That's great! Sure, I know Herman. I'm glad it's turning out so well. When LaVerne gets back, I want you two to get together."

"We will," said Dorothy. In about 30 minutes, Herman and his wife came over and took Dorothy home with them.

AND THAT'S THE BEGINNING OF ANOTHER IMPROBABLE STORY: In the week that followed, one of my junior bosses, and a very dear friend, James D. MacPhearson, just happened to drop by Herman and Frances's house. Herman and "Mac" were longtime friends. "Mac" was still a bachelor. He was introduced to Dorothy. They "clicked" with each other at first sight. Mac came back the next night and within a short time they were married. Isn't it wonderful, that all of that happened because Dorothy didn't write LaVerne and establish a date to visit. That's why sometimes life is just a "blast."—yet at other times, it's—but that's another story!

LaVerne came back from Alabama and we resumed out nomadic life together. We stayed on Zangs about eighteen months. Several more events happened while we lived there. I was on a special delivery route one day. It was a Saturday morning route and I had about thirty specials to deliver. I had been having a little trouble with pain in my back, as I did that morning. It was an Oak Cliff route and I went right by the apartment. I decided to stop and see LaVerne, as I always did if my route went near. My back was aching some when I stopped and I lay down on our bed, face down, to rest it. When I tried to turn over and sit up a very sharp pain hit my back. For several minutes I tried to turn over. It caused excruciating pain. LaVerne couldn't help either. Finally, I had to have LaVerne call our P.O. Special Delivery dept. and have them send another driver to finish my route. He arrived in about fifteen minutes. $2.70 (9 cents per letter) I lost.

Calvin "Roy" Darnell was our regular boss of the Special Delivery Department. I was preparing to deliver a route of specials one day in 1934 in the main post office, when Monetta Darnell, Roy's daughter came in. She later was renamed "Linda" by movie moguls. Monetta hung around until Roy could get away and "Speedy" Merrill could take over. I thought she was very pretty and looked older than twelve, her age then. She was active in the school dramatics classes and was a cheerleader for athletic events. Three years later she was "discovered" by Hollywood and life forever was changed for her and her family. Because I had seen her and was impressed by her beauty AND I worked for her Dad, I kept up with her later movie career, which was a very successful one as the leading actress with co-stars such as: Tyrone Power, John Payne, Henry Fonda, and Jack Okie.

"Linda" Darnell starred in such movies as: *Hotel for Women, Daytime Wife, Star Dust, The Mark of Zorro, Chad Hanna, Blood and Sand, Rise and Shine, Summer and Storm, A Letter to 3 Wives*, and about 40 more. She also starred in major TV shows from 1953-1956 and stage plays from 1956-1964. Unfortunately, she died in April 1965, at age 41 in a home fire. Her body was cremated and her ashes were kept in the office of a Chicago cemetery for ten years. Finally, her daughter, Lola, who lived in Pennsylvania, took her ashes and had them buried in the Adams family plot in 1975. Successful life? Yes, but in many ways a sad and tragic life.

In May 1934, ClydeBarrow and his female partner, Bonnie Parker, two desperate outlaws, were finally killed in an ambush on a country road in Louisiana by Texas Ranger Frank Hamer and his posse of 6. This included Ted Hinton, a Dallas post office employee. Ted worked on the night shift delivering specials. I worked days. I knew him since I would often see him in the special delivery room. Clyde and Bonnie and their gang had been robbing and terrorizing the small town banks and country stores in the Midwest and Southwest , especially North East Texas for the past two years. They had already killed several people. Ranger Hamer and his posse had been organized to track them down and put an end to their career. When Hamer got word that they were spotted near Gibsland, Louisiana, and their route was determined, the Posse rushed in to intercept them. They positioned themselves along one side of the country road. When Clyde and Bonnie came along, their car was riddled with bullets and both were killed.

Their bodies were brought back to Dallas. Clyde's was brought to Sparkman-Holtz-Brand funeral home at the direction off the Barrow family members where the public (estimates at 20,000) was allowed to view his remains on Thursday. Funeral and burial was the next day, He was buried in the Western Heights Cemetery. Bonnie's body was brought back to the McKamy-Campbell Funeral Home on Forrest Ave. Allen Campbell, part owner of the funeral home also was a post office employee. I knew him well. He gave LaVerne and me permission to view the body before the public viewing. I parked the car on Forrest Ave. and LaVerne and I were walking up to the entrance of the place. Suddenly, LaVerne stopped.

"What's the matter?" I asked.

"I don't want to see her," she said.

So we turned around and went back to our apartment. We were still living on Zangs Blvd. at the time. After thinking it over, I realized that she was right, Later that day the Parker family had set a time for viewing Bonnie's remains and a huge, but orderly, crowd filed by to view her. Reports stated that Bonnie was clad in a pretty blue negligee and a white veil over her face. Her funeral and burial was next day (Saturday). All the Barrow family attended. She was buried in the Fishtrap Cemetery. Later she was taken up and reburied in the Crown Hill Cemetery in Dallas. A sad ending to a pretty young girl that turned on a chance meeting one day when she went to a friend's house and met a nicely dressed young man. The young man was Clyde Barrow. As it happened, they "clicked" with each other and became inseparable companions. At the time Clyde was trying to find a good job, but it was the "Depression" and a past record of law breaking kept interfering. (A lot of facts about Bonnie and Clyde I learned from the excellent book "Go Down Together" by Jeff Guinn, published by Simon & Schuster Publishers, New York, NY.)

Another thing I remember that happened while we lived on Zangs: I had just had my brakes relined on my Ford and one morning as I was crossing the viaduct to go to work, I decided I'd test them to be sure they worked OK. It was early morning before the traffic picked up for the day. So I stomped hard on my foot brake. It stopped my little car "on a dime." Great! Just then I heard an awful screeching and honking. I couldn't imagine what it was. Then I looked in my rearview mirror and Horrors! There was a car right behind me. It was so close the driver looked like he was in my rumble seat. He backed his car a little and pulled around even with me. Then I recognized him. It was

Henry Parsons, on his way to the P.O. same as I. "What the hell's the matter with you, Robb? Are you crazy? I almost slammed into you." "I'm sorry, Henry. I was just testing my new brakes. I didn't know you were behind me," I lamely said. "Well, your brakes are 100%. I'll see you at the office. Maybe it was partly my fault. I was fiddling with my car radio." We had a good laugh when we met at the office. But I was more careful in situations like that in the future.

And another thing happened connected to that viaduct near that time: The viaduct that carried auto traffic from Oak Cliff to downtown was parallel to the street car trestle where both went over the Trinity River. They both left Oak Cliff from the end of Jefferson Blvd. late one night, after the bars closed, a young male drove to the end of Jefferson. By mistake, he took the street car tracks on to the trestle. He didn't realize his mistake until he was about 100 yards out over the river and his tires were chewed up by the cross-ties that held the tracks. He couldn't go forward (about another 1 1/3 miles) and he couldn't back off either. He managed to climb off the trestle and get home, somehow. Imagine the surprise the next morning for the first street car on the trestle. It took a while to get the car off the trestle and the morning traffic resumed. I don't know what the auto driver paid for his mistake but I'm sure it was plenty.

In 1935 the Post Office was given the job of setting up the new Social Security system for the Dallas district. Our Postmaster selected about seven to do the job. I was one of those chosen. As the information cards from the people of our district poured in, we alphabetically processed them. It was an interesting experience. I learned that almost anything you can think of, somebody is named that. It took us several weeks to get them sorted, boxed and sent to the Social Security Administration in Washington, DC.

I went "regular" in the summer of 1935 and the postmaster pulled me off Special Delivery and put me on eight hours per day, forty hours per week. I worked at the main post office substituting for carriers who were taking vacation, in the hot sandy streets of South Dallas and in some of the close-in areas. A mail truck would take several of us out to our routes and drop us off. When we were finished, we would catch a street car back to our P.O. station. I did this for about six months. Then I got a message from Mr. Rattan, the head of the money department, to come and see him. When I saw him, he explained that his dad, who was the postmaster of the Cooper office had told him to look me up. He had a vacancy in his department and offered it to me. I gladly accepted. So began my years in the post office financial department.

BACK TO OUR NOMADIC WANDERINGS:

We stayed about eighteen months at the Zangs apartment. Finally, getting tired of the traffic noise, we moved all the way back across Dallas to a duplex in the Oak Lawn community. We didn't stay long in the duplex in Oak Lawn either. It was a nice and quiet area. LaVerne had just found out that she was pregnant. About the second week that we were there, Bill Jones, Laverne's cousin from Birmingham, Ala. A boy about nineteen, and his sister came to see us. I remember that we wanted to do something to celebrate the occasion. Although we didn't have anything in the apartment, Bill said he had something in his car that would do. It turned out to be alcoholic. We made a toast of it anyhow, in fact, several. We had a radio playing, the conversation slowed down and we discovered that Bill was sound asleep. The girls, who only sipped the beverage enjoyed the visit with each other. I, who was not used to liquor, was so dizzy, quietly sat in a chair. We wondered when Bill would wake up. Finally, he opened his eyes. It was 1:00 am. Bill wasn't drunk. First, he had lost so much sleep on his trip that he couldn't stay awake. So LaVerne fixed him a pillow and cover and he went to sleep again on the couch. I made a bed on the floor and the two girls slept in the bedroom. We all felt fine in the morning and LaVerne fixed breakfast (Pancakes), and Bill and his sister left for their next stop. We didn't stay but two months in that apartment. The reason: LaVerne decided she couldn't stand the smell of the place. Plus, several days later she surprised a "peeker" at one of the windows. We decided to move. We moved back across town to 5215 Ross Avenue. There we had a room and kitchen privileges. It was a single family home. We stayed there about six months and moved to a duplex at 5308 Belmont Ave., also near Greenville Ave. Most of my work was at or from the main office instead of Young Street Station.

While living at Ross Avenue and Belmont Avenue I used to ride the streetcars to work so that LaVerne could have the car. I was "regular" and didn't need the car at work. Every streetcar had a little sign about the seats that read on one side "Whites Only" and on the other side "Blacks." I had never liked the restrictions on blacks, but not being into politics at the time, I just acceded to the current law. When Rosa Parks, the black lady, refused to give up her seat and move back to allow a white man to take her seat, I admired her actions. Since the days of slavery, the blacks have overcome a lot of racist discrimination. We still have a ways to go. And there are many others who struggle with poverty, heredity, education, and health that need attention.

In 1931, when I had been in the wreck on a special delivery route in my Oldsmobile, the damage to Mr. Collin's car was almost $120. I had paid him all but $50. When I sent the last payment, it came back marked, "No longer at this address" and no new address was shown. Not knowing where to send the last payment, I just forgot about it. I had plenty of other places to send or spend my money. About four years later (1935) I was married and living on North Zangs Blvd. in Oak Cliff. I was walking down Main Street in Dallas one day, when I started to pass a young man. I suddenly realized he looked familiar. Taking a second look as he looked at me, we both recognized each other. We stopped and I walked back.

"You're Mr. Collins' son, aren't you?" I asked, as I stuck out my hand.

"Yes, I am, and you're Mr. Robb," he replied as we shook hands.

"How's your dad," I asked. "I still owe him $50. I've lost his address."

"He died, Mr. Robb, in 1932," he answered. "He was 75. He had a heart attack." Tears appeared in his eyes and he took out his handkerchief and wiped his eyes. I had taken out $50 out of my billfold and was about to give it to him.

"Oh, I'm sorry. He seemed such a fine gentleman," I said, shocked at the revelation. "I still owed your dad $50 for the wreck I caused four years ago. Is his wife still here?"

"No. She died several years ago. That's alright, Mr. Robb. Just forget it. I wouldn't know what to do with it."

"Are you married, Mr. Collins?" I asked.

"Yes, I am and my wife just gave birth to a seven pound boy. It's our first child." He said, brightening up.

"Well, congratulations to you and your wife," I said. "Why don't you take this $50, put it in the bank and start a college fund for that son started by this $50 from his grandfather. I think your Dad would like that."

"Mr. Robb, I'll do that. I think Dad would appreciate that." He took the $50, we shook hands again and we both went on our way. I had just been paid and was lucky to have had that much in my wallet at that time. We'd be a little pinched on our spending for the month, but I was glad to get that $50 debt off my conscience. It was the last of the debts that the lingering depression had left me with. I was sure that my darling wife, Laverne, would approve when I told her about it.

Richard was born September 13, 1936 at St. Paul's Hospital in Dallas while we lived on Belmont Avenue. We used to put him out on the little concrete front porch for his nap in the sunshine and fresh air. It was a nice place but we needed more space so we moved to a bigger apartment on Congress Avenue, where Richard hemmed up a spider in a corner and ate it. We were worried but it didn't seem to affect him. We continued looking for our "Dream house" in the area. We found it (a little vacant cottage at 1921 Annex Avenue)! We quickly rented it. When we went back that evening to clean, we found it crawling with roaches. We had a choice of spiders or roaches. We chose the roaches and started a campaign to eliminate them, which we did in time. While we lived there (1938) LaVerne joined the Dallas Junior Women's Forum, which met on Ross Avenue nearby. Several of our friends were members. LaVerne was a member of the Garden Department. and won several awards for her flower arrangements at the Texas State Fair. While we lived there, on Nov. 13, 1937, Louise Martin and Delmon Smith were married at the Women's Forum. LaVerne, being a member, arranged it.

In 1939, while we were still living at 1921 Annex, LaVerne and I were looking for a house to buy. I was now a "regular" in the post office with a regular salary. Richard was almost three. We were shown a house at 5740 Palo Pinto Avenue that we fell in love with. It was a three bedroom, two-bath on a large 1½ size lot. It was empty, and we could buy it for $4600. The owner agreed to take $600 down and finance the rest. Mr. Clem of the Clem Lumber Company had built it as a wedding present for his daughter. I didn't have $600. Mr. Moore, the Realtor, agreed to hold it off the market for twenty-four hours for me to try to raise the $600. When children have financial problems, the first person they think of is Dad and Mom. I was no exception. It was too late in the evening to do anything that day.

The next morning I caught the 10 o'clock interurban to Terrell, Texas, where Dad, Mother and Marie had moved. I arrived in Terrell about noon. The return trip for Dallas left at two pm. So I had two hours to convince my busy Dad to loan me $600. When Dad heard my pitch, he readily agreed to help. He immediately wrote me a check for $600. I promised to pay him back at $50 per month. That's the kind of loyal Dad we had.

As I waited for the two o'clock interurban to come in, a tall man arrived, purchased a ticket and stood outside where I was nervously pacing. After a few minutes I went over to the shady area where he was, to get out of the hot sun.

"Do you live here, young man?" he asked.

"No. I live in Dallas," I replied. "Where do you live?"

"I live in New York. I was just down here to visit a relative in the hospital."

"I work in the post office in Dallas," I said.

"That's a good occupation. I have a good friend who lives in Dallas, Johnny Celmars, a former boxer. Have you ever heard of him?"

"I sure have," I said. "He and Sully Montgomery came down to my hometown, Cooper, once, to box a couple of our guys."

"Did you ever hear of Jack Dillon?"

"Yes I have," I answered. "He was Light Heavy Weight Champion. Do you know him?"

He laughed. "Yes I know him pretty well. I'm him. I'm Jack Dillon." I was completely astonished.

"Wow! You're Jack Dillon? I'm glad to know you. I'm Glen Robb. Do you still box?" I asked.

"No", he said. "I have a couple of training gyms for young boxers. You look like you have long arms. That's an advantage in boxing. Did you ever try boxing? It's a good thing to know. You don't have to be a professional."

"No," I said. "I've been too busy with music and other things." It was then that I noticed his big hands and long arms.

"I can see that your arms are much longer than mine," I said.

"Let's measure. I'll stand against the wall there. You stretch your arms along mine. We'll see," he suggested. We did. His arms were four or five inches longer than mine on both sides.

"You've got a pretty good reach, alright. You should try boxing," he said. "It's a pretty good thing for a young man to know."

"Music's my hobby," I said.

"I always wanted to play the piano," he said. "I never got around to it. You just can't do everything you'd like to do."

"That's for sure," I agreed. The interurban had arrived and he ran into the waiting room for his suitcase. We both boarded, but I didn't see him anymore.

There was a portico-chere at the entrance next to a large concrete covered porch. It had a huge combination living/dining room and a large screened porch just off the kitchen, where we liked to have breakfast while a mockingbird would serenade us from his perch atop a nearby telephone pole. The house was 2200 sq. ft. and built of cypress wood. There was a greenhouse attached to the back of the house. The lot in front was elevated about three ft. above the sidewalk. It had a one car garage in the rear connected to a one room and bath servant house. An alleyway ran back of it. The servant house was rented to a black lady (Octavia) and her husband. Both worked elsewhere at the time, however, Octavia helped LaVerne at times. A streetcar line ran just half a block away. Richard's school, Robert E. Lee Elementary, when old enough, was a close walk. We moved Richard and our clothes in (no furniture as our previous homes had been furnished. Our wedding present from Mrs. Dawson was our first piece of furniture, a Singer sewing machine. The Hart Furniture Store gave us a credit and we bought two beds, a table and some chairs and we were in business.

One way to meet your new neighbors when you move into a new house is to unintentionally damage their property. Such occurrences happened when we moved into 5740 Palo Pinto. Living on one side of us was Mr. and Mrs. Sticksel, their son, John, and grandson, Donald. Our chickens kept getting out and feeding in Mr. Sticksel's garden, which was a large productive one. It was the only problem that we ever had with our neighbors, except one with the neighbors on the other side. There was a long row of fig bushes along the right side of our backyard. They dropped a lot of large overripe figs that drew flies. I've never liked figs and I like flies even less. I decided to cut them down. They were about five or six feet high and there were about a dozen of them. So I was out one day sawing them down. I had downed the first one and was working on the second, when I heard the back door of the Flood's (our neighbor) house slam. I looked up, and here came Mrs. Stallings, Dick Flood's mother, running towards me.

"What are you doing?" she screamed. "Don't you cut down my fig trees!" That was the first time that I knew that the figs were not on my property. In fact, they were exactly on the line between the lots. I apologized and explained that I thought they were on my property. It was my mistake and we were friends all the time we lived there.

We didn't need but two bedrooms so we rented out a bedroom and bath over the years. Our tenants:

"Tex" Stephens worked as a Church of Christ youth minister for a year. He was a guy who coughed a lot, so we worried about him. He stayed two months

"Dixie" Adams, who played the piano and sang fabulously, stayed six months. She and her young daughter rejoined her husband in San Antonio. We were sorry to lose them.

Our last tenant was Miss Boyer, about forty years old, who taught at the Hockaday Girls' School on Greenville Avenue, which was only a block away. She stayed for several years and was a very good tenant. We rarely saw her.

When it rained in the winter our greenhouse addition would get filled in with about a foot of water, so we used it mainly for storage of equipment. Besides lots of room for flowers and watermelons, there was a good space at the back of our lot for chickens.

When the U.S. entered World War Two, one of the first things they did was to install rationing. Little round chips were put out by the OPA (Office of Price Administration).Red chips you could spend for meat. Blue chips were for certain other items. Each family was allowed a certain number per period of time, depending on the number of people in the family. Gasoline was also rationed. LaVerne and I decided that our best strategy was to raise baby chickens, so we ordered 100 from a large poultry farm and prepared an area at the back of our lot for them. They were cute little buggers. When they grew up they were all roosters. They started crowing about 4:30 am. The one that crowed the loudest we had for dinner that evening. We finally ate all of them except one, a huge white leghorn. We called him Buster. He grew so big that he had Richard buffaloed. When he ruffled up his feathers and strutted at you, even I shied away from him. We did get another batch of chickens and ended up with a group of about ten hens. Old Buster was still there and we had plenty of eggs. I don't recall what ever happened to "Buster." I suppose he just walked off to where big roosters go to seek their fortune.

We tried gardening on a little area adjacent to the house. LaVerne planted some flower seeds and I planted some watermelon seeds. My watermelons came up and began spreading. They grew fast. The vine had several little melons on it. It spread over into LaVerne's flowers, which were also doing well. In order to give my watermelon plants more room to expand, I began pulling up the flowers that were in the way—just as LaVerne came out of the back door and saw me.

"What are you doing?" she screamed. "Those are my petunias. You're ruining them!"

"I thought they were weeds," I said, backing off.

That's all the time I had to say anything more, as she ran around me and started to grab my watermelon plant. When I saw what she was about to do, I tackled her.

"Don't you dare!" I yelled. But it was too late. She had yanked it out. We both backed off and stared at each other. We both apologized and had a good laugh and hug.

We bought a used 1937 gold colored Packard while on Palo Pinto. It served us well for several years. We were happy in our big house. We were proud of our little son. When he was only two months old, we took him to the Texas Centennial at Fair Park, just so he could say that he had been there. We thought that he was the cutest boy in "Big D," and the smartest, too. We took him everywhere we went; church, movies, etc. LaVerne had several girlfriends who had small children and there was always a birthday party for one of them. Richard had lots of that kind of experience.

LaVerne was a good hostess. She enjoyed entertaining relatives. So we had a very busy social life. The Church of Christ that we attended had a very large membership and something was always going on there and among the members. LaVerne was a good cook, as were her sisters Mable, Shirley and Sue. We had lots of dinners and "42" parties at our house.

Charles Thomas and his wife Grace were our closest friends while we lived on Palo Pinto. They had a little boy younger than Richard. They lived only a few blocks away and we both attended the Sears & Summit Church of Christ in the area. We had many delicious dinners at each other's house.

Laverne discovered that her ETSTC music teacher, Miss Katherine Murray, lived just in the next block. They renewed their friendship and LaVerne often visited her.

Sisters, Shirley & LaVerne, in SF

Shirley came to visit us in 1940 after she had graduated from high school. We were in 5740 Palo Pinto that we had bought the year before. She soon found a job with the Haggar Slacks Co. There she met Fred Moses and before the year was over they were married and she and Fred moved into an apartment. Then came Pearl Harbor and soon Fred was inducted into the navy. A short time later little Freddie Moses was born.

Mrs. Dawson sold her house in Cooper and bought a house on Belmont Street in Dallas. Shirley and baby moved in with Mrs. Dawson and Sue. Then when I left for the navy in 1944, Shirley and Freddie moved back in with LaVerne and Richard.

I think it was the summer of 1940 that Ignace Paderewski came and gave a piano concert at Fair Park in Dallas. Eighteen years earlier I had first learned to play his "Minuet in G" during my piano lessons from Mrs. Berry. LaVerne had learned it earlier, too. When Paderewski played it at the concert, there was a special roar of applause from the crowd. He was also a past president of Poland, and was at the time about ninety years old. He died suddenly not long after the concert. He was buried in our Arlington Cemetery. Later his remains were taken up and reburied in his native Poland where he was loved and honored.

In 1940 when the presidential election was in full swing President Roosevelt came to Dallas to canvas for votes. LaVerne, Richard and I decided to try and see him. We were Pro-Roosevelt fans. We didn't try to go to the big event downtown. We knew the route his car would take from his "Special" railroad train parked at the Highland Park Station and we joined the crowd waiting on Ross Avenue. He would take this to his reception at a hotel downtown. After about a forty minute wait, here he came in an open top limousine, waving at the crowd of people standing five deep. It was a thrill to see him really in person. We wanted Richard to see him. The limo drove slowly along, Roosevelt waving and the crowd (including us) cheering, until he was out of sight. We hung around a few minutes talking to a few other people, then, we went home. It was worth the trouble. How many ordinary people like ourselves ever get to see our president IN PERSON. He easily was elected to a third term (and later to a 4th term). His route, I believe, was from Highland Park Station, which is no longer there, down Knox Street to Ross Avenue, then downtown. We stood on Ross.

After Mr. Rattan brought me into the financial department of the post office, he assigned me to the money order recording department. Each money order has an eight-digit number. We process paid money orders for the 10th Postal District (except for the larger first class offices). I think that's when I started wearing glasses. I would also occasionally work on the tabulator or the sorter. Gus Thornton was our boss there. There was about a dozen in our crew including Glenn Wrigge. After about 2½ years there, Mr. Rattan brought me down to the first class floor where I was put on the windows serving the public selling stamps and Money Orders. I enjoyed the window work. I like to interact with people. All kinds of people buy stamps. There were two stamp/money order windows, a postal savings and a savings bond window.

One of our postal service clerks came up short $500 one time. He had to pay it back. Window clerks had a set amount to operate on (from $400 to $500 for stamps, much more for postal savings). I came up short about $30 once and smaller amounts under $10 occasionally.

Another of our stamp clerks (It wasn't me) got in an argument with an obnoxious customer who cussed him out and challenged him to come out and fight. Our clerk was so mad, he threw up the window guard and crawled through the window to fight him, but the guy disappeared into a crowd in the lobby.

In 1941 when WW2 started, the Post Office Department started selling war bonds and war savings stamps. I was put in charge of the shipment of these savings stamp supplies to all the post offices of Northeast Texas, parts of Oklahoma, Arkansas and Louisiana, except the larger first class offices. I had a crew of three to help me. In 1942 and 1943 I also became the substitute for "Lightening" Paige, the First Assistant Auditor when he went on vacation. He handled the supplies of stamps. I needed to ship out the supplies of savings bonds he shipped to the offices of the 10th district. I also, when Paige wasn't available, substituted for Mr. Bradshaw, the Auditor, who was responsible for millions of dollars in wholesale stamps, bonds, and blank money orders. He also controlled the money that supplied all the window clerks their operating funds. I substituted for him once. Paige was much older than I. I could see my future as the Auditor of the Dallas post office someday if I behaved myself. But I considered it as a dead end for me for advancing to be the Postmaster. I had only limited experience in the delivery of mail (the carriers), except my Special Delivery time. Bill Hudson, the Assistant Postmaster was a young man and would be the next postmaster when the present one retired. I liked Bill Hudson and had a friendly relationship with him. Bill was an enthusiastic member of the Junior Professional Speaker's Club. Glen Wrigge, who was getting a lot of experience in the handling of the mail was influenced by Bill to join the speaker's club. The result was that they became very good friends, played golf together, etc. Wrigge was about a year older than me and a great guy. I could see that he would be the postmaster eventually if he wanted to. I began to wonder if I should think about a new direction.

Backtracking a little, on Dec. 7, 1941, Japan struck our navy base in Hawaii; I was working full time in the Dallas P.O. I was also attending a night class in commercial art. I had been pursuing an architectural curriculum at SMU and Dallas College with being an architect in mind. Commercial art was in the group of requirements. With the shock of the start of the war, when the term ended, I didn't register for any more classes. I figured that I would be called up for the military right away. However, every time my draft came up for induction, the postmaster would get me exempt, as he did with some others. Delbert, my older brother, had just been drafted. He had hoped to delay his induction until his wife, who was pregnant, would deliver, but the draft board said "No." He already had one son. I felt bad, being exempt and others having to go in my place, so the next time my draft was about to come up, I went down and volunteered along with my friend, Ray Moore. LaVerne supported me in my decision. Before I left I resigned my Supervisor Asst. Auditor job so that my friend, Jim Douglas could advance to it, otherwise the job would officially stay vacant until I got back from the Service.

So, in March 1944, Ray and I volunteered for the navy. While sitting in the Navy recruiting office with about twenty other recruits, the recruiting officer rapped on his desk.

"I need a couple of you guys to help me with a little job." No one answered.

"I'll help," I said.

"Same here," volunteered Ray.

by Tom Robb

The job was a simple one of alphabetizing a couple of hundred names on cards.

"I've got to divide today's recruits into those going to Camp Wallace at Houston, the camp at Great Lakes, Illinois or the camp at San Diego. I'll give you two a choice." Ray and I chose San Diego. We had a week to wind up our affairs before we had to report back to the recruiter and take the train to San Diego. My last day at the Dallas post office before I left, the "gang" in the money order department gave me a "send-off" party. Clara McBride brought a cake and as work for the day ended we had a cake cutting "goodbye" party. Our M.O. personnel were a special group and I appreciated their gesture.

I don't remember much about my leaving LaVerne and Richard. The last two days were so busy and fast. I tried to get in a little handbag all the things I thought I'd need in boot camp: sox, undershirts, shaving things, toothbrush and toothpaste, hair oil, comb, hairbrush, hand lotion, etc. I thought that I might get stateside duty after boot camp and our separation wouldn't be very long. We were all caught up in the excitement of the "moment" and not thinking much about the future. LaVerne dropped me off at the recruiting station and I was put on a train (also Ray) that left for San Diego. I was excited at the prospect of the events ahead of me but worried some about leaving LaVerne alone to handle everything in Dallas. And, I was missing her already by the time we hit the New Mexico border.

When we got to boot camp in San Diego, they interviewed me to determine my occupation, talents, etc. I told the interviewer: "Put me in someplace other than postal work. I'd like to learn a new job."

He smiled, "We'll see," he said.

I was made the company mailman. Ray, a of couple years older than me and the same postal experience, was given some other responsibility. I don't remember what it was. Most of the other recruits were in their 20's. I was thirty-four. We were a rag-tag looking bunch at San Diego as we first assembled at our assigned barracks. Our boss, Sergeant A.J. Cavallero, was a small man compared to his voice. He talked TOUGH! And he turned out to BE tough. The first thing he had us do was to get a haircut. He marched us to the barbershop. It didn't take long the way those barbers whacked off hair. Everybody got the same style. Next we were marched to the supply department, where a guy just looked at us and decided what size of everything we wore. It was a long service counter and we just pushed our accumulated bunch of clothing along until we had everything we needed, all except shoes. They were careful to fit those. They asked us what size we wore.

So the handbag and all the supplies that I had carefully assembled—sent back to my address in Dallas, including the clothes I arrived in. There was no problem later getting a right size of shirt, pants, etc. I think the first part, haircuts and clothing, were more a psychological introduction for first day recruits. It let us know as new recruits that we had NOTHING to say about the operation of boot camp. And if that didn't sink in; next morning after breakfast we were all assembled in front of our barracks.

"How many you guys from California?" asked the instructor.

"Yea!" yelled about fifteen guys.

"How many from Texas?" he asked.

"YEAH!" about twenty-five of us yelled, trying to outdo the Californians.

"OK. You guys win," he told the Texans. "You have the latrine detail for the week."

Sgt. Cavallero was tough and consistent. Our days were filled with classes on outdoor bleachers in the hot sun, or drilling on the grinder in the same hot sun. For a week we had been restricted from the supply store. I was sunburned pretty bad on my face and was starved for something sweet (candy bars, cokes, etc.). Luckily Delbert's friend, Chip, was still in San Diego and came by to see me. Delbert had written him that I was there. He bought me some sunburn cream from the ship's store. It really helped. After the first week we were allowed to buy what we needed in the supply store. After the fifth week we were allowed to leave the base and go into town, which most of us did. We went sightseeing, etc. San Diego is a beautiful city.

Cecil Reilly was in the Navy and was working in Navy offices on Coronado Island in the bay and had an apartment in San Diego. He was married to Sue; LaVerne's youngest sister. They invited me to dinner about my sixth week of "boot." She cooked me a delicious meal and I also got a lot of good advice from Cecil, who had gone through boot camp several months earlier. I was still in boot camp when the Allies, on June 6, 1944 invaded Normandy. It was exciting news.

USS Marcus Island

On one of the weekends while I was still in "boot," I was sitting at a table in the USO in San Diego, eating a sandwich and drinking a big shake, when Delbert suddenly appeared and sat down at my table. His ship, the baby aircraft carrier "Marcus Island" had just come in. I had no idea that he was in San Diego. We had a good visit until I had to catch the bus back to camp.

Finally our eight weeks in boot camp were finished. In a drill competition that is put on periodically, our company (#334) won first prize. Then after our pictures were taken, we each were sent to our various jobs. Ray Moore was assigned to a supply ship. After a simple test, easily passed, I was sent to the Fleet Records Office in San Francisco. I was also given tests for rifle marksmanship and recommended for assignment to Bofers anti-aircraft gun reserve crew aboard ship. I had been given instruction in aircraft recognition, bayonet use, boxing, swimming, etc. in boot camp. I was lodged in barracks in an old building on lower Market Street in San Francisco. Fleet Records was in the same area. In the meantime, LaVerne and Richard (eight years old) were left in the house on Palo Pinto. As soon as I arrived in San Francisco from boot camp, she rented the house out and she and Richard caught the train for San Francisco.

It was a risky move, but we were just like two magnets. We had to be together when possible. San Francisco was crowded with troops, etc. and apartments and rooms were scarce. There was a three day limit at hotels. I had managed to rent a room at the Ambassador Hotel in downtown and was awaiting the arrival of LaVerne and Richard. The manager of the hotel reminded me of the three day limit.

The Navy officer in charge of our barracks wasn't inclined to let me stay outside of our barracks, until I told him that my wife and son were already on a train on their way to San Francisco. He relented and said, "Good Luck!"

Ambassador Hotel

Chapter 5: 1944–1949

I MET LAVERNE AND Richard at the Santa Fe Station at 4th Street. and Mission (just below Market Street) and only a few long blocks from The Ambassador Hotel, where I had managed to rent a room. It was great to see them. We walked the few blocks to the hotel. I introduced them to the hotel clerk and we went up to our room. For the next two days we checked with the rental agencies and called on newspaper ads with no results. We were on several waiting lists as the weekend and our three day limit came up. The desk clerk was a good guy. He felt sorry for us and allowed us another day or two. He said that there was a good turnover of rooms and apartments, as military personnel were often moved about. Something on our lists should come up.

While at the Ambassador, located at the corner of Mason and Eddy Streets, just one block above Market, we began to get the "feel" and excitement of San Francisco. Our room on the second floor overlooked a bar on Eddy Street where the doorman stood outside chirping "Showtime" until 2 am.

San Francisco was a fabulous city. We were anxious to see as much of it as we could during our indefinite stay. On Sunday we went to church out at the Eighth Avenue Church of Christ. We met a lot of nice people including Mr. and Mrs. Bert Coop and family who were visiting from Redding, Calif. He managed a hotel there. They had left their San Francisco apartment on Third Avenue vacant, just in case he was drafted by the military and his family needed to reoccupy the apartment. When they heard our story, they offered to let us rent the apartment on condition of: if he were drafted we would immediately give it up. After church they took us by the apartment. It was a lower apartment in a four-plex. We quickly agreed and paid him the first and last month's rent. The next day (Monday) we moved into 434 Third Ave. What a lucky break! The apartment was between Geary Blvd. and Balboa, just two blocks from Golden Gate Park. The Geary streetcar line from downtown out to the Pacific Ocean was just a half block away. It also ran by the school that Richard would attend while we lived there.

Bike riders in Golden Gate Park

While at third Avenue, we regularly attended the eighth Avenue Church. Bro. Bernie Baucum preached. We met and became good friends with several Navy couples including Freddie & Ruthie Presnall and Walter & Mary Graves. Gardiner Blackmon, Chief Labor Negotiator for J. Paul Getty's Tidewater Oil Co., his wife Leona and their family were also good friends. We had picnics in the park among all its many wonders. It is truly a great park. We went bicycling where LaVerne relearned to ride one at the cost of a skinned knee. That was a brave effort for her as she hadn't ridden a bicycle since she was a teenager. We also took in the exhibits in the park including a huge twenty foot tall skeleton of a dinosaur. Out at the ocean, we never got tired of watching the seagulls, the white caps and the ships coming in and going out. We took in Sutro's Palace, the Fun House and had dinners at the Cliff House. We had many good times with those dear friends. Other friends were Clyde and Lillian Bynum and Althea Sims, an older lady who lived with them. They lived out about Twentieth Avenue. Clyde was an adjuster for the Internal Revenue Service. I remember we had dinner at their house once and Lillian took us to their basement to show us several male and female chinchillas they had just bought. She planned to raise them for their beautiful pelts. There was a hot demand for their fur at that time. We had dinner with them several times and it was interesting to see the little critters. I could almost see them growing. Lillian was very proud of them. At a certain age, they would be just right for the market. Later, after the end of the war and we lived in Berkeley, we saw the Bynums again and asked her how her chinchilla project came out.

"I got so attached to them that I couldn't bear to sell them to be killed.

Finally, for some reason, they began to die and Clyde persuaded me to sell them and I did," she said sadly.

At Christmas time 1944, LaVerne, Richard, the Presnalls (I'm not sure about the Graves) and I went up into the hills north of San Francisco to a "Cut-Your-Own" tree area for our apartment tree. After trudging up a rugged hill and finding just the right tree, we sawed it down (hand saw). We dragged it down to Freddie's car, "Bessie". LaVerne and I didn't have a car in San. Francisco When we got back to the apartment and before we had time to set it up, a nice tree was delivered to us compliments of Bert Coop & family, the owners of our apartment. So we had two Christmas trees that season. The next week, Freddie and Ruthie for some reason had to be out of town for a week and let us use his car. LaVerne, Richard and I decided to visit The Cliff House for lunch. Parking is hard to find anywhere in San Francisco. I let them out at the restaurant and started circling around the area. I finally found a spot on a residential street behind "Sutro's Hill" several blocks away. I parked and set my brakes, since the street was on a hill, and joined them at The Cliff House. After the meal and viewing all the curios they had displayed at nearby Sutro's Palace, we walked back to the car. I found a police ticket on the windshield, a citation for not cutting my front wheels into the curb. It's a logical law that I was ignorant of. With all the visitors in San Francisco, they have more than a normal amount of "run-a-way" cars. I gladly paid the $25 fine for my lesson.

3 buddies on SF street – Fred Presnall, Walter Graves and Glen (Tom) Robb

by Tom Robb

Besides enjoying our many friends while in San Francisco, I also enjoyed my work at the Fleet Records Office. I was on the 7 am to 3:30 pm shift. From our apartment on Third Avenue, I would take a streetcar to downtown. From there I had to walk from Market St. on down past Mission St. for about five blocks to our office on Brannon St. I often stopped in an early open coffee shop for a second cup of coffee and a doughnut, just to see the various patrons; policemen, taxi drivers, streetcar operators, stevedores, etc. Some were just getting off their shift, others, like me, on their way to work. I have always been a people watcher. It's very interesting. My work was mainly dealing with undeliverable mail. Military people were so mobile, being transferred from place to place, that their mail just couldn't keep up with them. A lot of it ended up at the Fleet Records Office. Our office was in a loft of a huge warehouse type building. About fifty of us sat at separate desks spending all our time trying to forward all kinds of mail to the latest addresses of our men, who were scattered all over the Pacific area. Some letters and packages had already been forwarded many times. Many packages were so beat up we had to re-tape or re-package them. Some had cake crumbs spilling out, probably months old, but we fixed them up and sent them on anyway, if possible.

Troop ship USS Lafitte

While working there, on Oct 20, 1944, we got the report that Gen. MacArthur and his forces had invaded Leyte Island in the Philippines. It was great news! I spent seven months working at the Fleet Records Office. I remember riding a streetcar on my way to work on April 12, 1945. At one stop a man got on and said that it had just been announced on the radio that President Roosevelt had died. Ten days later, on April 22, 1945, I received orders to go to Navy base #3964 at Tacloban on Leyte. It was a jolt, but I had known it was pending. So on April 24, 1945 I grudgingly, emotionally and excitedly packed my things in my duffel bag, said goodbye to LaVerne and Richard and caught the streetcar down to the barracks on lower Market Street.

Sometime earlier LaVerne had applied and been accepted to work at the United Nations Institution in San Francisco as a junior accountant. After I left she and Richard attended some of the United Nations beginnings in S.F. They had met and talked to Senator Sol Bloom of New York State, one of the delegates. However, when I got my orders to leave, LaVerne decided to go back to Dallas and requested the tenants at 5740 Palo Pinto to vacate. She and Richard went back to Dallas on May 16, 1945. The United Nations job was still not ready.

Sailor TGR sitting on wall in SF

I stayed at the barracks that April night and was transported the next morning to Treasure Island to catch my ship out. It turned out to be the USS Gen. William. C. Langfitte. I remember that by the time I had to carry my 100 lb. duffel bag up the gangplank of the ship, my back was killing me. But you do what you have to do and I made it. Finally I was assigned a bunk and fell into it. I was okay after a good rest. I wasn't able to communicate with LaVerne and Richard, but did get off a letter. The ship spent the night at T.I. and we hoisted anchor about mid-morning next day and headed out. It was an eerie mixed feeling as the Golden Gate disappeared behind us.

When we got out about forty miles off our coast we hit the Japanese ocean current that flows north, causing very turbulent conditions for our ship. It just happened that we hit at the time we were having dinner on the ship. The menu was spaghetti. It was difficult to hold the tray of food in front of you, with the ship rolling from side to side. I had never been on a ship before and soon after eating I began to get nauseated. I went up on top deck to get fresh air and there was a crowd of guys who were sick, throwing up spaghetti all over the deck before they could get to the rail to pitch it in the ocean. That sight and smell was the last straw. I joined the others at the rail. It was a mess, but we soon got through the cross current and the ship sailed smoothly as we all recovered. Because of the crowded conditions below deck, I spent some time on the main deck. I even slept there some nights because of the heat, when we got down around the equator.

An interesting sight on the way over was seeing the schools of flying fish, which looked to be about eight to ten inches long. They would propel themselves out of the water, fly just above the surface for eight to ten feet, then, drop back in the water. This was especially beautiful at night when the ship would be going through a patch of some kind of algae that glowed. The ship made a brief stop in Hawaii then began a thirty day journey to the Philippine Islands. At the stop in Honolulu, Joel Polite, one of my friends, managed to get a job helping in the ship's mailroom. We were all starved for sweets. When Joel was selected to take the bag of our mail to the post office ashore, Tom Fox, another of my friends, and I persuaded him to divide the mail into three bags so that we could go along helping him. On shore we delivered our mail to the post office and received back mail for the ship. Before going back on the ship we found a drug store and filled our pockets with candy bars, which we divided with some of our friends aboard ship, keeping three or four for ourselves. After leaving Hawaii, we headed south to the Philippines. We didn't go straight there because of the danger of Jap submarines that still prowled the Pacific. We passed the International Dateline without incident, although some of the regular crewmembers got "initiated".

Germany surrendered on May 8, 1945.

Bofors gun mount

We went on down toward Australia and came back through "The Slot" off Guadalcanal. We slowed once to set off a series of depth charges, which threw up geysers of water. One day I was on deck when the 5-inch gun crew set off several shots in practice. The decks were cleared, but I lingered just outside to watch. The shock waves really blasted my ears and I was deaf for several minutes. I had been assigned as a possible gunner for a Bofers gun crew and had practiced shooting them in boot camp. We zigzagged our way up to Guam, where we let a couple of men off, then went on to Navy Station 3149 on Samar Island, where most of us were put ashore to await plans for our duty at Navy Station 3964, Tacloban, which was the base of Admiral Nimitz's Seventh Fleet.

While at Samar (a hot, sandy, primitive island with dense trees, but wide beaches) we set up camp. It was the middle of May 1945. After several days of standing in long chow lines in the hot sun and being on details setting up tents, etc. Joel Reeves and I just "lost" ourselves and retired to a vacant tent on the edge of the jungle. Later a young reticulated python, about ten feet long, was discovered and killed near us. Pythons grow up to thirty feet and are equally adept in the brush, climbing trees or swimming. Joel found some parachute cord and material made from pineapple fibers. We unraveled the threads of it and made "hula" skirts out of it. It made a beautiful skirt, which I kept and brought home. It was ruined by rainwater flooding my garage, where I had it stored, about 1980.

I had not heard from LaVerne since I left them in San Francisco. Joel and I kept going to the Navy base post office on Samar, but they had no mail for either of us. Finally the mail clerk we were talking to said:

"We're doing the best we can. We're understaffed and swamped with mail. See that stack of mailbags? That's what we're working on." He waved his hand at a stack of bulging mail sacks six feet high.

"Wow!" I exclaimed. "I must have a dozen letters in there."

"How about letting us help you work through that. We're both postal employees in the states," pleaded Joel.

"Let me ask the Lieutenant," he said. He went and asked the Lieutenant In charge, who came and checked our dog tags and IDs.

"Sure," he said. "When can you start?"

"Right now," I replied. He cleared the matter with our company command and we started right away working on the huge backlog. While working there I found about three or four letters from LaVerne of different dates (out of sequence) that had been forwarded from Tacloban. The latest dated one stated that she was going into the hospital for a tumor removal. It was dated about two weeks earlier. I was very worried, as I didn't know anything about tumors. Joel and I worked there for about ten days before we were transferred to Tacloban. When we got to Tacloban we were assigned to "General Detail". We asked and were accepted to work in the base post office, where we found many more letters from our families. Joel was from Panama. I found out that LaVerne was okay. It had been about a month and a half since I had left them in San Francisco.

Just after midnight on July 30, 1945 a Japanese sub launched six torpedoes into the Cruiser USS Indianapolis sinking it in twelve minutes at a loss of over 850 lives, with 316 of a crew of 1200 surviving. The rest were killed, drowned or were eaten by sharks. It was the same area that we had come through only seven or eight weeks before. Not until August 2nd was the oil slick discovered by a Navy pilot. Fortunately, the Indianapolis had just delivered the components of the Atomic Bomb to the island of Tinian in the Marianas the week before.

Tacloban Bay, P.I.

I soon was reassigned to the postal depot, which was huge, as it was the receipt and distribution point for all of the area. Since Tacloban was the base of the Seventh Fleet, every ship and plane brought bags of mail and received bags for their crew and also bags for their next destinations. Our warehouse generally had mailbags piled eight or ten feet high awaiting the various ship's arrivals. Manila had a mail base like Tacloban's. We had a few prisoners-of war in a closed off area but did not work them. They were peaceful. I was assigned to lead a work detail (sailors awaiting transfer to other bases) one time to unload a lot of mail from an LSTV.

Our troops were still fighting to secure the area up north of Manila and in the south on the island of Mindanao. I was put on a draft to Manila but it was cancelled before they needed us. After a couple of months, I decided that I should try to get into the finance office since that was my training in the Dallas Post Office and I had handled lots of money in my finance job there, so I went over to the paymaster's office. As I walked in and up to the counter, a person got up from his desk and came over to assist me. Who, to my surprise, was it but my Boy Scout friend from Cooper, Tex., Howard Nolan! He still looked the same as when we were twelve years old. It turned out that he was second in command of the office. We had a happy reunion. I was okayed and transferred to the payroll department of the base, which was headed by Lt.j.g. J. L. Hegwood, Jr. Howard was a chief storekeeper. I became a "striker" for the rating. I spent the rest of my time there on the pay crew. We paid the base guys, some of the guys on small islands close by and many small ships' crews that came into Tacloban and were away from their pay bases. I usually paid out the pesos and Lt. Hegwood carried the only weapon, a pistol. There were about five in our pay group and we travelled by LSVP (a small landing craft).

TGR in Jeep

I was not much of a coffee drinker before I joined the Navy, but since I didn't like beer, I learned to be a confirmed coffee drinker in spite of the hot weather in the P.I. We kept the coffee urn ON all day. The only problem was, that most of the time we could only get Australian coffee, which I didn't like as well as American grind. We had a jeep assigned to our pay office and I used it to go up to the Officers' Club to get ice for our drinking water, thanks to the influence of our Lt. Hegwood.

The US Army had a base a Palo, a town about twelve miles in the country from Tacloban. Lt. Hegwood received orders to have our pay records photo stated. Since my hobby had once been photography, he sent me down to Palo in the jeep to do the job. Each day for about a week I took a batch of pay records to Palo and photo stated them. Odd, but we didn't have the facilities available there in Tacloban. I found out that the Army could get things the Navy couldn't. I enjoyed the trip seeing the country on my trips each day; farmers plowing the fields with caribou, small houses up on stilts (flood protection and shade for their fowls and animals), the large straw hats and the dress of the people. I couldn't tell the men from the women.

I ate my noon meal each day at the Army mess. I was surprised that they had "real" butter instead of margarine—purchased from the local farmers, I imagine. They also had good American brand coffee, which I loved. The five days passed quickly and I was back at the usual in Tacloban. We in the pay office liked to get early chow for our noon meal and were issued an "early chow" chit. We also had to use it for late night dinners when we had to work overtime to get a payroll list ready or were late getting back from paying a small ship's crew. One time when we knew we would have to work overtime getting the payroll ready, we decided to go in for early chow and work on payroll later. There was a new guy at the door of the dining hall entrance. "You can't use that chit for early dinner. It's for late night meals," he said. "I'm sorry, rules is rules. You'll have to wait another forty minutes." He was adamant. We went back to our office to wait. It wasn't Lt. Hegwood (who ate at the officer's mess) or me, but somebody searched out that guy's payroll file and dropped it behind the big iron safe. As a result, on payday his pay chart couldn't be found and he received only a token amount. About the third payday later his chart was miraculously found and he received his regular pay again. Nobody knew who did it. In fact, nobody asked. We didn't have any more trouble at the chow hall.

We had a good outdoor movie and I took it in regularly. There was a stage and one of the groups that came to entertain us was Kaye Kaiser, Frances Langford and Ish Kabibble.

U. S. NAVAL SHORE FACILITIES
NAVY 3964

P-A-S-S

1060

This is to certify that ROBB, Thomas G.
Ser. No. 938 95 54, Rate S1c is attached to
N. S. F. and is quartered in TACLOBAN. This pass
permits him to be on the streets of Tacloban between
the hours of 0800 and 2230 daily. This pass does not
authorize entry into native homes.

Date 18 JUN 1945

A. M. ALLYN
Executive Officer

USNAB NSF NAVY 3964
(COMMAND)

Disbursing
(UNIT)   (DIVISION) OCT 1945

(MESS HALL)

T. G. Robb   9389554
(NAME)   (SERIAL)

VALIDATING OFFICER.

NAV. S. AND A. FORM 380   GPO 16—35329 1

453

EARLY CHOW PASS

H. A. JENSEN
LT. (JG) USNR USNR

Early chow & Navy passes

On August 6, 1945 the U.S. Air Force dropped the first atomic bomb on Hiroshima, Japan. Only a week before the Indianapolis had been sunk, it had dropped off the bomb to our Air Force Base in the Marianas. Our military command demanded that Japan surrender. They didn't respond. Three days later, on Aug. 9th, a second atomic bomb was dropped on Nagasaki. On Aug. 14, 1945, the Japanese agreed to surrender. That was when it was announced in Tacloban. I was at a movie. I don't remember the name of the movie, but right in the middle of it an announcement came over the base alert system that Japan had surrendered. A huge celebration followed. We all yelled a huge "Thank God! Hallelujah", etc. and the movie was shut off. The ships in the harbor, about 100 of Admiral Nimitz's fleet put on the greatest display of fireworks I had ever seen; cannons, anti-air, star shells, flares, etc. It was great!!!

USS Ticonderoga

Next day we all started thinking of how soon we could get back to the U.S.A. The Navy had a system of discharging us on "points" earned. I was lucky that I hadn't taken the storekeeper's exam. Those with that rating were frozen and would be the last to go home. I qualified to go, but it still took the Navy three months to get me home. I and several thousand others were sent to San Francisco on the aircraft carrier Ticonderoga. It's a beautiful ship. I was put on a "break out" crew and several times we brought up supplies from the lower levels. Instead of using the hanger elevators, we passed the supplies, hand to hand up ladders from several decks below. I think it was partly to keep some of us busy. When you're in a line of about five guys on each ladder section, and the guy below you is trying to hand you a fifty pound sack of flour at the same time as you are trying to hand the guy just above you another fifty pound sack of flour, you're pushed to the limit and you feel like your arms are about to come off. Only the guy at the bottom has it easy.

When we hit the Japanese current out beyond San Francisco, there was a kind of storm going on. The huge waves smashed in one of the hanger doors on the second deck and some of the guys lost some shoes & stuff. But we eventually made it to the beautiful Golden Gate and Treasure Island. I was taken along with a lot of others over to Oakland where a Santa Fe troop train to Houston was being made up. It was about fifteen cars long. When we got down into New Mexico it was very cold, below freezing. The train crew stopped the train next to a little country town. When they tried to get started again they found some of the train's wheels were frozen, or something else had. Anyway, we were stalled there for about twelve hours. During the stall, a crap game got started in my car and one of the train porters relieved some of the guys a lot of the pay they had drawn when they started home. At least he had both fists full of bills, as I stepped around him on my way to the head. There was a small grocery store near where we stopped. The guys kept jumping off the train and going to buy stuff there. Finally, as the train started again I looked out the window and back at the store. I knew some of the guys were still in there. Suddenly, as our train began to gather speed, two guys rushed out the door of the store. One wasn't carrying anything and made it okay. The other had his arms full of a big sack of something, most likely beer. He ran as hard as he could and when he saw he wasn't going to make it, he dropped the beer and made a last ditch effort to catch it as his buddy and a lot of others were yelling for him to run faster. He barely made it as the guys on the end of the last car grabbed him and pulled him aboard. He lost the beer but I'm sure he was glad of the sacrifice. Another guy who ran from the store late, ran a ways and gave up as we disappeared down the track. I'm sure he got home somehow.

When we got to Camp Wallace in Houston, we were discharged. It was Dec. 23rd. I immediately caught the Rock Island Zephyr to Dallas the next morning and made it home on Christmas Eve 1945. What a happy ending of my military experience. LaVerne and Richard looked wonderful!!!!

by Tom Robb

I went back to work in the money order department on the stamp and money order windows. Gradually everything got back to normal. LaVerne resumed her piano teaching of a few students. She also began taking lessons herself in popular music. First from a man who had a studio downtown, then from Georgia Ruth Pearson, who wrote beautiful arrangements.

I have always liked to walk. I used to walk to work sometimes from our house on Palo Pinto to the main post office, at Ervay, St. Paul and Pacific Streets, a distance of about two miles. Also I would sometimes walk downtown for lunch to one of the restaurants there. One day, I think it was in 1946, I had gone for lunch downtown and was on my way back to work. As I neared the main entrance of the post office, I became aware of an odd group of people scurrying around and ducking behind cars. As I crossed the street and approached the entrance of the building, I heard a shot and realized that it was a gunshot. I ducked behind a car with another person as three or four more shots rang out. Chips flew off the steps at the front of the building, not more than fifteen feet in front of me.

"What's going on here?" I asked the man hunched down in front of me.

"Some crazy guy is sniping at people around the post office. He hit a carrier, who came out to take a look. He's shooting from up in the YMCA building there in the next block." There were no more shots and we got the word that the police had found him and had him in custody. I went on into the building to my work. There, I learned that the carrier had died. It was just a crazy event that happens sometimes. I was very lucky that I saw the other guys behind the cars. I don't remember what happened to the sniper, except that he had a mental problem, and of course, knew neither the unlucky carrier nor the others he was shooting at.

In 1945 and 1946 LaVerne was an instructor at a private girls' camp, Camp Audubon, in the mountains above Boulder, Colorado Her training in photography was the basis of her duties there. She taught photography including the developing of the negatives into the final pictures to the girls. They took plenty of pictures. LaVerne had other duties including helping with horseback riding. Remember, LaVerne grew up on a farm and these girls were mostly city girls. There were about a hundred or more girls at the camp owned by a lady from Ft. Worth.

In 1946 Richard and I met LaVerne at the end of the camp and we went on up to see the big annual Cheyenne Rodeo, The "Daddy" of all rodeos. We checked into a motel and drove around the town. This was Friday. The big part of the rodeo was the next day. There was already a mob of people there. One of the most interesting things we saw on Friday was a huge steam locomotive at the Union Pacific Station. It had been used to help pull long strings of freight cars over the mountains between Chicago and San Francisco. Sometimes there would be a mile long string of a hundred cars, with a second engine in the middle and a third one pushing at the end. The engine on display was an enormous one. The next morning LaVerne wasn't feeling well but we did see the big parade. We decided to skip the rodeo and the calf roping. Sunday morning she felt better and we headed home to Dallas. Although we missed part of the event we were happy to be together after the three week Audubon Camp.

We had been on the waiting list at Hope Cottage to adopt a baby for at least four years (even before Pearl Harbor). LaVerne was unable to get pregnant and our doctor suggested adoption. After I came home from WW2 we renewed our application. Dr. John Young, who was a dear friend of ours at Sears and Summit Church of Christ, was on the board of directors at Hope Cottage. LaVerne talked to him and he took it up with the nurse in charge and things looked hopeful.

In 1947, LaVerne, Richard and I took a long vacation trip through Colorado, Utah, Wyoming, Montana, Idaho, Washington, Oregon and down to California, then back to Dallas. On this trip, while we were in Washington State, Jane was born back in Texas and was put in the Shriners' Hope Cottage on Welborn Street in Dallas for adoption. On this trip, Richard riding in the back seat, spent so much time reading his "funny" books that he missed half of the interesting scenery. We tried, "Hey! There's a haystack on fire!" etc., but he soon caught on to that ruse. On our way to California in 1948, we stopped in Cloudcroft, New Mexico to see our friends, Grace and Charles Thomas, who were vacationing there. They had been so much help to LaVerne while I was in the Navy. Charles was in the process of taking his CPA examinations, which he later passed. Just before LaVerne and Richard came out to be with me, right after my boot camp, Charles had mowed our steep front lawn and helped her get the old Packard running and sold it for her. They had invited us to spend the night and when we arrived at their cabin, they started finding places for everybody to sit. Grace sat on the lower of the double-bunk bed, Charles insisted that LaVerne and I take the two main chairs and he pulled up a small child's chair.

"Let me sit in that and you take this chair," offered LaVerne.

"No. You sit there. This is fine for me," he said.

Charles weighed about 220 lbs., and when he sat down in it, the chair completely collapsed, depositing him on the floor. He wasn't hurt and we all, including him, had a good laugh. Later when it came time to go to bed, Richard was assigned the top bunk and Cordell, their young son, the lower. Cordell protested. He wanted the top bunk, Richard didn't object, but Cordell had never slept in a top bunk before. After a bit of argument, Grace allowed Cordell to climb up and be tucked in. Cordell was about 8 yrs. old, Richard 11. LaVerne and I slept on a folding single bed in the living room. So we all got comfortably snuggled in bed and the lights were turned out. It must have been about 2 or 3 o'clock in the morning when there was a loud THUD and Cordell let out a yell and started crying. He had fallen out of the top bunk. Now everyone was up and the lights turned on. He wasn't hurt, but Grace insisted the lower bunk for Cordell. Richard climbed into the top bunk and we all settled down again for the rest of the night.

The next morning, after breakfast, we resumed our trip. Interesting things that relieved the dullness of the long stretches of level roads were the signs along the roads, tumbleweeds that rolled across the road and were trapped along the fences and the Burma Shave signs, each different. After we left Cloudcroft, which is near Ruidoso, we went through Raton Pass into Colorado. We viewed Colorado from the top of Pike's Peak, then on to Denver. From there, to avoid the high mountains to the west of Denver, we went on north through Ft. Collins, Laramie, Rawlins and Rock Springs, Wyoming, where we spent the night, The next morning we headed out toward Seattle, Washington. The first good-sized city was Pocatello, Idaho; then Idaho Falls with the beautiful water falls. In Butte, Montana, we were surprised to see a huge open pit iron ore mine almost in the center of town. From there, we drove northwest through Missoula, Montana to the pretty little city of Coeur de' Lane, Idaho. It's like a diamond in the rough. I would be a really nice place to live. We decided we needed to hurry on and our next stop was Spokane, Washington, the location of Gonzaga University and their very good athletic teams. Finally, our turning point, Seattle, was our next objective. Barring a grizzly attack or some other disaster we'd make it. The next day we arrived, intact, in Seattle.

When we got to Seattle, a city much like San Francisco, with much of the downtown built on hills, LaVerne and I wanted to do some shopping. Richard was so bored with the idea, that we dropped him off at a movie house that had something that he thought he would like to see. It was in the middle of the afternoon and we promised to pick him up at exactly three hours later, which would be 6 pm. He went in and we left. Two hours and forty-five minutes later:

"We'd better go and pick Richard up. I've seen plenty of things I like but can't afford to buy," mentioned LaVerne.

"Let's see," I mused. What was the street that theater's on?"

"I don't remember. I guess I didn't notice. Gee! How are we going to find him?"

"It's over in this direction," she said, pointing to the right. I headed the car in that direction.

"I hope the movie isn't over early and he's waiting out front and we don't find him right away," I worried. We drove all over the neighborhood that we thought the theater was in. We were very worried, but knew that Richard would stay right there. If we could only think of the name of that theater! It was getting dark and the streetlights were now on. The lights of the theater should be on by now.

"There's a 'glow'. It may be a theater." She pointed out. I drove around to the next block. It was THE theater and THERE was Richard standing in front.

"Where have you been? I've been standing out here for an hour," he complained.

I guiltily admitted that I had forgotten the location. I don't think it bothered Richard, but it was a good lesson for me. We enjoyed our short visit there; a beautiful area; busy like an ant hill. From there we went down to Portland and the wide and beautiful Columbia River. There were a lot of boats on the river. We drove up the river on the highway that runs up to Bonneville Dam. At the dam there was a ladder where the salmon could jump up the falls. It was amazing to see them attempt the jump. They looked to be about 1½ to two feet long. About half succeeded on the first try. I think most of them made it on up to the headwaters to spawn. There would be one trying it about every three or four minutes. It was exciting.

From Portland we decided to take Highway #1, which runs along the coast with its gorgeous views of the Pacific Ocean. It seemed that the highway was either turning to the right or the left it was so crooked. I think I almost wore out my tires on that stretch of highway, but it was worth it. If you're in a hurry, Highway #5 inland is faster but not as scenic. I remember stopping to spend the night at the spot where the Rogue River empties into the Pacific Ocean. When we got to the bridge over the Rogue, there was a gorgeous sunset over the ocean. We stopped on the bridge to view it. That was THE perfect spot. The sky was filled with scattered golden clouds that gradually darkened as the sun sank lower. We went on into a small town where the only hotel was an older frame two-story affair. Our room for the night was on the ground floor. The wooden sidewalk that ran along the street was just outside our room and the tramp of boots on the walk and the conversation of the people passing by made them sound like they were coming into our room. We kept the shade on the window that looked out on the walk pulled down, especially after we went to bed. The next morning we resumed our journey South again on Highway #101 (at times Hwy 1), which ran along the coast. About 200 miles south of Eureka the two highways split again and we took #101 toward the Bay Area. Since we were getting a bit travel weary and had spent 8 months together in San Francisco during WW2, we decided to skip it on this trip. We switched over to Highway #99 through the San Joaquin Valley to Bakersfield. From there we went to Barstow, Needles, Kingman, Flagstaff, Winslow, Gallup, Albuquerque, Santa Rosa, Clovis, Lubbock, Abilene and finally Dallas.

It was great to get back home! On unloading the back of our car and taking out our prize memento, the tumbleweeds, we found them infested with earwigs. We got rid of them both really quickly, killing as many of the insects as we found. Our prize "weeds" we put in the garbage in the alley. In case you're disappointed that we skipped San Francisco, here's a list of interesting sights to see when you go there: Golden Gate Park-the ocean with its seagulls, ships, the morning fog, the Cliff House and seal rocks, Telegraph Hill, Alcatraz, Coit Tower, Grant Avenue, and Chinatown, Union Square, the cable cars, the wharf area with all it's great restaurants (DiMaggio's), the Merchandise Mart, Market Street, the crookedest street in the world, the

Giant's new ballpark, Mt. Tamalpias, Muir Woods and many others not mentioned.

Then one day we got a call from Hope Cottage to come out for an interview. We thought it was odd since they had thoroughly checked us out; even came out and inspected the house. So we went out for the interview. What they wanted was to show us a little girl, six months old (Hope Cottage let no babies out for adoption younger than six months). We immediately fell in love with this beautiful baby.

"When can we take her?" we both asked anxiously.

"Today, if you'd like," the nurse announced. So we signed some papers and they let us take her home. LaVerne had brought a little blanket, just in case, but we didn't have diapers or anything else and Jane (named her later) was wet before we got home. I scurried around to get diapers, bottles, baby food, etc. and by the time I got back with them, Jane was crying to be changed. But we were ecstatic. When Richard got home, I think he was surprised and pleased as well. Jane's natural mother had insisted that she be adopted by a Church of Christ couple. We were very lucky!

We had lots of friends at Skillman Church of Christ, which supplanted the old Sears & Summit site, and for the next few years Jane and LaVerne had lots of happy occasions there with parties for the little ones. The Colemans, Tinsleys, Thomases and others had children of Jane's age. On one occasion that I remember, we were visiting Grace and Charles Thomas. After a delicious dinner, we retired to their living room and the kids were sent to bed. Jane, about a year old, was put to bed in their master bedroom and was soon asleep. After about an hour of conversation by the adults in the living room, LaVerne decided to check to see that Jane was okay. What she found was Jane sitting upright in the middle of their big queen size bed. She had found Grace's cosmetic box and was having the greatest time putting lipstick, perfume, etc. all over her face and hair. It was a riot of a scene. After deciding against just putting Jane through the washing machine, LaVerne scrubbed her up good and we kept her in the living room until we were ready to go home. As far as Jane's curiosity and ingenuity are concerned, they are good traits to have.

We had many good times while we lived at 5740 Palo Pinto. LaVerne was a very good hostess and a good cook. Most of our friends were church friends, but not all. I had lots of post office friends and LaVerne had a lot of others, also. We seldom went downtown without seeing someone that we knew. LaVerne and I had taken bridge lessons but most of our friends from church liked to play "42", which is similar to bridge, except it is played with dominoes. We had many domino parties. One of our domino couples was Richard Meggs and his wife. Richard had a cork leg and kept his sock pinned up with thumbtacks. He owned an automobile tire company near downtown.

In 1948, after much discussion between LaVerne and myself, I decided to complete my college degree. I had more than two years so far. I planned to try for a degree in real estate. Only three colleges had a complete program with that major: University of California at Berkeley, Northwestern in Chicago and MIT in Massachusetts. Since I had spent time in the Navy in California during WW2, we chose U.C. Berkeley. I sent them my letter of application along with my records from SMU and we waited their reply. We were very confident of an acceptance.

In the meantime: We had sold our house on Palo Pinto. The buyers, who had sold their house, were urging us to vacate. Cecil and Sylvia had rented a house on Rosemont Street in Oak Cliff. He was getting a promotion with the Burlington Lines Railroad and was preparing to move to Portland, Ore. We were waiting to occupy their house, so we moved in with LaVerne's Mother until the Rosemont house was vacant. Houses to rent were scarce at the time. Cecil let us know as soon as he knew the date of his departure and we went down and arranged to move in, making a smooth change and no rent loss to the rental company. So the shuffle worked out well for all. I was still working at the post office and we quickly settled in at 915 Rosemont in Oak Cliff and awaited the university's reply. Richard's new school, Winnetka Elementary, was only a few blocks away. We had sold the old upright piano and bought LaVerne a new Baldwin Acrosonic Baby Grand and she started teaching piano again using the name of Bobbie Robb.

A few things I remember happening while we lived at Rosemont:

That winter, the whole Dallas area had the worst ice storm that I have ever seen. It was also the most beautiful. Already most trees, except the evergreens, had lost their leaves. The temperature day and night was freezing. The day before, there had been a slow drizzle of rain that soaked everything, then froze. It had left the branches of the bushes and the evergreens' branches hanging low. I remember going up the street to a little grocery store, about a block away from our house, for a half-gallon of milk. The owner was about to close. It was very cold and customers had stopped coming. It was 11:00 pm and he decided to close after I paid for the milk. The drizzle had stopped several hours earlier and the clouds had rolled away. The cold moon cast an eerie glow on the half-dark scene. I shivered. I should have worn my heavy jacket. About half way home, I heard the sharp crack of an evergreen limb breaking and the thud as the whole limb hit the ground. The misty rain had turned to heavy ice. I pulled my sweater up tight around my neck and hurried on. Our warm bed would feel good tonight, I thought. The next morning, what a beautiful sight! The bright early morning sun on the glistening ice covered branches shown like thousands of diamonds. There wasn't a breath of air; just a cold ethereal scene. I hastened to get LaVerne to take a picture of it before it started melting. She did, and the temperature stayed down and we got many pictures of the ice and the snow that followed later on. There was so much ice and snow that fell on the streetcar tracks that the cars didn't run that day. But in a couple of days, the temperature did edge up and things returned to normal.

Finally, I received a letter from the University of California. In the admitting office's answer, they questioned one of the subjects that I had listed. They doubted that it qualified as one of the subjects that U.C. required. I knew the two subjects in question were the same. SMU had a different name for it. I took the letter out to SMU and they agreed with me. They promised to send a letter to U.C. explaining the subject. I then sent a letter to U.C. explaining the subject and another letter advising them of the forthcoming letter from SMU and stated that I was on my way to Berkeley to enroll in the September term.

Let me give some credit here to LaVerne. She, like me, was not afraid to take a chance. We were both healthy, as were Richard and Jane (12 & 2). We had just sold our house on Palo Pinto and had about $8000 in cash. We had, as always, discussed the pros and cons of my attending Cal. We had complete confidence in each other, so we were both looking forward to a new exciting adventure in California. I had informed our post office officials several weeks earlier regarding my plans to leave and now I gave them my resignation. It was taking a chance but I was confident that we could work out any problems when we got there, so we got really busy to move. I bought five or six big flour barrels. Anything that we couldn't put in those barrels or in our car, we sold or gave away. The only thing that caused a problem was LaVerne's recently purchased Baldwin Acrosonic Baby Grand piano. She loved it! She had been teaching several students in the area. It was the only really nice piece of furniture that we owned. LaVerne had made do with second-hand upright pianos all her life. It would cost too much to ship it and it was too big to go in our car. The only choice was to sell it, which we reluctantly did.

"I'll never get another as nice, I'm afraid," she sighed. As it was sold and taken away, big tears filled her pretty eyes. Later when we lived in Danville, we bought her a beautiful dark brown baby grand piano.

The last day at Rosemont was a hectic one. The flour barrels were picked up by a transit company and what little furniture we had was sold or given away. We were supposed to leave the house vacant. At the last, just before we got in our loaded car to go, we deposited the last things just over the back fence into the alley, where they would be picked up by the garbage men. LaVerne had told our next-door neighbors about it and we saw a couple of them looking over the "leavings" in the alley on that last day. We had been at Rosemont about ten months.

As 915 S Rosemont faded from our sight we felt a peculiar feeling of elation, sadness, thrill, chill, excitement, anticipation, a little bit of worry, confidence, etc. Whatever the outcome, we were on our way!!!

An interesting event that later happened in Dallas as I recall it: One day Mrs. Dawson walked up to the Lakewood State Bank near where she lived. She made a deposit, then, walked over to a table in the lobby to put the receipt in her purse. A man slyly watching her as she came in apparently said to himself: "She just made a deposit to her account. She's elderly, probably very thrifty and likes money. A good try." He had just gone to the cashier to change a $20 bill to justify his presence in the lobby, watching out for the bank dicks. There was no one near her now, so he approached her.

"Pardon me, Lady. I'm Mr. Mora. I've got a problem and I need help. You look like a kind and responsible person. Would you help me?"

Mrs. Dawson: "What's your problem? I'm in a hurry. I've got to get back to my house."

The man: "I've got $5000 being held by a bank in Livona, Italy. The court there has approved its release to me as soon as I forward them $500 in court costs. Then they will wire the money to me. I have just 48 hours to send the court the $500 or I'll lose my $5000. I need the money. My wife's not in good health and needs to see a doctor."

Mrs. Dawson: "Where is your wife?"

Mr. Mora: "She's with my mother in El Paso right now."

Mrs. Dawson: "Do you live here?"

Mr. Mora: "I've just moved here from El Paso. I have a job with the City of Dallas starting next month. My wife will join me then. I live in an apartment on Ross Avenue. Where to you live Mrs.–? I've forgotten your name. I'm sorry."

Mrs. Dawson: "I live on Belmont St. I'm Mrs. Dawson."

Mr. Mora: "As I mentioned, I've got to raise $500 in 48 hours and if you could help me by putting up that amount for just 48 hours, I'll give you 40%, that's $2000 earned commission, and you'll get your $500 back from me at the same time. It's a great investment for you. It's like the stock market."

Mrs. Dawson: "I don't keep up with the stock market. Hmm. I know they make a high percentage sometimes."

Mr. Mora: "Yes, they do. There's nothing wrong with people like us making a good investment, too."

Mrs. Dawson: "Mr. Mora, as I said, I'm in a hurry. I'll need to think about it a little."

Mr. Mora, seeing his pitch about to be wasted: "I agree with you. You go home and think about it. Let's see, its 12 o'clock now. I'll come by your house in a couple of hours and we'll figure out the details. You said you lived on Belmont St. What's the number there, Mrs. Dawson?"

Mrs. Dawson, reluctantly: "Its 6263, Mr. Mora."

Mr. Mora: "I'll see you then at 2:00, Mrs. Dawson." Mrs. Dawson walked home. On the way, she thought about what had been said. It would be nice to increase her savings by $2500. It would take a long time for her to save that much on her meager income. However, something just didn't seem right. She didn't like to be rushed into anything, especially if related to money, which was so hard to get. When she got home she called LaVerne and told her about the proposal. LaVerne immediately realized that it was an attempt to embezzle money from her mother. She told her sister, Shirley, and they called Sue. All three sisters planned how to get Mr. Mora arrested. They were convinced that Mr. Mora was a fraud. Mrs. Dawson agreed. So they called the police, who outlined a strategy to trap Mr. Mora with the incriminating evidence. At 2:00, Mr. Mora rang the doorbell. Shirley ran and hid in a utility closet and Sue hid under a bed in an adjoining bedroom that was close enough to hear what was said. Mrs. Dawson opened the door and ushered Mr. Mora inside and into a chair.

Mr. Mora: "Then you are ready to make the investment?"

Mrs. Dawson: "Yes. As you say, it's like the stock market. Everybody does it."

Mr. Mora: "I'll get back to you as soon as I receive the $5000 with your $2000 and return your $500."

Mrs. Dawson started writing a check for the $500.

Mr. Mora: "I'd prefer cash, Mrs. Dawson, if you can do it."

Mrs. Dawson: "Okay. I'll have to give you a check, but I'll go along with you to see that you have no trouble cashing it at my downtown bank."

Mr. Mora: "I think that will work okay. You are making a good deal, Mrs. Dawson and my sick wife will appreciate it."

Mrs. Dawson: "Do you want to ride downtown with us, Mr. Mora. "

Mr. Mora: "No. I have my car. I have some things to do after we're through at the bank."

So they all, including the police and a bank detective, met at the downtown bank.

Mrs. Dawson gave Mr. Mora a $500 check written on the bank. Mr. Mora cashed it with Mrs. Dawson's okay given to the cashier. Mr. Mora accepts the cash, counts it and puts it in his wallet.

Mr. Mora (to Mrs. Dawson): "You're a very fine lady, Mrs. Dawson. I really appreciate your help."

Mrs. Dawson: "Give my regards to your sick wife. I hope she gets better soon."

Bank detective, in plain clothes: "You are under arrest, Jack Rusolini, for embezzlement from this lady, Mrs. Dawson. He put the handcuffs on Jack (Mr. Mora) and took him away. Mr. Mora (or Jack), as he was led away: "I should have known better. Never trust a female; especially one from Texas."

Sather Gate, University of California at Berkeley

Chapter 6: 1949–1975

When I arrived in Berkeley, California and enrolled in the University of California, I used my G.I. benefits for some of the tuition. Because I came from out of state, I paid a higher fee. And I had other expenses, such as books, student athletic fees, etc. I was using a lot of money.

RICHMOND ERA:

We found that apartments and vacant houses were scarce. The University, however, controlled some low-cost multiple housing in Richmond, which was adjacent to Berkeley. They rented us a two-bedroom apartment on the upper floor of a four-plex. Jane and Richard's only place to play was the space between the buildings and a space behind. There were a lot of kids.

Across the hall from us lived a family named Rossi. They had a son, Donald, several years younger than Richard. The father worked at some job (he wasn't a student) and got paid every Friday. He usually went to a bar after work and stayed until they closed at 2 am. Then he would come home, if able. His wife would be so mad at him that she wouldn't let him in the apartment. He would bang on the door (waking all of us and others) until she finally let him in. Then they would fuss, yell and throw things at each other. Their two small girls would be crying in the background. Finally, they would quiet down and we could get back to sleep. The walls between apartments were thin shiplap and plasterboard and we could hear every word they yelled. The next day they would act as if nothing had happened.

Mrs. Rossi had a piano in the apartment and used to bang on it. She thought she had a great voice and wanted LaVerne to play the piano and she would sing. But, LaVerne didn't want to get involved with her.

While living in the apartment, we met and became friends with a young couple who lived in the ground floor apartment below the Rossi's. They were both students at U.C., and married, but she went by her maiden name.

131

She was Ruth Rosenkranz and he was Melvin Cadwallader. We enjoyed the limited time we spent with them. They had us down once to a "candlelight" dessert, where we all agreed, after much discussion, that we were all "middle-brows"; not "Low-brows" or "high brows". Ruth later went back to New York and became an artist. Melvin stayed on the West Coast and became a professional in the field of psychology. I don't know how it happened, but I still have her driver's license.

I was using a lot of our money from the sale of our house in Dallas, so I decided that I should get a part time job to help out. In inquiring around, I found that Craig Oil Co. hired part-time workers for their gas stations. I checked with them and they had a student leaving a graveyard shift, 9 pm to 1 am, at a station nearby on San Pablo Avenue in Richmond. That was just what I was looking for. So, I took the job.

I was taking four subjects at U.C.; two of them were lecture classes. In addition to attending the lectures, I could buy "Fybate Notes" of each lecture for forty cents. The notes were made by a graduate or upper classman who attended the lecture and made a report on it, which was published the next day. They were very good and helped me a lot.

"Cal" had 24,000 students on campus that year, 1949, and the two lecture classes had 1,000 to 1,500 students in each class. You were expected to attend class, but no check was made. If you didn't pass the exam, you didn't get credit for the subject. I usually attended and made my own notes and still bought the "Fybates". I passed the courses OK.

Back to my job at Craig Oil: The filling station was a nice large one on a major road and business was good. There were two or three other employees there until midnight. I was by myself until 1 am. Then I would close, lock everything up, go home, wake LaVerne and fall in bed.

At 7 am LaVerne would wake me up, stand me on my feet, feed me breakfast and shove me out the door to meet my 8 o'clock class. Two of my classes at U.C. were at opposite sides of the campus. One class was on the West side, near the business district; the other was on the East side, near the stadium. I was always late for my second class, but I passed the course.

In 1949 there wasn't much business at the station after 11 o'clock and I spent my time hosing down the driveway and cleaning and resupplying the bathrooms. It was an easy job. Only one incident happened in the four months that I worked there. It was just after midnight. I had just finished hosing down the driveways. The big Gulf Oil truck that supplied the station had just left. It was a cloudy, gloomy kind of night. I was tired and sleepy and was about to shut down and head for home. The streetlights danced, as the breeze caused their light to flicker on the wet pavement. As I was preparing to turn out the lights and leave, an old four-door sedan struggling on missing cylinders pulled in and up to the pumps. A crowd of about five or six young black kids piled out of the car and headed for the restrooms.

"Give me five gallons," said the driver. I started the gas into his car.

"The bathroom is locked," called one of the girls. I finished putting in the five gallons and went over and unlocked the restrooms. Then the driver decided he needed to go to the bathroom, and did. All the others came back and climbed back in the car. When the driver returned and started getting in the car, I yelled, "Hey! Wait a minute. You haven't paid for the gas!"

"Some of you guys pay the man," said the driver, turning and speaking to the two couples in the back seat.

"I ain't got any money left," one said. There was an embarrassing silence.

"Come on," I said. "I don't want to have to siphon it back out! How about taking up a collection? I suggested.

"Yeah," said the driver. "Everybody chip in." All contributed, even the girls, and I finally collected the $1.75 total (gas was 35 cents a gallon). They left, laughing and still in a celebrating mood. I re-locked the bathrooms, the pumps and the office and went home. I worked at Craig Oil for four months, then, I went to work part-time in the real estate office of Mr. H.E. Russell, in Richmond. I didn't have my real estate license yet, but he and his secretary, Mrs. Robinson, went out of their way to help me learn the business. I showed property, listed property, made a lease deal, etc. It was a small office, but Mr. Russell was a long time successful Realtor and I learned a lot from him and his staff.

The Church of Christ in Albany met in a store-front on Solano Avenue and we started attending there. Later, when we bought a house at 973 Curtis St in Albany, we put our membership in at the Church of Christ at Prince & Fulton Streets in Berkeley. Our house on Curtis was a three bedroom on an upgrade, 50 X 50 foot lot. It had a two-car tandem garage underneath and a small den and laundry room, also underneath. We bought it through Jack Frost, a realtor who was a member of the Church of Christ. He had an office on Solano Avenue in Albany.

Richard and Jane were both able to play on the Marin Elementary School playground, which was just across the street. We could just look out our front door to check on them. Richard attended Albany High School and graduated from there in 1955.

Jack Brunelle lived several blocks away from us, on Richard's first paper route, and became a friend of his. To this day, Jack is like one of our family. His parents were both deceased and he lived with his sister and her husband.

Our lot sloped down toward the street, and though small, had plenty of space for flowers. LaVerne and I have always been eager gardeners when spring comes calling. We had our little flowerbed in front and a little plot on the side for flowers and veggies.

I bought a nearly new Chrysler from one of our next-door neighbors. Richard and Jack decided to try it out the first night. While driving it around, they decided to "do" Marin Avenue, from top to bottom where it ends at a little flower garden. That stretch of Marin is very steep and straight and called "Suicide Hill." Once you start down, you'd better have good brakes. I never could get the "straight" of what happened when they got to the little flower garden at the bottom. If you are lucky, you can slow your vehicle down enough to curve around it. If not, it's a bath in the fountain in the center. I don't know whatever else you can do. I didn't think to check if their clothes were wet. Their report: "The brakes are not very good and the clutch is in bad shape." I didn't pay them anything for their report. Soon, I got a new clutch put in and the brakes relined. I'm just glad I wasn't with 'em! (Perhaps the truth is best left unsaid.)

One summer Noble and Mary Dawson's daughter, Sharon, came up to visit us from Hollywood. Noble was LaVerne's half- brother. Sharon was about Richard's age and we thought the two would have a good time together. She stayed about a week. She was a real cute girl. Several years later she was killed in a car accident.

One year we had a Halloween party in our basement. We put about two to three inches of wood shavings on the concrete floor, LaVerne and Jane decorated it all scary with shaded lights and we invited a bunch of our friends and their kids. We had a spooky good time.

Our next-door neighbors, the Strobel's, were Jewish; they had two little boys, Allen and Brucie. On the other side, in a corner house lived a lady who was a wino. We never really got acquainted with her. She was pretty queer. She would walk by all dressed up on her way to the store a couple of blocks away. She'd soon be back. A little later, here she'd come by again, all dressed up in a completely new outfit, going to the store again. She never spoke. Down the street on the Strobel's side lived the Whitmores; Mr. Whitmore was a former mayor of Albany.

One summer Richard's college roommate from Abilene, Gene Coleman, came to visit. As soon as they arrived, Richard found he had a job waiting and was off to work each day. Gene was drafted into painting the house while he vacationed with us.

Richard had been studying violin since the 4th grade. In high school he had a very accomplished teacher who decided he didn't have the enthusiasm to progress further and suggested we were wasting our money and her time on lessons. There were plenty of other pursuits in high school. Richard worked at various jobs: paper route and McCallum's Famous Ice Cream. He played basketball and managed the track team. During this "era" he participated in the teen "style" of that day- not letting his jeans be washed until they were stiff enough to stand up in a corner without falling over. LaVerne didn't subscribe to the trend. It was a 50–50 success at our house.

After graduating from high school in 1955, Richard enrolled in Abilene Christian College in Abilene, Texas. The following summer he spent traveling all over Texas selling aluminum cookware. He'd run out of money sometimes and write or call us. We would send a money order to where he said was his next stop. About half the time, the money order hadn't arrived, and he would have to go on and "make do" somehow. We would get our money order back stamped "Unclaimed at General Delivery".

LaVerne studied and passed the real estate salesman's exam and worked for Jack Frost Realty. She was about to take an offer on a big house on Marin Ave. when she got sick. By the time she recovered the house had been sold to someone else. When Mr. Frost closed his office on Solano, LaVerne didn't try real estate sales anymore. She got a substitute teacher's license and worked in the Albany school district. One day she was hanging out clothes on our circular clothesline and stepped wrong on a garden hose; that produced a broken foot. She had to wear a plaster cast on her leg—quite a handicap. About the same time we bought our first black and white TV set.

I finally graduated from U.C., along with about 2,000 classmates, in June 1951, with a BS, majoring in Business Administration and minoring in Real Estate. I looked around for a job as a real estate salesman. Because of my college credits, the State of California did not require the usual two years of experience as a salesman before taking the broker's exam. So, I took the broker's exam and passed.

I applied for a job with Coldwell Banker Real Estate Company, the leading realtor in the Oakland area. I was offered a job as a salesman (broker) in the Richmond territory. I had worked in Richmond in my student days with H.E. Russell Co. and decided that I couldn't make enough money to live on there. I thanked them and declined.

Next, I contacted the Wulfing Company in Oakland. It was a large office on Grand Avenue with about twenty salesmen. I was accepted as a Broker/Salesman. When Matt Wulfing took me around his office introducing me to the other fifteen or so sales personnel, one salesman's name seemed familiar:

MATT: "This is Tom Robb, our new salesman. Tom, this is Harry Weir."

ME: (trying to place the man)–"Hmm, Harry Weir. Where are you from, Mr. Weir?"

MR. WEIR: "I came from Minnesota."

ME: "Did the town happen to be Duluth?" (I began to remember a pen pal from Duluth when I was twelve.)

MR. WEIR: (with a quizzical smile) "I grew up in Duluth."

ME: "Do you happen to remember a pen pal from Cooper, Texas when you were about twelve years old?" (I sensed a miracle evolving.)

His mouth flew open and he looked me square in the eyes. "You're Glen Robb! I can't believe it," he said. We shook hands, hugged and patted each other on the shoulder. This was truly an extraordinary coincidence. It had been thirty years since Harry and I had corresponded as twelve year olds. Harry and I became lifelong friends, and both did well in sales there in Oakland, until the 1953 recession hit our economy and Mr. Wulfing closed his office on Grand Avenue and with two commercial salesmen moved to an office downtown. Harry and I opened an office on Claremont Avenue in Oakland for several months, then, he moved his office to his home on Broadway. I moved my office into the Acheson Building on University Avenue in Berkeley.

Harry died of a heart attack not long after moving his license into his home on Broadway. At the present time (2010) Lou Dobbs, the former newsman on CNN looks almost exactly like Harry Weir did.

My biggest sale while working in Oakland was to trade a four-plex for nine units and then selling the four-plex, both in the Lake Merritt area. My most noteworthy client I had in Oakland was the author of the book, "How to Run $1000 Into a Million." He had a clear property on the coast south of San Francisco that he wanted to trade for apartments in Oakland. I found eight units in a good location that he liked, but both were looking for a real "steal" from the other and I gave up on them.

The recession was still on and after two months I had only made a lease, so a friend of mine and LaVerne's invited me to share his office in Berkeley. Hobert Powell had been in the real estate business in Berkeley for a long time, but he was now in poor health. The Bishop Ranch, between Walnut Creek and Dublin was quietly on the market. It was several hundred acres. Hobert had talked to some investors in New York City that he'd dealt with before. He had not been able to get them to come out and inspect it. Because of his health, he asked me to take over those clients and he proceeded to wind down the rest of his business. I realized the immense potential for development of the Bishop property. I tried by letter and by phone to get them to come and inspect the ranch. I explained that Mr. Powell was ill and had asked me to help them. I could never convince them to take a look. I sent pictures, estimates, etc., but was unsuccessful. The Bishop Ranch was sold soon after that and today is covered by thousands of homes and apartments.

About a month later, Mrs. Powell called us, excitedly; she thought Hobert was having a heart attack. She had already called for an ambulance. LaVerne and I rushed over to their house, but there was nothing we could do. The ambulance crew had arrived but couldn't revive him. They took him away and we stayed with her until some relatives arrived. His death was a shock to me. I kept his office open and tried to wind up any business that I could, mainly notifying his customers of his death.

As far as I know, LaVerne grew up a healthy and normally energetic girl. She had the normal childhood illnesses. The first health problem that I knew of was in 1951, when our little son, Phillip T. Robb, was born in Kaiser Hospital in Oakland. He was a "blue baby" and lived only one day. Poor circulation was the cause. The hospital staff tried to save him, but failed. It had been a difficult pregnancy. The doctor feared for LaVerne's life and suggested they may have to abort the baby. LaVerne wouldn't agree. She insisted on the birth. The doctor found a lot of polyps that restricted growth. LaVerne was never able to get pregnant again. Phillip was flown to Dallas for burial with family in Cooper. On the way, Fred, Shirley, Cecil and Sue were hit by another car and Sue was thrown into the windshield, cutting her face badly. It left scars for the rest of her life. Phillip's body is buried in the Dawson plot of the Cooper cemetery.

I loved to sell real estate. I especially enjoyed the personal final dickering that has to be done to close a deal. If I found a property that my buyer really liked, I could almost always get the buyer and seller to conclude a sale.

But the recession of 1953 was too much to get through. After closing Mr. Powell's office, I made application for reinstatement in the post office, in Berkeley. I was accepted. I worked in the Berkeley station as a sub for two years, then, became a "regular" in 1955. I retired from the Post Office on December 30, 1965.

When we first came to California, Berkeley didn't have good clothing stores. We shopped for clothes in Oakland and San Francisco. I bought my suits in San Francisco until Berkeley got a good store on the Shattuck triangle downtown.

In 1950, on a trip back to Dallas, we called Grace and Charles Thomas to see if we could come out to see them. They had just moved into a beautiful new house on Cripple Creek in Trinity Heights. They said "come on out." We arrived and after a gracious welcome, they invited us to tour their new home. It was a large one-story house of about 3,000 square feet. After touring the kitchen, dining room, and four bedrooms, we started back to the living room. I know that ladies are always interested in closet space. As we were coming up the hall on the way back to the living room, we passed a closet. LaVerne, out of curiosity, stopped and opened the door. Out poured a flood of stuff around her feet – a vacuum cleaner, mop and bucket, a couple of folding chairs, a small throw rug, etc. Our reaction was comic.

Charles (laughing) – "I should have warned you not to open that door, but you had it open before I could say it. When you called, I didn't have time to put everything away, so I crammed it all in there." We had a nice visit with them. Their lot was huge and sloped down to a tree shaded creek (Cripple Creek) The Thomas's had two boys, Cordell and Brad. Charles is the first one I ever heard say: "It's like a lousy calf; live through the winter, and die in the spring." That was one of his favorite sayings.

In late 1953 and 1954, I was a sub in the Berkeley Post office. Since my working hours were in the late afternoon, I had time to supplement my income by other means. Ed Feeley, another P.O. employee and I teamed up buying older run down houses, working them over and selling them for a profit. LaVerne and Mary, Ed's wife, worked along with us on the houses.

We bought a lot on East 23rd Avenue in Oakland that had two small houses on it. The lot was fifty feet wide. We made application to the city to divide the lot into two 25 foot lots, each with a house on it. It was in an area that had other twenty-five foot lots. Our application was approved and we set about remodeling each one. We dismantled the old gas ceiling light system and had electricity installed. We scraped, sanded and painted woodwork, sanded and waxed floors, upgraded the kitchens and bedrooms. We hauled a truckload of junk from the small basements and the yard, and planted some flowers and shrubs in the yards. LaVerne and Mary worked daily along with us. The two separate houses were finally ready to sell. Both houses sold quickly at a modest profit for us.

We checked out other houses for sale and looked at several until we selected one that needed a good amount of work. Ed and I went downtown to the listing office to make an offer to buy it and left a $500 check on deposit. The house was vacant. After a week they hadn't been able to get an acceptance of our offer, so we cancelled it. They promised to send our check back in the mail. Several days passed and we hadn't received our check back; Ed and I decided to go by their office and pick it up. When we walked in there were three people in the office, the man we figured was the owner, another salesman and a secretary.

"We came by to pick up our deposit check for the house on 27th Avenue. We cancelled our offer by phone last week," I said.

"Oh, you're Mr. Robb and Mr. Feeley; that property on 27th? Just a minute," he said, as he disappeared into what looked to be a back room to the office. We waited. In a couple of minutes the secretary and salesman left by the street door. We waited another five minutes and still the owner didn't come back.

"Hmm, I wonder what's holding him up?" mused Ed.

"I don't know," I said. "Maybe something happened to him. I'll take a look in that back office. I really need to get to work at the post office right away." I took a quick look in the room into which he'd disappeared. It was just a storeroom, a short hall and a bathroom. There was a door at the end of the hall that led to the area outside the building. He was nowhere to be seen.

"He's not back there, "I announced. "He must have left by that back door."

"I'll bet he cashed our check and is out trying to get the money somewhere to pay us," suggested Ed.

"That beats all!" I said. "I guess business is not very good for him right now. We waited another fifteen minutes and no one re-appeared.

"Let's go," said Ed. "We can come back tomorrow. Maybe he'll have the money by then." We left.

The next day we went back. He had the cash. He apologized and we left.

Ed and I took in a hillside lot as part payment on one house we remodeled. It was a nice area in back of the Claremont Hotel, which straddles the line between Oakland and Berkeley. The night after we took title to the lot, a heavy rain caused the lot above ours to slide over ours and on down the hill, leaving our lot a mess. We were stumped. It looked useless. A few years later we did sell it to someone who cleaned it up and built on it. It was in a choice location and few lots were left in the area.

TGR family of 5 on Curtis St.

In 1955 Richard graduated from Albany High School; I went regular at the Post Office; John was born in the French Hospital in San Francisco. Ruthie Presnall found out through the attorney who had handled the adoption of their son, Marvin, and called us. We called the attorney, Mr. Trefts, and he arranged for us to adopt him. We paid him a fee, which included the mother's hospital expenses. We picked him up at the hospital when he was only a few weeks old. We were thrilled. He has always been a great little son and a leader. He has always had lots of friends, both boys and girls.

With a new baby, we needed a larger house, so we started looking for a suitable house in our price range. We contacted a local real estate lady. She had been trying to list a house on Colusa Avenue that she thought would be good for us. An older man lived there by himself while he worked in Alameda. He had let the place get run down and you could hardly see the house for the overgrown shrubbery. We liked the inside and made him an offer of $13,500; he accepted. That was in 1956. After we moved in we took out most of the old landscaping and replanted. We took out a partition between the breakfast room and the kitchen. We added a tile shower in the second bathroom, and did lots of scraping and painting. We did all of this ourselves. LaVerne worked along with me doing all of this. She was my favorite helper. She even helped me a lot to tear out and replace the foundation baseboard which was rotten and anchoring it to the concrete foundation. This was done in a crawl space off one and a half to two feet. It was slow work and rough on the knees. But, we did it!

We lived on the corner and Mr. & Mrs. Drucker lived next to us on Capistrano Street. He owned a tobacco shop on Solano Avenue. Across the street from us, on the corner lived Mr. Whittemore and his bachelor son. The elder Whittemore was a retired refrigeration engineer. He took all the fallen leaves I raked up and put them around his house for mulch. Next to us on Colusa, toward Solano Avenue, lived the Spaugh family. Their son, Donald, was a little older than John. The father worked for the State Agricultural Experimental Lab in Albany. (Our house on Colusa was in Berkeley.) Then there was Percy and his wife Margaret. She was an heir in the Manning Coffee family. Margaret received a monthly allowance from her trust fund. She was very nice, well-educated and a poet, but suffered from Parkinson's disease. Percy's last job was driver for Goodwill, but now devoted to caring for his wife. He spent all he could spare accumulating antiques.

While living there, LaVerne taught piano. She had yearly recitals for her twenty-two students. One of her male students eventually became Associate Director of the Berlin Symphony Orchestra in Germany.

Meanwhile, we enjoyed our association of friends and the activities of the Berkeley Church of Christ. Several events happened I'll mention: In the summer we liked to have picnics at Kiest Park. On one occasion, while the ladies were assembling the food on the tables, several of the young boys were throwing rocks at the Jay birds in the trees. One of the rocks hit LaVerne on her arm near John's head. Too close for comfort! The rock throwing stopped. One year we had a new preacher, Brother Elbridge Lynn. We liked him. He was about sixty years old. One Sunday he was in the middle of his sermon when he started to step down off the rostrum, he fell forward flat on his face. Everyone was horrified! He was helped up, evidently not hurt and insisted on climbing back on the rostrum and finishing his sermon. He apologized and explained that he had Multiple Sclerosis (MS) and a seizure just hit him at the wrong time. He left in a few months (no more seizures) and went into semi-retirement.

Later we hired Brother L.V. Pfeifer as our preacher. He was a young man and a good preacher, who had recently returned from missionary work in Italy. He and his wife, Maxine, lived in an apartment above the classrooms. Maxine had our family over for dinner one evening. She was just finishing setting everything on the table except the baked hen, which was cooling a bit before it was sliced and served. I noticed a peculiar smell when I first got there. When Maxine took it out of the oven, the smell became much more evident. I could see Maxine was worried about something when she whispered to her husband. But, she carved the hen, put the pieces on a platter and passed it around. Everyone took a helping (but not a big one). We had a blessing then looked around to see if anyone had taken a bite. No one had. I took a bite and everyone followed suit. It was awful bitter! I realized that Maxine had forgotten to take out the gallbladder before she cooked it. Everyone had politely taken a small bite of it, then, quickly switched to the vegetables, etc.

Maxine slammed her fork down on the table and said, "Don't eat any more of that hen. I apologize for whatever is wrong with it. I have plenty of other things in the refrigerator." She got up and brought out other dishes and opened the window to air the room. By the time dessert was eaten we had forgotten about the poor hen. LaVerne and I knew what the problem was and I think Maxine did, too, but sometimes a little thing will ruin a big event. We all loved L.V. and Maxine. He later became director of Mission Studies at Harding University in Arkansas.

Another event happened in the late 1950's. We liked to go camping in Yosemite National Park. One year that we were up there, Jay and Lula Graham, and son Lee, were camped next to us. We both had tents. John was a year old and Lee was tow. Lee kept biting John. Finally, Jay fixed them separate pens next to each other. We thought we had the problem solved—

but, Lee would still bite John through the separating barrier. I don't remember how it all was solved. I think Lee got a good spanking.

The congregation at Berkeley, for a time, had a family night together each month. We had a fellowship hall and each time, a selected family would put on a "skit". It was fun and some were pretty good. This was when John was about five. When it was our family time, we worked up a skit copying the old tent show story: A crooked banker trying to foreclose on the home of the poor widow. I was the villain, LaVerne was the poor widow and John (riding a broomstick horse) rushes up at the critical moment and in a gun battle defeats the villain and saves the widow's house. Our skit was either too good, or too bad. The skits were discontinued after that.

After all the renovations on Colusa, we had a large family friendly house. We lived there for ten years, during which time our three kids grew up a lot. John was enrolled in Mrs. Carson's pre-school for a couple of years (ages three & four). There he became good friends with Jeff Tieslau. Jeff and John were inseparable friends until an awful accident occurred. Jeff's dad operated a tugboat on San Francisco bay, steering big vessels in and out to the ocean. Jeff often was taken along. One day Jeff was with his dad on the tug when a large wave rocked the boat and Jeff fell overboard. His dad immediately jumped into the water to save him. The weight of the implement belt of tools and his clothing weighed him down so much that he was barely able to find and hoist Jeff back onto the tug. His dad was so exhausted that he sank and was drowned. Jeff was saved. After the funeral of her husband, Mrs. Tieslau decided to move back near her parents in an Eastern state. LaVerne and I helped her get their house ready to sell; painting, papering, etc. The house, which was on the side of Albany Hill, had a good view of the bay and San Francisco. It sold quickly and they left Albany. John became friends with Donald Spaugh, who lived next door.

Jane had several girl friends that she spent a lot of time with while growing up. She was a Girl Scout and was an excellent swimmer. Her swimming coach's daughter had trained for the U.S. swimming team, and urged Jane to train for competition. Jane had other plans.

In 1964, LaVerne and I, Jane and John took a trip up to Yellowstone National Park. I was still working in the Berkeley Post Office, Jane was in Berkeley High School and John was eight and in about the third grade. We drove from Berkeley to Salt Lake City. What a beautiful setting. It's no wonder the Mormon pioneers ended their search there. We descended from the mountains around it and found a motel for the night, anxious to explore the city the next day. We took a swim in the Great Salt Lake, where the salt content buoyed you up and it was easy to float. The water stung my eyes and the "salty" feeling made me want to get a shower as soon as I got out of the water. We stopped at a pretty park and spread a blanket for a picnic. LaVerne was wearing shorts. After eating we were lolling around enjoying the sunshine and a policeman stopped and addressed LaVerne:

"Lady, you're not allowed to wear shorts in the park. It's a considered indecent here. I assume you're a visitor in our city. Please, no shorts while you're here." He was very courteous and went along. LaVerne changed to a dress the rest of the time we were there.

The next morning we headed out north toward Jackson. From Jackson we traveled along just east of the beautiful snow covered Teton mountain range. That brought us to the south entrance of Yellowstone Park. We drove through the southwest corner of the park to a hotel in West Yellowstone, which is just outside the park. The next couple of days we toured and took in the many features of the huge park, such as "Old Faithful" that erupts every so many minutes, the hot bubbling colored pools of steaming water and the picturesque Yellowstone River deep in a canyon that it has dug over the centuries. An awesome sight! We saw a moose grazing along the road. A lot of people were taking pictures of it, being careful not to get too close to it. We stopped and LaVerne took a picture of it.

The next day we stopped at a souvenir shop and John and I went to the restroom. While there, I suddenly became very nauseated and weak. I just had to lie down on the floor. John quickly alerted LaVerne and she had an ambulance called. It quickly arrived and took me to the park hospital. John rode with me in the ambulance while LaVerne and Jane followed in our car. By the time we arrived at the hospital and I saw a doctor, I was feeling normal again. The doctor could find nothing wrong with me and after a couple of hours he let me go. I've had the same thing happen to me several times since and always the quick recovery and no reason found. After a nice vacation, we left Yellowstone and returned home.

Odd things happen on travels, sometimes. I'm reminded of another occasion when we were returning from our trip in 1947. We were driving through a mountainous section of open country outside of Globe Arizona. Suddenly we came upon a long line of cars stopped ahead of us. The highway department was dynamiting along the road ahead. After a while, Richard walked up the line of cars to see what they were doing. He came back in a few minutes and said: "Mother, there's a couple up ahead that say they know you!" LaVerne and I walked up about twenty cars and found two of our friends from church and their daughter. They had been traveling, like us, and were returning home to Dallas.

After graduating from Berkeley High in 1965, Jane entered Lubbock Christian College in Lubbock in 1966. She finished nursing school in 1968 and took a job at Abilene Christian College, where she met Henry Norton.

Henry graduated from A.C.C. in 1970. They kept in touch and were married at the Church of Christ in Orinda, California on January 4, 1973. LaVerne enjoyed planning and helping in the wedding.

Apartment Building in Alameda

In 1964 LaVerne and I bought a twelve-unit apartment building in Alameda. Most of our tenants were married couples from the nearby Navy Base. They were good tenants. It was a four-story building, three stories of apartments and a full basement that included a laundry room, storage area, four garages in the rear and an entry mezzanine in front. LaVerne did most of the managing. I concentrated on repairs and cleaning. LaVerne helped on that, too. Mr. Kilgore, the seller had been reinforcing the foundation. I helped him finish it.

I retired from the Post Office on December 30, 1965. I had worked for the post office a total of 32½ years. After being unemployed for a couple of months, I got "antsy" and went to work for Mason McDuffie Real Estate Company in Walnut Creek. For the first year I commuted from Berkeley. Then we bought a house at 247 Greenbrook Dr. in Danville. We sold the house on Colusa in Berkeley to Mr. and Mrs. Loobkoff for $33,950. We had paid $13,500. On Greenbrook, we were one of the first to buy in the Greenbrook subdivision. Our friends, Frank and Gwen Brindel bought a house near us on Waterman Circle. John helped us a lot putting in the new landscaping, while attending the Charlotte Wood Elementary School in Danville. From there he attended Danville High; transferred to Ygnacio High for a time, then San Diego Military Academy. From there he joined the U.S. Marine Corps.

In August 1967 my mother developed pneumonia following minor surgery. I flew to Texas to visit her in the hospital. For the first time in my life, I told my dear Mother, "I love you." She was too sick to answer. She died soon after I saw her, on August 20th. Ever since, I have wondered why and regretted that I didn't tell her more often. Maybe that's one of the reasons I often assured LaVerne that I loved her (as she responded in kind.)

I think it was in the summer of 1968 that I was in the office of Mason-McDuffie Company. At the time there were five or six other salesmen in the office. I was doing "floor duty", which means I was to serve any "drop-in" customers looking for a house to buy, or had a house to sell. Also, any customers answering our ads were my customers. If I went out with a customer to show houses, the next sales person "up" took the floor or phone calls. It had been a slow morning for me, until the secretary brought me a letter addressed to the firm. The secretary had opened it, seeing that it was regarding the search for a house, gave it to me. The first thing I noticed was that it was an airmail letter from Japan. The letter was typed and in English. It was from a Mr. Akio Limb He stated that he and his family (wife and three daughters) were moving to the area and wanted to look for and buy a house, new or newer, of four or five bedrooms, in a good neighborhood. He requested that I call him in Japan, acknowledging the letter and what prospects were of finding a house for him. He stated that he would pay whatever the market price was in the Walnut Creek area. Then he stated that he and his family would be arriving by plane at the San Francisco airport on a date that he would tell me when I called him. I quickly surveyed the possible houses for sale in our area that I thought met his need. I checked the time zones and found that Tokyo was seven hours earlier than Walnut Creek. I waited until it was 9 am in Tokyo and dialed the number listed in the letter. There was a short wait and then a faint sound and I knew the receiver in Tokyo was open. But, no one said "Hello?" or anything. Only silence.

"Hello, I said. "Anybody there?" (There was a giggle, evidently by a girl.)

"This is Tom Robb calling from California." (There was more giggling; sounded like I had just told them a good joke.) Then another person took the receiver and uttered a question in Japanese.

"This is Tom Robb in California. May I speak to Mr. Akio Limb? I asked hopefully.

"Oui, oui," (or, something like that.) I heard a "clack" as she laid the receiver down. There was a lot of excited chatter. I was about to give it up as a jinxed effort when Mr. Limb came on the line.

"I'm sorry for the delay, Mr. Robb."

"That's OK," I said. We discussed my efforts to identify several houses that I was ready to show them. I assured him that we could search until we found a house they liked. He told me the date of their arrival in San Francisco and I promised to meet them there and get them settled in a hotel. We could look at houses the next day, if they were ready. He agreed and we hung up the phones. I made reservations at a good hotel and set about planning their tour of the three best houses I had selected for them. It still would be ten days before they arrived. On the day off their arrival I was waiting for them to emerge from arrival gate. It was a sunshiny day and their plane was listed to be on time. I had not seen any of them and I hoped I could recognize them when they arrived. Everything, so far, had worked out right and I had a good mental picture of a young Japanese family. Finally, their plane came in and docked. The people started streaming out. I knew the girls were young, about four, five and seven, but I didn't see any group like a young Japanese family. I was worried. Then a well-dressed young Japanese man followed by three of the cutest little dark-haired "Cupie-Doll" type girls I'd ever seen appeared. They were followed by their mother; not a Japanese, but a beautiful American lady. I knew it was the Limb family, immediately. I introduced myself and welcomed them to the U.S. Shirley, the mother, had met and married Akio on one of his business trips and had gone back with him to Japan to live until they decided to make their home in California. While in Japan, the three little girls had been born. After getting their bags, they waited while I went for my car. I took them to Walnut Creek and left them at their hotel. They were tired. It's a long trip from Japan. I promised to call them the next morning to see three houses and left.

Next day we started the search for a house that they could occupy right away. We soon found one, a new four bedroom house in a good neighborhood with good schools. I helped them with the purchase, got the utilities turned on and they settled in. One unusual thing that surprised me, before entering the houses that I showed them, they would all remove their shoes before entering, leaving them in the entrance, a Japanese custom. I quickly did the same. I still have a small embroidered dresser scarf that the girls made and gave me. Besides Akio's business as a factor, he was an excellent speaker.

Mason-McDuffie Real Estate was headquartered in Berkeley. It had about six sub-offices in the East Bay; Walnut Creek, where I worked, was one of them. Bob Brickel, in the Berkeley office, was in charge of production. He regularly helped our salespeople with company-wide seminars that featured top national sales experts in rented auditoriums in Oakland, and speakers at dinners, etc. All this to keep us knowledgeable and enthusiastic. We had weekly bus tours of new listings. Mr. Brickel's office kept in touch with the big Eastern U.S. companies that were likely to be transferring employees to our area. A lot of the sales people were long time employees and they got most of the transferred house buyers, especially in Berkeley, Orinda and Lafayette.

I was lucky to be recommended by someone to a Mr. Robert Kramer, who was transferred into our area. I sold him a house in Lafayette. He was pleased with the service and recommended me to his brother, who worked for IBM in New York and was about to be transferred to the Bay Area. I followed up with a letter to his brother.

I sold his brother a house in Lafayette and three more transfers from the company. To cap it off, the last IBM employee I sold was the best. I sold him a house on 1/2 acre in Orinda for $500,000. As a result I was awarded a Certificate of Achievement for top sale of the month (our area.) The Commissioner of Real Estate came down from his office in Sacramento to hand me the award at a breakfast our group had during one of our regular weekly sales meetings. I think it equaled my top sale at Wulfing's when I traded a four-plex in on an eight-unit apartment, then cashed out the four-plex.

I like to work hard to be the best at what I choose to do. But I am not a leader. I don't like to tell fellow workers what they <u>have</u> to do. I am not good at saving money. LaVerne was good at that. I was always fortunate to make enough money that we could live a moderate lifestyle. I was so in love with and proud of LaVerne that I would buy her anything she wanted. Just before we took a trip to Hawaii in 1971 to visit Richard and family, we were shopping in Walnut Creek. In their display window, the I. Magnin store had a beautiful many-colored wrap-around dress. As we passed, LaVerne stopped and gazed at it.

"That's beautiful," I said. "It would look great on you."

"Yes, but it's probably too expensive," she said. There was no price tag visible. I could tell that she really admired it.

"How do you know?" I asked. "It may be a 'leader' or on sale. Let's go in and see."

"Alright," (there's that word again) "You'll see. It's probably $300. Or more," she countered. We went in and were directed to the third floor where a saleslady approached us.

"I'm Alice Moss. May I help you?"

"What's the price of the dress you have in the window downstairs?" I asked.

"I'll get it for you," she said. Before we could protest she was gone. We sat down and waited. Soon she returned with the dress from the window.

"I'm sorry to be so long," she said. "Let's try it on you."

"How much is it?" asked LaVerne.

"It's been reduced from $199.50 to $99.50. We had three, each a bit different. This is the last one."

LaVerne agreed to try it on. When they came back from the dressing room, LaVerne looked gorgeous in the dress. I could tell from her smile that she felt happy in it. She flashed a questioning look at me that asked: "What do you think?"

I knew that she wanted the dress.

"I don't want you to ever take it off! Ms. Moss, we'll take it," I said. LaVerne was thrifty, but liked to buy quality clothes.

"I'll box it for you," she said. "When you came in I immediately thought: "There's the girl for that dress in the show window downstairs. When you asked about it, I knew I had to get you in it. That's why I went down and got it off the mannequin." Ms. Moss soon had it boxed. I wrote a check and we left.

"Do you think we should have bought it?" LaVerne asked.

"Of course!" I replied. "It'll be twice as pretty on you. Lucky dress!" I said, as we crossed the street to our parked car.

In 1971 LaVerne and I took a trip to Hawaii to visit Richard, Sandra and family. They lived in a house in the seaside community of Kailua on the island of Oahu. Richard worked in Honolulu. He met us when we arrived and took us to their house. It was great to see them. There were Hibiscus and Plumeria in bloom all around. The house was only about 100 yards from a sandy beach on Kailua Bay.

Richard and Sandra had planned a lot for us to see. After a day at their house, we started on a busy and exciting tour. We joined the crowd on Waikiki beach in Honolulu to hear the very popular singer "Emma" Veary give an early evening concert of popular Hawaiian songs. I loved her singing. After returning to California, I ordered several of her records. I also ordered two records by singer Nina Kealiiwahamana in concert with Jack de Mello and his orchestra.

We also went to see the Pearl Harbor Memorial over the sunken battleship U.S.S. Arizona. We had a lot of fun playing in the ocean surf on the almost private beach near their house.

We visited Paradise Park, where the monkeys and birds were loose in a gigantic arboretum. I bought some popcorn at the entrance and started eating it and feeding some of the birds. A pretty Macaw flew over and landed on my shoulder and bit my ear. I gave it some popcorn and it flew off. Several others landed on my shoulder; I knew what to do before I got another "chew" on my ear. The main attraction there was a group of trained Macaws and Cockatoos doing their routine. They would climb up a ladder to a little platform where they boarded a small trolley that then took off down a wire that carried them to another little platform. There they were taken off by the attendant. Evidently they hadn't learned to climb back down yet. And the monkeys were as amused at us as we were with them.

One day we visited the Polynesian Cultural Center. Students from all around the South Pacific Islands manned authentic little exhibits of their home cultures and performed live music and dances from the various islands: Samoa, Tonga, New Zealand, etc., all dressed in their tribal garb.

Richard took us to a unique restaurant called "The Crouching Lion" on the North Shore. There, we were served a delicious dessert named "Banana Bisque" It was so good that after returning home I wrote them for the recipe. I got a letter back saying," We're sorry, but we can't give it out. Thank you for letting us serve you." We went to many other fine places that I don't remember just now. We went to a small Church of Christ on Sunday where Richard and family attended. Going to dinner someplace we had to traverse a ramp of some kind. Remember that wrap-around dress from I. Magnin? Well, a gust of wind came along and whipped that wrap clean off before you could say "Jack Robinson" I turned around and LaVerne was walking up this ramp in panties and stockings. Fortunately, she'd caught the hem of the dress in the nick-of-time and was pulling that wrap-around back around. We had a good laugh over it! It wasn't because of that, but we left town the next day.

We had been with Richard and family for a week. LaVerne and I planned to take a quick look at the other main islands before flying home. So, the next day Richard took us to catch an Aloha Flying Service plane to the island of Kauai, where we spent the rest of the day and night. I remember the hotel was located in a large coconut grove. It was a beautiful setting. We enjoyed the quiet, relaxing atmosphere after the busy one we had spent on Oahu. There was pretty waterfall and the Fern Grotto not far from the hotel. The approach was a forested climb through lush underbrush and trees. LaVerne decided she preferred the rest, so I walked up the trail to the falls. It was a pretty scene. Kauai is called the Garden Island. I don't think they were talking about potatoes and tomatoes. All these islands are the tops of a range of mountains that are mostly under the ocean water.

The next day we took a plane for Maui. We stayed in a hotel in Kahului, near the airport. I don't remember much of what we saw on Maui. It's bigger than Kauai and has a lot more space for agriculture. I think all the big islands grow pineapple and fruit for juices. I think we took a tour bus around part of the northern shore. I remember seeing a huge banyan tree and a scene along the beach where the tide rushed through what they called the "Blow Hole".

The following day we flew to the big island of Hawaii. We landed at Kailua on the Kona Coast. We registered at the Kona Beach Hotel. They were full, but had some cheaper cabins adjoining the golf course. We took one of these. No sooner were we comfortable settled in the cabin than there came a downpour of rain. The guys playing golf didn't stop; they just played through it. The rain only lasted a few minutes.

This time I rented a car and we started touring that side of the island. We drove down the coast, stopping at various scenic spots. At one place we came to a street that led back toward the volcano, Mauna Loa, and the center of the island. It was a dead-end road that was blocked by a lava flow, according to our map. We drove only a short distance and came to the blockage. It was a huge mass of lava, still smoking and apparently still advancing very slowly. I dropped a quarter at the base of it, thinking that in another million years some funny looking guy will break it out of a chunk of black lava and find my quarter. He'll deduce that long, long ago there was a leader named George Washington who worshipped a big bird named "E PLURIBUS UNUM." Mauna Loa's lava streams have reached the ocean in more than a dozen places. It erupted again in 1975. The next day we drove across the island to Hilo, where we left the car and took a plane back to San Francisco.

I retired from Mason-McDuffie Co. in 1973. Laverne and I decided we wanted to have more time together, do a little traveling and to lead a more relaxing life. Her health was not as good as it had been, and the apartments were taking more of our time. When I retired, our boss, Grant Shaw, took me, and all the office personnel, to lunch at the Alamo Restaurant as a goodbye gesture. I was happy with the affair. He told me that if in the future I wanted to come back to selling real estate, he would have a place for me. I had worked in the Walnut Creek office for eight and a half years.

In the summer of 1974, LaVerne and I decided to go to Victoria in British Columbia, Canada. We wanted to see the famous Butchart Gardens. Others had told us how beautiful it was and we were both eager gardeners. We drove Interstate Highway 5 up to Olympia, Washington, and from there to Port Angeles. Then we took the ferry across the Strait of Juan de Fuca to Victoria, which is the Provincial capital of British Columbia and is on Vancouver Island.

In Victoria we watched the State Parliament in session. We watched from the balcony as members sat around long tables. When they wanted to cheer a compatriot who was speaking, they would just pound on the tables. It makes quite a noise. At home I often watch the British Parliament in session in London. While their seating arrangements are different, they are more "into" the arguments as they proceed, than our own Senate and House. It's an interesting comparison.

The Butchart Gardens are thirteen miles outside Victoria. There is a lot to see. The estate is comprised of 130 acres and gardens occupy twenty-five of those acres. The Butchart's large home adjoins the Gardens. Plants bloom there continually, replaced with freshly blooming ones from hot houses. There is special lighting for night viewing in the Spring to Fall seasons.

Mr. and Mrs. Butchart are world travelers and have collected many exotic and rare plants. The original site was a limestone quarry and they have used it very well as pools, elevations and sunken areas. We spent a whole day there. There is a coffee shop, gift shop and restaurant on the premises.

On leaving Victoria, we drove north to Sidney, then by ferry through many small islands to Anacortes, Then to Burlington, Washington. There we caught Highway 5 again, and getting a bit tired, we scooted back home.

I had been working with the church group that was building the Sierra Children's Home for orphans and needy children on a twenty-acre farm near Vacaville, California. I was a member of their Board of Directors and was helping to get permits from County and State officials, hiring the Superintendent and the House Parents for the first house. (There were five or six houses planned.)

On May 15, 1975, when the first house was finished and occupied by the house parents and children, we scheduled a barbeque at the site to celebrate the occasion. Orvil Lee had been hired as Superintendent. My two-year tenure as a director was soon up and I didn't seek re-election. Instead, I recommended that Jim Smith, a member of our Orinda congregation of the Church of Christ, replace me. He was elected.

There were several important things that occurred in the early 1970's I'd like to mention here:

We were in a war in Vietnam.

January 11, 1969—Kelsey was born to Sandra and Richard in Cambridge, Massachusetts.

November 6, 1970—Chelsea was born in Honolulu, Hawaii.

May 1971—LaVerne had a mild stroke. It affected her face, but soon faded.

December 10, 1973—John and Jean Holm married.

December 29, 1974—Dawson was born in Honolulu, Hawaii.

January 17, 1975—John (now in the U.S. Marines) was injured in a parachute jump and had to have knee surgery.

February 19, 1975—Aaron was born to Jane and Henry Norton.

April 26, 1975—LaVerne and I attended a "Hillbilly" party at Merrill and Lucille Smith's. LaVerne wasn't feeling very well.

July 1, 1975—John had his second knee operation (7.5 hours) at Balboa Hospital.

The church at Orinda planned a Bible School campaign, with classes for children and meetings and lesson in the evening for adults. A half dozen or so young people from outside our area were invited to help in the two week campaign. LaVerne had helped plan it and offered to provide a room and meals for two visiting teen black girls. The event was to last from July 26 to August 15th.

June 18, 1975—LaVerne and I had dinner at Panchito's restaurant in Oakland to celebrate our 42nd wedding anniversary.

June 25, 1975—LaVerne had a mild mouth problem, again.

July 26, 1975—the Bible School campaign started; Jennifer and Mary arrived to lodge at our house.

August 8—LaVerne went to Kaiser Hospital for advice about her medications and the "mouth problem." She saw Dr. Williams and Dr. Malone. I don't think they found anything to change, since she was not having the problem at that time and she was to see Dr. Olwin the next week.

August 14, 1975—Shirley and Fred, and friends of theirs from Monroe, Louisiana flew into San Francisco. They stayed at a hotel over there, but we got together with them as often as we could. It was especially good for LaVerne to see her sister, Shirley. And, of course, Fred and the couple with them.

August 15—the Bible campaign was over and we took Jennifer to the airport for her flight home.

August 18—we took Shirley, Fred and their friends to the airport for their flight home.

August 22—LaVerne was instructed to increase the Lecithin that she was taking from 1 tsp. to 1 tbsp. per day.

August 26—LaVerne saw Dr. Olwin again.

August 29—Lois Crow treated us to dinner at the Elegant Farmer Restaurant in Oakland, with the Bert Irbys who were also our friends.

September 1—(LaVerne's 63rd birthday) Bob and Julia Gadberry had us to dinner to celebrate her birthday. Bob and Julia were two of our dearest and long- time friends in the area.

September 7 1975(Sunday)—we went to church, both morning and evening services. On our way home in the evening, we went by our apartments in Alameda to check that all was OK. LaVerne stayed in the car. She was thirsty and I stopped at a little store and bought each of us a cold drink then went home. We went to bed about 10:30 pm. About 12:30 am she woke me up. She was feeling bad and was worried.

"You'd better take me to the hospital," she said. I immediately rushed to get dressed and got her into the car and we rushed off.

"Hurry," she urged. There was not much traffic and we to downtown Kaiser Hospital pretty quick. She was admitted, but they were busy and she had to wait a little bit before she could be placed in an examination room. Dr. Olwin happened to be on duty and he soon came and checked her over. It was after 1:00 am and he came to me and said that he wanted to keep her in the hospital for a couple of days as a precaution. She seemed to have been stabilized somewhat. The nurses had given her a shot of something.

She was put in a room in the emergency section and had requested that I be allowed to be with her, so I stood by her bed. She didn't seem sleepy. Her heartbeat was being monitored on a screen nearby. It was now about two o'clock. There were two nurses that checked on her periodically.

LaVerne lay quietly, but seemed to still be anxious. She complained that it was cold in there. The heart monitor showed a regular beat, but the beats sometimes got further apart. I wasn't familiar with such measurements and kept watching the nurses as they checked her vital signs. They gave her another shot and adjusted her pillow. They added a blanket over her.

The monitor on the wall began to be more irregular. The nurse in charge called on the intercom for a doctor to come to emergency.

"Hold my hand," LaVerne said. I had been standing just at the foot of her bed. I immediately took her hand and held it.

She had just told me that it was "so hard to breathe." In a few minutes she looked at me and said: "I love you."

I replied, "I love you, too."

She settled down like she was going to try to go to sleep. I kept holding her hand and watched the heart beat monitor screen on the wall.

The screen showed her heartbeat to be irregular. As the minutes passed, the beats grew farther apart. One of the two nurses in the room gave her an injection in her arm. It didn't seem to change the heartbeat.

The nurse called on the intercom for Dr. Olwin to come at once. LaVerne's heartbeat went down to a level with no beat.

I was like in a trance. I realized that it was very serious, but I had complete faith that LaVerne would recover as soon as Dr. Olwin came. The nurses worried and gave LaVerne another shot.

Dr. Olwin appeared and asked me to step outside, which I did. I heard Dr. Olwin twice give LaVerne blows to her chest. He talked briefly with the nurse and left. I was still just outside the emergency room. The nurse came out to me and said:

"I'm sorry, Mr. Robb." I could tell that she was very moved. She continued: "You've been here all night, maybe you should go to Vila's for coffee or breakfast and plan on who you should call."

I was speechless. I couldn't answer her. That's when it hit me that LaVerne, the most precious thing in my entire life, was dead!

I had watched her die and didn't realize what was happening. I went back and looked. They had pulled the sheet up to cover her face.

I then went outside and stood, trying to decide what to do. It was like being on a wonderful trip on a train. The train stops and you are shoved off in a desolate area. No houses. Just cactus and sage brush as far as you could see.

The "other nurse" in the room with LaVerne came out the door and hesitated, as if to say something to me. But she didn't, and walked away.

I was too upset for coffee, or anything else, and went home. Although it was very early in Texas, I called Richard and told him about LaVerne. Richard caught the first plane out and arrived that afternoon. He took charge and helped me make the decisions and arrangements for the funeral, burial, etc. I couldn't have done it without him. After LaVerne's death, I was just lost. I'm 100 now and have never gotten over losing her.

She was buried in Oakmont Memorial Cemetery in Lafayette, California. From her grave, which is on a broad hill overlooking a big valley, you can see all of Mount Diablo to the Southeast and the Sacramento River to the West. It is a beautiful spot.

The other church members at Orinda were wonderful, having me out to dinner, etc. I spent a lot of time in church activities, but never felt like I did when LaVerne was with me; more like a sixty-five year old "visitor."

I think it was incredibly fortunate that I arrived at my music lesson just as LaVerne Dawson was finishing hers on that day in 1922, when I was twelve and she was ten.

And when Mother spoke up and asked Dad, "Why don't you write your friend, Charley Raney, and ask him how he likes the country out there?

But don't you, dear reader, go away. I'm still out on that awful, desolate, cactus covered desert, and it suddenly is getting dark. What has happened to us? Why? What can I do now?

———————******————————

AN AUTUMN BREEZE BRINGS MEMORIES
Words and Music by Tom Robb

The autumn breezes wafting thru;
The stars are bright and clear
I sense a faint perfume like dew—
And dawn will soon appear.
Sweet mem'ries from across the years—
Come softly back to me,
When music filled our happy hearts—
And we were young and free.

I close my eyes and see your face,
Your eyes, your hair, your smile.
I can't forget; they thrill me yet
Your kiss, your warm embrace.
We shared our dreams, our crazy schemes. We never—
Thought that life had heartaches too.
And tho' our story had to end—
I'm still in love with you.

The past is now our history.
Some things were meant to be,
And something happened to my heart—
When you first smiled at me.
Tho' autumn breezes come and go, with starry
Skies above.—and we're apart;—
Somewhere, someway, sometime, somehow—
We'll meet again, Sweetheart!

Chapter 7:   1975–2010

AFTER LAVERNE'S FUNERAL AND burial; Richard, Jane and John stayed with me about a week, then they each left to get back to their jobs. I realized that I needed to find something to do to occupy my time and mind. I busied myself with other things as much as I could. I was invited to dinners with a number of friends and received phone calls and cards from a lot of others. LaVerne had a lot of friends in a lot of places. I did chores around our church in Orinda like taking turns in cleaning, repairing and painting the outside stairway, restriping the parking area, etc. I still had the apartments in Alameda to take care of.

The following month (October) I volunteered as a driver for Meals-On-Wheels, a national organization that carries a midday meal to people who are housebound. The meals are made up by a hospital kitchen or other such facility with emphasis on nutrition and low cost. The meals are still hot when they are delivered. I drove for the Walnut Creek station, which had about ten routes. Each route delivered twenty-five to thirty meals contained in a closed, special container that kept them hot On Fridays we carried an extra meal for Saturday. No meals were delivered on Sundays. The customers were charged very little above cost and in some cases the meals were free. We tried to get the meals out as quickly as possible, usually taking about 1½ to two hours. I spent eleven years driving for them usually two days a week. I enjoyed the contact with the people, some of them living alone and barely mobile. They became good friends, almost like family. Sometimes I'd go back after the route to do a favor for someone who was unable to do it themselves, like getting some item from a store, hanging a broken window shade, etc. In one case I spaded up a bed and planted flowers just outside a picture window for an older, invalid lady. One of my customers, a lady about forty, lived by herself in a room over some stores on Main St. in Walnut Creek. She was blind and I had to give a "special" knock on her door for her to open it and receive her lunch. She was friendly. I'm sure that she had someone who kept constant check on her. She was on my route for about six months. Over the eleven years, I carried most of the Walnut Creek routes. It was a rewarding experience.

Since I was twelve years old music has been a very big interest in my life. After LaVerne died, I found that my church activities were just not enough. I felt that I didn't fit there anymore, being single. No one could take LaVerne's place, but I needed a group that met a personal need by having more single people near my age that shared mutual interests.

Conn organ

A few weeks after LaVerne died, Jack and Diane Brunelle invited me to their home for dinner. Jack had just bought a new electronic organ. I enjoyed the evening and Diane's home cooked meal, but especially hearing jack play the organ and trying to play it myself. I was thrilled to play once again. I had not played the organ since 1929 when I was in Kansas City and had the opportunity to play on the huge organ of the Loose family of the Loose-Wiles Biscuit Co.

Later, in Feb. 1976, remembering my visit with Jack and Diane, I noticed an ad in the newspaper about an organ concert the next Saturday at Boundary Oaks Golf Club auditorium in Walnut Creek. I went. Registering at the door, I was given a program. I sat down among a large crowd. The organist played a lot of beautiful numbers and it brought back memories of the programs I used to hear at the beautiful Palace Theater in Dallas back in the 1920s, when I was single and just started working at the post office. I was enthused. Chaney's Organ Co. in Walnut Creek, the concert sponsor, lost no time in inviting me to come down and look at their assortment of organs. I was sold anyway and stopped there the next week. Paul Funston, their salesman, soon had my signature on the sale of a small spinet with the choice of trading for a larger one later on. I was invited to attend their midweek night organ class, which I joined.

Earlier, on Dec. 20, 1975 I went to Texas to spend Christmas with Dad and all my relatives there. I stopped on the way in Carlsbad, Calif. to see John and Jeane. John was in the Marines, but living off base. Jeane was expecting their first baby to be born any day. I went on to Texas and when I came back through Carlsbad a couple of weeks later, little Shawn was there. He had been born Dec. 23, 1975. On March 20 1976 Chaney's delivered my spinet organ. Within a couple of weeks I realized that it was too small. Since they had a policy of trading up for full value on newer models, if it were their sale, I exchanged my spinet for a larger one. Over the years, as newer models came out, I upgraded to the newest model, such as #651, which had the professional footboard, large keyboard, rhythm unit, chimes, large speaker, etc. I decided, "This has got to stop!" I didn't buy the #652 when it first came out. Chaney's wouldn't offer me enough in trade for my #651, so I decided to keep it and we negotiated a fair price for the new #652. I rented a U-Haul trailer and took the older one to Richard in El Paso. As it turned out, the next year's was the last one put out by the Conn Organ Co. before the company was merged with another organ company. The trumpet that Dad bought me when I was 12 was a Conn.

June of 1976 Richard, Sandra and family visited me for about a week and we took in the sights around the S.F Bay area. I really enjoyed their visit. When I took them to the airport to catch their plane back to Texas and was about to park, Richard noticed an airport sign that noted "Oakland".

"Is this the San Francisco Airport?'

"No, this is the Oakland Airport. Isn't this where you leave from?" I asked.

"No! We leave from the San Francisco Airport," he said.

"Well. We don't have time to get you to San Francisco now. You'll just have to spend another night with me. I'll take you to San Francisco tomorrow," I promised.

After the shock of the error, we all thought it was funny.

"I didn't do this to trick you into staying longer, but it's a nice kind of consequence for me. I hope it's not a bad one for you," I admitted.

"We'll adjust," he said.

I got them to the San Francisco Airport the next day in plenty of time. As they disappeared from sight, that awful sadness and uncertainty returned.

I went home. I could feel the emptiness. It wasn't a home anymore, just a house. LaVerne had been with me for forty-two years. Of course, there was Pepe, our dog and all the favorite plants to care for, but I needed something else to help me get out of this terrible funk. Someone had said, "The sun will shine again. Flowers will bloom again." People! Yes, it has to include girls, like LaVerne. Why are they so important, really necessary? I had avoided them as much as I could until I was twelve. That's when I saw LaVerne at a music lesson at Mrs. Berry's. The disease didn't hit me until she beat me in the spelling match at the high school. That's when I got a bad case of infatuitis. There's not much you can do about it, but it is one malady that's an awful pleasure to have, it you have a partner. I took the group classes at Chaney's for a while, then, started taking night group classes at the Oak Park Adult School. Ellen Orsi was the teacher and what a great teacher she was and still is. She really drilled us on the basics of scales, chords, etc. After three years of night school, I took eight years of private lessons at her home studio. I also took piano lessons from Bob Athade of Lafayette on music variations for a couple of years and concentrated on making my own compositions of popular songs.

I have composed and copyrighted sixty-five of my songs in two folios. The melodies of all my songs were written first and the lyrics added later. I joined the Nashville Songwriters Assn. for a year to enter a song or two in their evaluation process, but they required a tape of someone singing the song. My voice would probably have ruined the song. My playing the song on the organ wouldn't qualify. So far I've not been able to interest any popular singer to look at my songs because they write their own songs and their labels have their own writers. The only addresses I can find are not the singers' personal ones. Even so, I have heard from a few with a hand written "thank you" comment, a few pictures or a "not planning a new album at this time". But I'm not completely discouraged. As soon as I finish my "memoirs", I'll get back to writing more stories and promoting my songs.

A little over a year had passed after LaVerne's death when I got a letter from Bro. Mel, a Church of Christ missionary in Italy. He was a longtime friend. He stated that his sister, Cleopatra (not her real name), recently divorced, was living alone now in Santa Ana, Calif. and he was worried about her loneliness. He wondered if I would drop in to see her if it were convenient. He hadn't thought about the consequences of putting two lonely people together, especially two who had recently lost or separated from a partner in marriage. Even before LaVerne's death we regularly went back to Texas to visit our relatives once a year and I had planned to go again in December, 1976. So, just before my trip I called Cleopatra, explained who I was and that I had heard from Mel. I asked her if I could stop by and see her on my trip. She agreed and we set the date.

On my trip I got into Santa Ana about the middle of the afternoon and put in at the Ambassador Hotel. I had her address, which was in a very nice neighborhood, and rang her doorbell. She answered and invited me in. Cleo was a very attractive young lady about eight years younger that I; dark hair, about 5 foot4 inches and very trim. She was operating a kindergarten-care place for about twenty little tots; a very efficient and nice looking place. I liked her from the start. After about thirty minutes of getting acquainted we went out to a Mexican restaurant for dinner. Then back at her house for a couple of hours of chit chat and I went back to my hotel. The next morning I headed out for Texas. I did stop in Albuquerque and wrote her a "thank you" note expressing my appreciation for her seeing me on such short notice and "out of the blue" like that. Later I drove down to see her about every two months and stopped to have dinner with her on my trips to Texas. She made one trip up to Walnut Creek to see me, staying at the Walnut Creek Motel. We spent the next day (Saturday) on a ferry trip to Sausalito. We went to church on Sunday and after dinner I took her to Oakland to catch her plane home. Our dates had gone on for about eighteen months. I went down to see her and take her some yellow iris plants from my yard that she had admired. She told me that she had received a letter from Mel reminding her that the Bible warns against divorced persons marrying again except for certain circumstances. I don't know what her aspirations were but Mel was her brother. I think the letter bothered her a lot. We had not discussed marriage, but if things had been alright we probably would have.

The next time I went to Texas, I didn't stop by on my return trip as usual as I had a very bad cold. In fact when I stopped at Richard and Sandra's in El Paso on my way home, he thought that I should see a doctor. He called his doctor who, although it was a Sunday, came down and opened his office and gave me a shot of penicillin. It cured my cold, but I broke out all over in a rash. That is why I skipped seeing Cleo in Santa Ana. I drove straight home, non-stop, from Tucson, Ariz. I called Cleo when I got home and explained. She said that she and her daughter were leaving on a two-week vacation trip to Colorado. I think that's where her ex-husband now lived. Two weeks later as I prepared to take my usual trip to Texas she didn't answer my call. I stopped, as usual, at the Ambassador Hotel. There was still no answer from her phone. I believed that she and her ex-husband had made up. I hoped so. It would be the logical solution to the problem. I wasn't ready to get very serious about marrying again. I was also very involved in writing my songs and getting them published and I was trying to get better on my electronic organ. Cleo was a very fine lady and I enjoyed her company very much. I have never been a "loner" and have always had friends, both male and female, especially when LaVerne was with me.

Homer Ray and Flo used to give me a sack of pecans (sometimes shelled) before I returned to Calif. It was such a welcome gift that I decided since no one seemed to grow walnuts in Texas, the folks back there might like a few from Calif. So, before my next trip to Texas, I bought 100 lbs. from a walnut farm near me, packaged them in five and ten pound sacks and gave them out back there. I didn't get away with it. Besides the delicious dinners, I brought back pecans, cookies, etc. It proved the old maxim: "If you give, you will receive" or something like that. I spent the night at the Ambassador Hotel in Santa Ana.

The next day was Sunday and I drove on into Los Angeles, planning to go to church there. I knew a family that attended the Riverside Church there in the past, so I checked a phone book, located the address and headed there. Arriving at the building, I found it vacant and boarded up. Checking the phone book again, I found two more Churches of Christ listed. They were both on Riverside Dr., but, farther out.

I selected the nearest one and set out to find it. It was about 10:45 am when I entered. I walked in and sat down near the middle of the auditorium. The man who greeted me as I walked in was a black man. He gave me a visitor's card to fill out. I didn't think anything of it since most Churches of Christ near San Francisco had a few black members. In a few minutes they collected the visitor's cards. I noticed another white couple in a seat just ahead of me. I spent a few minutes reading the weekly church bulletin. Then as the song leader got up to make a few announcements, a distinguished black man, came and whispered to me: "Mr. Robb, would you like to lead our prayer just before the sermon this morning?" I was surprised but knew that many churches honored visiting members, but usually visiting preachers. I was used to leading prayer at our church in Orinda. I had to think fast. I had to do it. "Yes, I'd be glad to," I said. I followed him to a room back of the pulpit where those who had other assignments assembled. Then we all filed out.

The preacher, the Sunday School Superintendent and I sat down on the rostrum and the four men and boys that would pass the collection plates sat down on the front bench. As I sat down, I noticed that the white couple that had been sitting just in front of me had left. There was a sea of black faces. "That was kinda "chicken" for them to leave," I thought. I was glad that I had stayed. I led the prayer without a problem. The preacher gave a good sermon. The members of the congregation were very friendly, inviting me to come back. I learned that the "white" church was the one farther out on Riverside. After I found a restaurant for lunch, I headed out for Texas.

Looking back, LaVerne and I had lots of friends during our lifetime together and regularly entertained them at our house. After her death, my friends were usually members of the church, my organ club, music classes or our dance class and group. I just didn't have time or occasion to meet many more. During the activities of the above events, I found many other friends. After buying my first couple of organs and learning to play it a little, I joined the Treble Shooters Organ Club. We met once a month, usually at a member's houses. I was president of it for several years. We had about 20–25 members (some were wives or husbands who didn't play). At the meetings, each of us would perform with a prepared rendition of a song or two. Our club, along with others was a member of the Pacific Council of Organ Clubs that annually sponsored a grand festival at the Asilomar Conference Grounds, a state park, on the ocean near Santa Cruz, Calif. The affair showcased the newest organs by the manufacturers, played by the popular professional organists of the day, who went about the country putting on concerts for the various clubs and retailers. Lodging and meals were provided on the grounds.

While I was president of our local club, I arranged for Larry Vannuchi, a nationally known organist, formerly pianist for Glenn Gray and his Casa Loma Band, for a concert at our Boundary Oaks Golf Club auditorium in Walnut Creek. It was co-sponsored by Chaney's Organ Store in Walnut Creek. Several of us from our organ club used to go each month to the meeting of the Tamalpias Organ Club across the bay. It was bigger than ours and usually had a guest performer including Larry Vannuchi and others. Chaney's put on a competition sponsored by Yamaha Organ Co. for the members of their store teacher's pupils. I wasn't eligible to win but I played a solo, my eight-page arrangement of the "Limestone Blues".

During this time I was adding to my collection of records, especially piano and organ recordings; Fats Waller, Frankie Carle, Guy Lombardo and many others. I would listen for the runs, fill-ins, endings; anything that sounded pretty or different and would include them in my own compositions. There were others, but Fats Waller was my favorite. Fats wrote hundreds of songs in the 20s and 30s until his death on Dec. 1, 1943 on a train while travelling to New York City from Los Angeles. It's reported he had a wife in each place. He died from a heart attack, following having the flu and exhaustion. From his base in Harlem, he wrote a steady stream of popular songs like "Ain't Misbehavin", "Honeysuckle Rose", "I'm Gonna Sit Right Down and Write Myself a Letter", "The Jitterbug Waltz", "I've Got a Feelin' I'm Fallin", "Keepin' Out of Mischief Now". His style of playing was called "Stride Piano":—Left Hand: a single note on count one of the chord, then a two note chord (1&7) on count three or any variation up or down as long as you emphasize counts one and three. Three count could be a third, a fifth, a sixth, a seventh or a ninth, even an eleventh. —Right Hand: it is free to carry the melody and the runs and variations that the song lyric is built on. Try this next time you're relaxing at a piano.

Fats and others used to have "jam sessions" in Harlem just to hear what other pianists had that was new and to pay the rent of some needy family. The others included George Gershwin, Ira Gershwin, Eubie Blake, James P Johnson, the Dorsey brothers and Cab Calloway. They would sometimes have a "cutting contest", where someone would start playing a song for eight or sixteen measures, then scoot to the left of the bench while keeping playing and another guy would sit down by him and take over the song, picking up the melody with his right hand and as the first player left also taking up with the left hand. The second guy would give up to a third and by the time it was stopped they had played several songs with a lot of new stuff. The host who lived in the house would serve up a good meal of beans, cornbread, etc. and the guys would take up a collection to help pay the rent.

There were other organ festivals during the year sponsored by organ manufacturers and their retailers. I attended two besides Asilomar— the Organ Holiday at Santa Cruz and Bill Irwin's Organ Workshop in Santa Rosa. Bill was a performer and a teacher at some of the main festivals. I have several of his books on organ playing. Some other things I'll mention that occurred during the late 1970s and early 1980s:

2/22/1979 I picked up Kenneth Kersey at the San Francisco airport from a business trip to Australia. He flew Quantas Airline.

2/27/1979 I met Mabel Martin at the Amtrak station in Oakland. She had arrived from Los Angeles. Since she was a fellow organist, I took her to one of our organ club meetings.

7/20/77 Emily Norton was born to Jane and Henry.

7/8/1978 I attended my fiftieth high school reunion.

Our 1928 Cooper, Tex. High School class held its tenth anniversary reunion in the summer of 1938 at the Delta Country Club. There was a good turnout, about twenty-five or so, if I remember. It was fun. LaVerne went with me. The next one that I attended was the thirtieth in 1958. Laverne and I lived on Colusa St. in Berkeley and I worked at the post office there. We drove to Texas. LaVerne and our kids, John and Jane, stayed at Mrs. Dawson's while I went to the reunion. What a difference from our tenth. Everyone looked like strangers at first. Then in about thirty minutes, they looked like my old classmates. It was great to see them again. They had borrowed a trumpet for me to play, but my lip was so out of shape I completely flopped on the try. Then in 1978 we had a fiftieth reunion, shared with several other classes. About a dozen of my class attended. LaVerne had died in 1975 so I flew alone from California. Richard met me and took me around to see Dad, Aunt Lula and other members of my and LaVerne's families. Then I flew down to see Jane and Henry for a couple of days and then back to Dallas I returned home on July 13th.

11/12/1979 I had a gastrostomy at Kaiser Hospital in Oakland. My parts keep wearing out.

7/19/1980 Cecil Kersey died in Chicago after a hard fight with cancer. Too young!

Early in 1980 Riley Metcalf died while playing golf at the Boundary Oaks Golf Club. He was my very good friend who worked along with me at Mason-McDuffie Real Estate Co. in Walnut Creek. We took care of each other's clients on vacations, etc. He was a very good salesman.

7/29/1980 John had an accident on his motorcycle and was taken unconscious to the hospital and had to have reconstructive surgery later.

3/30/1981 President Ronald Reagan was shot by would be assassin John Hinckly. It wasn't fatal and when Nancy Reagan visited the President at the hospital, he said, "Honey, I forgot to duck." Reagan was showered with many gifts during his recuperation including flowers, a goldfish, a ten pound box of chocolates and a fifty-five pound glass pig filled with jellybeans.

John, Cheryl and girls moved to Clements in the country, with goats, chickens, ducks, a tractor but no crops. I enjoyed visiting the girls, Jessica three and Crystal five, I think that my times seeing them helped a lot getting over LaVerne's death. It was like the enjoyment that LaVerne and I had seeing our kids grow up.

I had sold the apartments in Alameda. The Alameda Naval Air Station nearby had moved elsewhere and the Navy Couples, who had been the source of most of our tenants, soon moved elsewhere and the new type tenants were less stable. They were constantly moving out on short notice, owing rent. I didn't have a resident manager and I was spending more time cleaning and with repairs. The profit from the operations became pretty slim, so I sold. After deducting the 1st and a small second loan, the income tax and the selling commission, I think I made about $100,000. I had recently spent a lot on upgrading the apts. by adding a new roof, new and more attractive windows in the front, new carpets in the entries stairways and the three hallways, new washers and dryers in the laundry room and a renewal of the intercom system from the lobby to the apartments. And, I had the entire outside of the building repainted. I think that was $28,000. The building was now in tip-top condition.

August 12, 1981, I played the organ for the wedding of David Carney and Dawn Schindler in Benicia. David is the grandson of our friends Frank and Gwen Brindel. He is the son of Jim and Barbara Carney. Barbara is the daughter of Gwen and Frank. The new couple made their home in Arizona.

And, then one day I got a call from Lee Metcalf. "Tom, I'm having a small dinner party. Would you like to come?" I had dated Lee several times since Riley had died when one of us needed a partner at some affair or were just bored.

"Sure. I'd love to come," I replied. So it was, that a new, exciting era of my life was about to begin. But first, let me give you a little background: I have always liked to dance since Dad found me behind the player piano doing a "jig" when I was about four. When I was in high school, Marion Thomas, one of my classmates, used to have friends to her house to dance, but I couldn't dance so I wasn't invited. Geraldine and Kathleen Hooten who lived across the street from us used to have their girlfriends over to practice dancing. I'd hear the victrola playing and the girls giggling and squealing and wish that I could dance. Even Sylvia was over there sometimes with them. But I would never mention I'd like to dance, too. I was busy with my own music and learning to play the trumpet. I was timid with the girls. I did ask my cousin Nadine Robb one time if she would teach me a few steps. She was visiting us and I knew she was a good dancer. She didn't answer. I was sure that she heard me. I didn't mention it again, but I didn't forget it either.

One of my favorite programs on the radio was Guy Lombardo and his orchestra on WGN in Chicago and Ted Lewis and his band on WEAF in New York playing dance music in the big hotels. Later, after I was working in the post office in Dallas, I still had the yearning to learn to dance. I answered an ad in the newspaper for a dance studio. I paid $10 for three introductory lessons. A young pretty teacher taught me three or four steps of the Fox Trot, but I wasn't making enough money to continue. It was during the Depression. About the same time a friend, Roy Cox, who was a regular post office employee, promoted a few "spec" dances up in a conference room in the second unit of the Santa Fe building in Dallas. I operated the spotlights from the balcony, but didn't get on to the dance floor. Then just before LaVerne graduated from East Texas State she invited me to a dance on the campus. Red Buttons and his orchestra was playing. LaVerne was a good dancer and a very popular girl. I managed to fake my steps except for the Fox Trot because I remembered the four steps I had learned in my lessons in Dallas. Other guys were often cutting in (a tap on my right shoulder) and I had to give her up.

But I had a good time faking it. Laverne, the good sport that she was, was a true friend helping me.

After we were married we often danced in our apartment to the good music on the radio. Benny Allmon, a post office employee, started a small dance band during the Depression, when we were working short hours in the post office. I played the trumpet. I remember we played several weekends at an outdoor dance floor in Oak Cliff. We made $50 per night. For the six of us, each made about $9 per night. LaVerne stayed with Lucille at our apartments for those, but she did go to one that the Oak Cliff carriers put on and at which we played. I had to quit the band when I bought a car and started shooting specials. After Richard was born we were too busy with him and doing other things, so I laid my trumpet aside.

Now back to Lee's invitation to a dinner party. At the party, there were six people. Lee, now a widow having lost Riley a year earlier was with Al Walker. I was paired with Ruth Pattison. I don't remember the names of the other couple. It was a good dinner and we all enjoyed the evening. I liked Ruth and we began dating regularly. In February 1981, Ruth invited me to a banquet being put on by her singles class at the Presbyterian Church. I accepted. Since Ruth had to help with preparing the setup at the church, I met her there. I found a very friendly crowd of people. Ruth and I were seated at a table with two other couples. After a program, put on by two competing groups, we were served our food. Something I had eaten for lunch had begun to make my stomach queasy even before I got there. Just after I started eating, I suddenly felt sick without any notice. I rushed out, past many tables of diners, into the hall, where I was so sick I just lay down on the floor. Ruth quickly followed me out and someone called an ambulance and I was taken to Kaiser Hospital. By the time we got there, I was feeling much better. I didn't vomit. Ruth took me home and the next day took me to retrieve my car. I remember a similar attack in 1964 when John, LaVerne, Jane and I were on a trip to Yellowstone Park. What a way to impress a new girlfriend!

A couple of weeks later Ruth, who was taking dance lessons at Dance Masters Studio in Orinda (DMO), invited me to their regular Friday night dance, where the students were able to practice what they were learning in their lessons. It was so much fun and such a friendly group that I signed up to take lessons. I was assigned to Jill Cogan, one of the dance instructors. The owners of the dance studio were Steve Williams and his wife, Rita Bonel, both former professional competition dancers.

TGR and partner dancing, #1

Now for a few more comments about the DMO. Besides our lessons during the week, on Friday nights we had general dancing at the studio. Sometimes we brought desserts such as cookies, pies, hors d'oeuvres and a big bowl of ice-cold juice of some kind. Everyone was free to dance with everyone else and we did, so that we would be accustomed to dancing with different people. One thing I'd like to mention is that no one in our group was into drinking alcohol. It just wouldn't work considering all the steps in our routines. Steve and Rita were quick to counsel anyone who happened to come to our dances "under the influence". At our Friday night parties, for refreshments we always had a big bowl of fruit juice, ginger ale and something to give it a little "tang". I never knew what that was. Rum? It wouldn't affect me even if I drank half the bowl. Of course, a lot of us would have a cocktail at other places, myself included; at a good restaurant, for New Year's or for other special occasions. I rarely finish the first glass. The friendliness and encouragement of Jill, the other staff and the students was just what a lonely man who was drifting aimlessly, as I was, needed. I worked hard to be good at my new hobby, as I always do at anything I enjoy.

After a year, I was invited to join a group of about twenty of DMO's competition dancers, who normally went to at least two or three competitions each year. I was 71 years old. On a Friday night just before we were to go to a competition somewhere, we had a dress rehearsal at DMO. The men in our troupe wore their tuxedos and the ladies wore their gorgeous dresses. We danced the dances that we had practiced for the competition. The next weekend we would be at Portland, Oregon. We were supposed to be ready. It was the Oregon Star Ball at the Red Lion Inn. We competed there three different years; 1982,'83 and '84.

On one of our trips there, Mt. St. Helen's, which had erupted in May 1980 could be seen from our hotel, still smoking a little.

When you and your partner are out on the dance floor doing your "solo" dance, there are usually three or four judges standing along the sidelines with pad and pen judging you on your performance, according to your category. They don't miss much. You are judged on a lot of things besides your appearance; your steps (heel down first and at other times toe down first), how you hold your head, that your fingers are together, where you put your hand and arm at her back, alertness, if you are leading, your entrance and your ending. It's complicated, but a lot of fun. You and your partner (usually your teacher) are out on the huge ballroom floor all by yourselves and 150–200 other dancers or spectators are sitting at tables all around the dance floor with their eyes fixed on you—AND your steps are supposed to interpret the music that you have provided. But it's a thrilling experience! After our competition in Portland, Jill left DMO, as she and her husband were soon to start their family. Susan Conway, another young teacher took over my lessons. About eight months later, in March of 1983, I had practiced many hours with Susan, taking two lessons a week getting ready for our next competition.

On March 30, 1983 our dance troupe of about twenty-two dancers checked in at the Marriot Hotel on Canal Street in New Orleans. It was a five day competition called "The Winner's Circle". I was scheduled to do five dances. I had done well in Portland with Jill as my teacher and partner and she had been awarded "Top Teacher" in Portland. She had other students in the competition besides me. In New Orleans, Susan Conway, my new teacher, was my partner. We were to do the Fox Trot, Rumba, Waltz, Tango, West Coast Swing and a group dance. I was worried about the Tango as it was the last dance that I had learned. In preparation for my dances, besides the one or two practice sessions a week at the studio, I had done some practicing at home. In my house, my breakfast area and the family room, when empty, were a good-sized are to practice in. I stood the sofa up in a corner and put everything else in the hall and dining room.

A dance routine is usually about three or four minutes long, the same as a popular song. Most of the time we danced to the music of a song altered by Steve to exactly match the music that Rita had selected for our particular type dance plus an entrance and a closing flourish of some sort. A solo dance is made up of a number of 8–10 or more combination of steps, some repeated, such as an underarm turn, a back step, twirl, glide, spin, and walk around, all connected and synchronized with the music. The man is the leader of the dance and the lady follows. If I happen to skip a step or forget what comes next or fall behind the music, it is a disaster. The teacher or partner may take over and get me back on track but it doesn't fool the graders, who will list it in my grade sheet. I remember one time, when I skipped a series of steps, Rita practically lifted me off the floor and into the proper series. I got a second instead of a first on that dance.

Competitions are serious efforts for most. Sometimes, just before the action starts, there would be several couples out in the hall (Rita or Susan and I included) practicing the dance that we were scheduled to do. It's stressful. After all, you and your partner are out there all by yourselves before a large crowd of spectators and the judges with their notepads along the sides. Besides all the practicing I've mentioned, I did the same in my hotel room on any dance I was a bit not sure of. To remember the correct sequence of five different dances takes a lot of practice and a good memory. I give Rita, Susan and Jill a lot of credit for any success I had. I have a wall full of pretty trophies we received in eight years of competitions. I was active in that from 1981 to 1988 at the ages of 71 to 78.

I started telling about our New Orleans competition in March of 1983. I was so anxious after practicing my tango in my room and with Susan in the hotel hall that I had a headache. When I began to get dressed for my scheduled tango, I discovered that I had left all my cufflinks at home. I rushed out of the hotel to find a jewelry store. As I crossed Canal Street at the traffic light, my eyes got blurry with dots racing around. I got safely across the street and was lucky to see a jewelry store in the block. I had forgotten what I wanted there, but I went in and walked over to a long display case. I scanned the articles on display; necklaces, watches, and rings. My blurry eyes fell on a case of gold cufflinks. That was it. "What will you have, Sir?" asked a clerk. I couldn't think of the word "cufflinks". My head and eyes felt pressured. I pointed at a pair of the gold ones and he got them out. I took $25.00 out of my wallet, paid him and left with the little box in which he had put them. I hadn't said a word. He probably thought that I was dumb. By the time I had walked back to the hotel, everything was back to normal, except that I still had a dull headache at the base of my head. About 7 pm, when I did the Tango in the competition, I did it perfectly. Susan and I had practiced it one more time in the hall just before out time to go on without a problem.

About the eye/speech/headache problem. Pressure? Bright lights? I even had the same thing happen a couple of years ago, just as I was on my way to a doctor's appointment. Mercedes was with me. The doctor suggested that I go to the emergency room in Walnut Creek. By the time I got back to my car, I felt normal. I have never figured it out. The doctors think that it was a migraine.

As something different, the dance director proposed a new kind of group dance. All of the dance teachers in attendance who volunteered, about twenty, lined up to pick a partner out of two bowls of student dancers, male and female, who were participating that evening. When Debra Melito's, (a teacher from Houston) turn came, she pulled out my name as her partner. Judges were appointed and we danced about four different kinds of dances. I had no problem so far. There were about twenty couples on the floor. The last dance announced was a Mariachi. I had never heard of it, but Miss Melito knew it. I just followed her moves as best I could. Surprise! We won the event and I have a silver trophy for it. When not scheduled to dance, some of us enjoyed visiting the shops and sights of Old New Orleans. I had visited New Orleans with LaVerne one time when Jane and Henry lived there.

Dancing, with Rita #2

DANCE COMPETITIONS
Aug. '82 Portland—Red Lion Inn–with Jill, Oregon Star Ball
Mar. '83 New Orleans—Marriot Hotel–with Susan
Sep. '83 Portland—Red Lion Inn–with Susan
Nov. '83 San Francisco—Cathedral Hotel–with Susan, Gene Jennings
Apr. '84 Santa Clara—Marriot Hotel–with Susan
Apr. '84 Las Vegas—MGM Grand Hotel–with Susan
Jun. '84 San Francisco—Hilton Hotel–with Susan, International Grand Ball
Oct. '84 Portland—Red Lion Inn–with Susan, Oregon Star Ball
Apr. '85 Las Vegas—MGM Grand Hotel–with Susan
Oct. '85 Acapulco, Mexico—Princess Hotel–with Susan
Apr. '86 Las Vegas—MGM Grand Hotel–with Rita, Victor Dru
Jul. '86 San Francisco—Hilton Hotel–with Rita, International Grand Ball
Oct. '86 San Francisco—Cathedral Hotel–with Rita, Autumn Classic-Jennings
Oct. '87 San Francisco—Cathedral Hotel–with Rita, Autumn Classic-Jennings
Apr. '88 Palo Alto—Hyatt Hotel–with Rita, California Winter Fest
Feb. '93 Pleasanton—Hilton Hotel Ballroom–20th Anniversary party for Steve and Rita, including a brunch and dance. It was a surprise party attended by present and former members of their dance troupe. It was nice!

We competed five times, 1983–1987 in San Francisco, three times in Gene Jennings' "Autumn Classic" and twice in the "International Grand Ball" at the New Hilton Hotel downtown.

After you have had about five or six years of instruction, you can advance from Bronze to Silver. Then comes more instruction and you get into the Mambo, Jive, Salsa, Mariachi, Paso Doble and the lifts, etc. that you see in some of the "Dancing With the Stars" shows of today. I was just beginning to learn a few of the Silver steps when I became ill in 1988 and had to stop.

We did two more competitions in 1983, four in 1984 and one in Las Vegas in 1985. On October 10, 1985, we went to Acapulco, Mexico and the beautiful Princess Hotel on the Pacific Ocean. The interior of the hotel is elegant. The star-studded ceiling is three or four stories high over the huge lobby. My room (Rita always gave me a separate room) was on the third floor and I had a view of not only the lobby from my "catwalk" type entrance, but also the ocean surf from a small balcony off my room.

Adjoining the hotel was a nice outdoor restaurant, canopy covered, and a short walk down the beach (about 100 yards) was a Mexican Bazaar, also covered, which I think was controlled by the hotel, where hotel patrons could buy souvenirs, clothing and necessities.

Virginia Jenkins, one of our group and a dear friend, hired a taxi and took four of us on a tour of the city. We had refreshments at a café that overlooked the ocean cove where divers dived about 100 feet down into the water. It is one of the special events for which Acapulco is famous.

We also stopped and browsed in the city's largest department store. We bought a few items. I found that the locals were very friendly and helpful. Our trip to Acapulco was a very interesting and enlightening one

On July 13, 1984, Thomas James Robb, my Dad, died, while asleep, during the night. I flew to Texas for his funeral on the fifteenth. He lacked only one month and nine days of being 102 years old. He was a great Dad and I loved him very much.

Just two days after I arrived back from Acapulco, I caught a Pan-American plane on Oct. 17, 1985 for London, England. We arrived at Heathrow Airport the next day, Friday, after about twenty hours of flying. The trip over the great circle had been uneventful and a bit boring. We flew over Greenland and Iceland.

Richard and Dawson were there to meet me. After retrieving my luggage, clearing customs and exchanging $237.61 of American money for 200 Pounds British money, we took off for their home in the country about forty miles north of London.

There, we met Sandra, Chelsea, their four cats and "Blackie", Kelsey's dog. Kelsey was at work and I saw her when she got home.

I'll have to say that the forty mile drive north was a lot more unnerving to me that the 8000 mile plane trip from San Francisco, with Richard driving on the left side of the road and our getting out of the "merry-go-round" circles at the crossroads. I was glad when we finally arrived.

I did notice, on the way, the beautiful rolling countryside, the stone fences and the neat white plaster and brick houses with their slate and thatch roofs.

I don't remember the order of things the next week, but it went by in a hurry. Richard had to work some of the time and Sandra took me to see some of the sights in that area. Chelsea and Dawson were at school and Kelsey was at work. We visited the huge ruins of the castle at Kenilworth, the Ely Cathedral, Mildenhall and RAF Feltwell. We had lunch at a neat little basement diner called, "The Happy Eater", where I had fish and chips.

Also on that first week, either Richard or Sandra took me on tours that included Warwick Castle, a national treasure that is in tip-top condition, fully furnished, staffed and on display. We toured Kenilworth Castle, which is in total ruin. It's just as huge and has been in ruins for hundreds of years. It's just as exciting to see. You can see where some of England's fascinating history transpired during the War of the Roses and the struggles from the year 1066 until modern times. It's exciting to see where these things happened.

If you enjoy reading exciting history, I urge you to read the books of Jean Plaidy, who wrote about a dozen books on the English wars and the deathly struggles during the 15th and 16th centuries about such characters as Queen Elizabeth I, Mary Queen of Scots and Henry the VIII. Two of her books are "The Murder in the Tower" and "The Haunted Sisters". You'll have a hard time putting these books down.

After about seven days gawking at the sights north of London, we went down on Friday to see the huge city of London. Richard had made reservations at the Columbia Hotel, just across the street from Hyde Park and Kensington Gardens in central London. For the next two days we toured and experienced the big city.

We rode the "underground" to Westminster Abbey to see the rig-a-ma-role that goes on at Buckingham Palace, sipped tea at the Savoy, enjoyed, "Evita" at the Prince Edward Theatre. The next day we saw "42nd Street" at the Drury Lane Theatre. We explored Harrods huge store and the Thames River bridge area. We didn't view the tower inside, as we just couldn't see everything.

We snapped lots of pictures, ate fish and chips in a crowded pub, where the favorite sport (besides eating) was playing darts.

After the second day was almost over, we joined the crowd of cars on Route 12 going north and headed home. It had been an exciting and fun two days.

Some of the days I was there, I want to note. I don't remember which days, but Richard took me to Stratford-On-Avon, the little town where Shakespeare had lived. There is a famous theatre there that puts on his plays. We went through several towns on the way there; Acton, Kersey, Lavenham (Elizabethan half-timber building), Long Melford where there is a famous church, Clare and Newmarket (horse racing town.) All were quaint, clean, little towns.

When we got to Stratford, we found that the theatre was sold out, so we didn't get to see, "The Merry Wives of Windsor" that was being played. After spending the afternoon in the shops and museums, we spent the night at a bed and breakfast home, enjoying the evening in their parlor and their company. There were a few other people staying there, also.

In the morning we set out again. Richard found the ruins of a 500 AD old Anglo-Saxon settlement. Just the walls were standing. It was built in a small circle. This was outside the little town of Lackford.

We also found the ruins of an old church that was several hundred years old. It was just a long rectangular building with only the walls remaining and a dirt floor. Both were off a rural unpaved road and were not being cared for.

We drove on Southeast, bypassed London to Dover and its beautiful white cliffs. We then took a ferry over to Calais, France. At Calais, we drove around the city, not going too far, since we planned to catch a ferry back in the late afternoon.

I had a slight cough and we stopped at a store near the wharf to buy some cough drops. I didn't know what the French word was for cough drops, so I just asked for it in English. The clerk shook his head and waved his hands, indicating that he didn't understand English. I couldn't make him understand so I had to forget it. I think that he just didn't like English speaking people. I was sure that he understood what I wanted.

We boarded the next ferry to Dover and from there hightailed it back home.

On Sunday, Oct. 27, we toured the four Cambridge Colleges and went to Fagin's on the Cam River for dinner, after going to church that evening. On Monday we relaxed.

Early on Thursday, Richard and Dawson took me to Heathrow and I flew back to San Francisco. It had been a very fascinating two weeks.

I found the English people to be very friendly, but a bit reserved, not in a rush, inclined to be more relaxed and ready to enjoy a little fun or humor. I'm happy to admit them as part of my ancestry. There is so much to see in England, but the same is true of the US.

BACK TO MY DANCE COMPETITIONS:

After Acapulco and my England trip, we had a four-day competition in April of 1986 at the MGM Grand Hotel in Las Vegas, with Victor Dru as the producer. Rita was now my teacher and my partner. Susan had moved to Santa Rosa, were she had bought a dance club and where her husband, Ron, was now employed. They had just recently been married.

One of the places that I enjoyed very much was Las Vegas. We competed there three times (1984–85–86) at the MGM Hotel. I think you catch the excitement when you arrive there and you settle down and relax only when you leave. It is an exciting place.

One reason that I enjoyed these competitions so much was that our group performed so well for them. I think we all had confidence in not just ourselves but in our group and especially our partners (teachers). The stress for me came before I performed. After I began a solo dance, I concentrated and I didn't have time for worry until it was over.

A lot of dance studios don't enter competitions. The ones that do, I think, are pretty well prepared. I have seldom seen a couple in their solo dance get so confused that they just stop and walk off.

Our group had practiced so much together, and had been together at DMO with lessons and Friday night dances, where we switched partners often, that we were very much like a family.

At a competition, most of the time, there would be about 100 to 200 dancers, depending on the time of day, sitting around the dance floor at tables arranged for the 15 to 20 groups for the various studios competing. There was usually a full house at night for the pre-pro and professional dancers' performances.

At night, periodically, there would be a break from the competition for general dancing to a song or two, which was very popular. It was a nice relaxer and a chance to ask some new person that you had not danced with before to dance.

Occasionally a lower category dancer and their partner would be asked to repeat the dance they did earlier in the day for the night crown. Rita and I were asked to repeat one of our dances one night.

As we were leaving the ballroom for the night, a gray haired lady, probably in her late 50s, approached me.

"I'm Martha Graham," she said. "I want to compliment you on your dancing. You did very well."

"Thank you," I said, and she merged with the crowd leaving. I wondered about the name. Was that the famous classical dancer of that name?

The next morning as I was sitting at a table just outside the hotel restaurant waiting for Virginia Jenkins to come down and join me, Victor Dru, the man sponsoring the competition, spied me and stopped by my table.

"I'm Victor Dru. How are you this morning?" he asked shaking my hand.

"I'm fine," I answered.

"I want to congratulate you on your dancing. I've watched you. Keep it up," he said as he left. Rita and I had been asked to repeat our waltz of the night before for the evening crown. I was 75 years old. Maybe that was why they thought it was noteworthy. I didn't feel that old.

In the solo dance (usually three or four minutes long), you are competing against a perfect score set for your grade. The grades are beginner, bronze, silver, gold, pre-pro and professional. I was a high bronze and was just beginning to get into some of the silver steps. About half of the dancers at the competition were in the bronze category.

Everyone except the pre-pros and the professionals did their dances beginning at 10 am until 6:30 pm. The pre-pros and the pros did their dancing from 8:00 until 11:30 pm. Some dancers who competed were nationally known, even some from Canada and New York. Portland drew dancers from

Seattle, Salt Lake City (Mormons are good dancers), and the San Francisco area.

The dance system that we learned at DMO was the Fred Astaire system. Other studios used the Arthur Murray system. I think they are very much alike.

Often a newspaper reporter will contact the studio to supply dancers for a TV or advertising background scene. Rita called on Ruth and me to pose for a newspaper covering the Portland Star Ball and another time for a bay area TV station featuring one of our dance couples, whose hobby was ballroom dancing. Jean Means and I were also selected to pose for a full-page picture in the Diablo Country Magazine. Rita and I had our pictures in a photo shot of one of our dances on the wall of our studio the last year that I was there. I thought that was a great honor considering the many very good dancers from DMO.

Our dance group from Dance Masters of Orinda always got reduced rates at the best hotels, the Hilton in S.F., the Marriot in New Orleans, the MGM in Las Vegas, and the Princess in Acapulco. I competed in 15 competitions.

Our teachers, Steve Williams, Rita Bonel, Susan Conway and Jill Cogan very often earned top teacher and top studio. Our main studios in our area were one from San Jose and one from San Francisco. The Los Angeles area had its own competitions, which we did not go to while I was there.

Blackmore, England has an international competition each year. Ballroom dancing is popular in Europe, and is now making a comeback in the US with the popular TV series "Dancing with the Stars".

Dancing is great fun if you learn half a dozen steps. Different dances have different rhythms and different steps as well as some of the same.

My last competition was "The California Winter Festival in Palo Alto, California, April 24-26, 1988. The last day I was scheduled to dance two "solo" dances with Rita. Before the second dance I was feeling awful.

"Maybe I should skip it," I said to Rita

"You did the other well. I'll cancel if you want. It's your last scheduled dance," she answered.

"Let me walk outside in the hall a bit," I said. I walked around in the hall and got a drink of water. I felt better and went back in.

"I feel better. Let's do it," I said.

We did the rumba. Rita helped me a lot by co-leading. She knew the routine so she didn't wait for me to go into a new step. It was not a problem. In the judges' report, it stated that I appeared to drag a bit at times. I got a second on the dance.

After getting back from the competition my physical problems didn't get any better. So on my regular lesson on May 22, 1988, I told Rita that I had to stop until I felt better. As it turned out, that was my last dance lesson.

On June 15, 1988 Jane and Henry arrived. After my complaints, she put me in the hospital. My doctor, Dr. Tu, after a bunch of tests and the cooperation of his associate doctors, diagnosed my problem as Crohn's disease. Symptoms include loss of energy, extreme fatigue and in my case the inflammation of my lower intestines. Also, a bile duct was almost stopped up.

While waiting for the test results from the doctor, a nurse came in. She had blonde hair, dark eyes and was really good looking.

"I'll be your nurse for today," she said as she took my temperature, got me a glass of water, fluffed my pillow and left.

"Wow!" said Henry. "How do you rate that? No wonder you got sick."

"You're just jealous, I replied. Soon, I looked around and Henry was gone.

"Do you think he followed the nurse out?" I asked Jane.

"No," she said laughing, "He's probably down in the street trying to get run over so he can get back up here as a patient and be taken care of by Miss Darling." Soon Henry came in.

"How's the traffic down in the street, Henry?" Henry looked puzzled and looked from Jane to me. I told him what we were laughing about.

"Hey, that's a good idea. Maybe I'll try that," he said.

I dated two very dear ladies from our dance group at different times, both irregularly for several years. Ruth and Virginia are mentioned elsewhere in this story.

I had dates with several other ladies at other times and other occasions until 1995, when I was eighty-five and quit driving a car. It was about time, don't you think? Since then I've concentrated on writing my stories, plays and my memoirs.

In September 1996 Dave and Diane Megnin from Florida stopped by visit John and Mercedes. After chatting a while, Dave brought in a bag from their car. He opened it and pulled out a boa constrictor about six feet long. Diane coiled it around her neck, explaining that it was a pet.

Immediately, our cats left the room. The dogs went in "alert" mode and cautiously sniffed it (but not too close) and stayed close to John. After explaining its habits, feeding and history, he put it back in the bag and in the car. I didn't hear anyone from our house say, "I want one".

In Paris, Texas one afternoon as Dad and Mother were sitting in their living room, a strange man suddenly walked in the front door and walked past them to the back part of the house. They sat in surprise for a few seconds.

"Who is that?" asked Dad, looking around in the direction that he had disappeared.

"I don't know him," she replied. "I think he lives down the street. I've seen him pass by."

"He's an old fellow. He's just in the wrong house," said Dad, as he got up. He found the old guy at the back of the house standing, trying to figure things out.

"Aren't you in the wrong house?" asked Dad. When the man didn't answer, Dad told him, "You live down around the corner on the next street."

Dad escorted him back out the front door and directed him toward his street. The man thanked him and left. Early Alzheimer's?

Another event as told to me by Marie:

I was working at the post office in Dallas. Aunt Ney, at age ninety-six, was visiting Dad and family in Cooper when she suddenly died. The employees from the funeral company came to the house to get her and they embalmed her there in the living room. They drained the blood from her body and put in the preservative liquid right there.

They didn't notice, but Marie, five or six years old, was standing in a corner of the room and witnessed the whole ghastly procedure. Aunt Ney's body was then sent to Oklahoma for a funeral and burial.

I learned to read early. I think Aunt Ney helped me get started one time when she was visiting and helping Mother make quilts. By the time I was in the fifth and sixth grades, I was reading books from our school library, as well as the cheap magazines that I could swap or buy at the store. That's when I made my contact with Harry Weir, another twelve year old, in Minnesota as I reported earlier.

In high school I continued my love for reading with authors like Zane Gray, Booth Tarkington, and Mark Twain. Later it was Charles Dickens, Agatha Christie and Sir Walter Scott and still later I moved on to Nathanial Hawthorne, Edgar Allen Poe, Kipling, Cooper, Dumas and Tolstoy.

When LaVerne and I married, we were so busy with our kids and doing things together that I only read a few books not required in college or my real estate business. After her death, books were one of the things that helped me get along without her. Those authors and many others have set the stage for my urge to write stories; as playing my trumpet with bands and the Cooper orchestra and years of playing my organ, influenced my composing and publishing my two folios of music.

So it's natural that I enjoy writing stories and plays myself. I realize that I'm not an accomplished author yet, but most people don't start at the top. As I spent almost a lifetime involved in music, I have been studying and working on my writing since 2003.

For several years I had toyed with the idea of writing stories and plays, and had kept a folder labeled, "Ideas for stories". After getting temporarily stymied in getting some singer to look at any of my songs, I turned my attention to writing stories and plays.

My first idea was for short stories like in the Reader's Digest, true stories. I soon found out that I really enjoy the efforts, in fact, writing a story as much as reading one from the library. So I subscribed to "The Writers' Magazine" and "The Poets' and Writers' Magazine" in 2003 and started to school myself about the subject.

In Dec. 2004, I mailed two 2-act plays to a Diablo College competition for area writers. I live within five blocks of the college and had taken a music class there. I waited, but never heard a word from them. The local newspaper did publish the names of the winners, but Tom Robb's name was not mentioned. Looking back the six years since then, I can understand why. I have learned a lot since then.

I don't get that feeling of rejection on my stories anymore, for I know I have plenty of good competition, and the magazines get hundreds of entries. I find it's a lot of concentrated work but I love the challenge.

After my disappointment with the 2-act plays, Chelsea Robb offered to help me with my stories. She is an avid reader herself and works at a bookstore in the Seattle area. Each time I finished a story, I sent it to her. Soon I'd receive it back with her noted criticisms and suggestions. I give her a lot of credit for making my stories much more interesting and professional.

One Florida publisher, Eton Publishing Co., wanted my story "Try," but wanted $1200 for the publishing and promoting. I felt I didn't need to pay an advance fee. He dropped the fee to $800, then $600. I didn't agree and canceled the contract.

I have had many compliments, but not any offers, from the editors of magazines and publishers and a few agents. My biggest handicap seems to be that I have not already had works published successfully. There are already plenty of successful writers who are sending them stories and books. It's also a tough racket for the "outsider." That is exactly what I found in the music business. So I published my two music folios at Kinko's for $1200. Quality paper was the biggest cost in publishing my music.

A play, for me is more complicated to write because everything in the story must be revealed to the audience by what they see happen and what they hear from the stage. Income from staging a play is limited and theatres are cautious. That's why they tend to stage a lot of repeat, well known plays. The smaller theatres do stage more of the newer plays.

With seventy million people in the country who grew up reading the kind of stories that I write, I need to find a way to let them know what's on the market now.

Richard and Chelsea have just succeeded in getting my first book of stories and plays published. I am very pleased and thankful to all who helped. I have other stories in progress

My book of stories and plays, "That Magic Night in Hawaii and Other Stories and Plays" was published by iUniverse in April, 2009 and is on the Internet for $19.95. It can also be ordered through Barnes and Noble Bookstores.

That's all I can think of right now, Folks!!! I went into the living room and sat down in my favorite chair. "My book's published. My book of memoirs is finished. What do I do now?" "Have you ever experienced that?

"Well, that's all the good things I can say about myself. Now I'll tell you all the bad stuff. "What? You don't want to hear it? Well, whatever you say. So long!

Glen, Glenmore, Tige, Thomas, Tom Robb

Afterword

I have been having a peculiar problem for the last year or so. I have been hearing steam escaping from somewhere behind my head. The sound seems to come from about six feet back of my right ear. It comes on when I'm lightly concentrating on something. I just happen to recognize that it's spewing. Doesn't bother me much but it's non-stop until an hour or two later, I realize it's off. I think it is called tinnitus. I have been into music since I was twelve years old (trumpet, piano, electronic organ). Since my wife, LaVerne, died I have taken it up again since I have started playing the organ. How did I write my 65 songs in my two music folios?

Here's how I composed most of them: I had music going through my head a lot of time when I was asleep. A new strain of four or eight measures that I did not recognize would wake me up and I'd grab a notepad and write it down. The next day, I could construct a complete 32 measures of a new song. This has been so until recently. Now, the concerts that I used to hear only in my sleep, are on and off at times during my waking hours, usually in the evenings. They seem to come from my right side and from across a large ballroom. The music is beautiful! Not only do I hear some of my own songs, but strains from songs that I recognize from "The Great American Songbook".

I'll attempt to explain how I write a song:

A typical 32 measure popular song is constructed by taking 4 measures (waltz or fox-trot), repeating it, then, repeating that. That's 8 + 8 = 16 measures.

Now add 8 measures of just about anything; "God Bless America" or "Thanks for the Memories" will do. Then finish by repeating the first 8 measures. That's a complete song. Try it yourself sometime. That's how I came up with most of the melodies of the songs that I wrote. I'm sure most popular songwriters use the technique.

And, then there are the really great composers whose songs are much more than the basic 32 measures. I go beyond the basic 32 measures by making arrangements that are longer, move to other keys, or maybe into a medley of another song or two. It's fun!

In the last six months, the music that I heard in my dreams is now coming on in my head in the daytime. It is like a string band a short distance away. It's there when I'm concentrating on something else like reading a newspaper. It's beautiful! It will come on during the day and entertain me by its slow 2/4 or 3/4 time or sometimes I won't hear it at all during the day until late evening and there it is!

Some of the songs are older and slower. One is playing while I'm writing this. It's an "oldie" and beautiful. Sometimes I hear one of my own songs. I recognize the song that's playing now, but I can't remember the title. I did write down the basic 8 measures of two songs today that I didn't recognize. I'll check tomorrow to see if it's from a song already listed. If it's new, I may build a song with it (melody then lyrics), if I find the time.

I could listen to it for hours like background music, except that it repeats 8 or 16 measures over and over and over. I can change it as it plays by concentrating on it. If I am interrupted by something, I find it's gone. Later I suddenly realize it's on again. So much for that.

I joined an organ club, the Treble Shooters Organ Club, as I mentioned earlier. We met once a month for twenty years, then because of age, members moving away, etc. we finally disbanded it. During that time I regularly attended the annual California Organ Festival at Asilomar, Calif. and other concerts held by the professionals.

AND NOW INTO THE WILD BLUE YONDER

I don't remember dreaming much before LaVerne died, especially about people I know. Since she died in 1975, I have had several very vivid dreams that I considered at the time, and since, about being specifically about her present life. They have caused me to believe that she is now alive in another life here on earth.

It's an odd thing, but since LaVerne died in Sept. 1975, I have seldom dreamed about her, while I would like to dream about her often. In the thirty-odd years since she has been dead, I have dreamed about her only a few times. Four of these times, I have related in the following:

Example 1: On August 25, 1979 while asleep, I was suddenly very clearly conscious in what I understood was a dream of a young girl running toward me and very anxiously repeating to me the name of Lila Vanderskeldt and the name Burdick, Australia. She repeated both names three times as she ran toward me. She immediately disappeared and I awoke wide awake, I was so startled. This was about 2:30 am in the middle of my night's sleep. The girl looked to be less than 10 years old, slender and as I remember was blonde and nice looking. It was very unusual, but I didn't tell anyone about it. I had never heard or known of anyone with that name or family. I checked my Goode's School Atlas and there was no town named Burdick listed, but there was a Burdekin River and valley at 20:30 S. Latitude & 147:10 Longitude. Could the girl have said Burdekin instead of Burdick? At any rate, I was certain in my mind that the message concerned LaVerne. Could Shirley MacLaine be right? I quickly turned on the light and looked for something to write down the information that the girl recited. The only thing handy was the top of a box of crackers on my nightstand. I tore it off and used it. I didn't trust my memory to wait until morning.

Example 2: On December 18, 2000, a long time later, another dream. In the early morning, before my usual time of waking up, I suddenly dreamed that I was somewhere with a group of people in a house and someone called me to the phone. It was LaVerne. She said, "Glen, come home." That was all, and I woke up. It left me with a very odd feeling. I didn't know what to think. I couldn't go back to sleep for a while.

Example 3: On September 11, 2005 I had a very curious dream. I was lost in a rough, unfamiliar country. I was exhausted and had lost my shoes. I had to walk a long way on a road very rough on my feet. I finally was on a street and recognized a familiar building. I walked up some stairs to an apartment that I recognized as our home. I opened the door, looked and walked in. There was the person that I recognized as my wife. She was dressed in worn clothes, more like a gown. In a sort of offset to the room was a bedroom and a man was in the bed in what looked like pajamas. It looked like I was in the wrong place. My wife and I looked at each other for a long time, neither speaking. Finally, she went back into the bedroom and came back to the room I was in, through another door. She had changed clothes. She came up to me, put her arms around me and gave me a loving kiss. That's when I woke up. I felt like it was something special. I don't know how. In my mind the lady was LaVerne, although she looked like only a resemblance of her. In the thirty years since LaVerne's death, I have dreamed of her only a few times, although I think of her still almost every day. I have, though, dreamed often of being lost in mountains and dangerous territories. Since I believe in reincarnation, I'm not sure, but that these dreams are somehow connected. I may try to write a story about it. I have often dreamed that someone has stolen my car from where I parked it.

Example 4: On October 25, 2007 at about 5:15 AM I dreamed again. The name and a picture of a man, his wife and 2 kids flashed in my mind. The name was Jerry Nathan. The children looked to be about ten to twelve years old, the man and his wife were in their 30s or 40s. That was all. It woke me up and for some reason I thought it concerned LaVerne. I didn't know, nor have I ever known anyone by the name of Jerry Nathan. Weird! Isn't it?

I might add that I dream scattered, short dreams all the time. Usually, I dream about my various activities and about people, whom I don't know; not the pinpoint subjects as the ones above.

If I should meet a friend, who revealed to me all these odd, quirky things about himself, I might think that he's a little sub-normal. But the truth most likely would be that he is normal plus having had the time, or taken the time, to wonder "why" and "what if". I like to do that.

BONSOIR!
TGR

Appendix 1: Pigeon Drop

Editor's Note: Regarding the money scam related in Chapter 5, following is corroborating remembrance from the only surviving witness to the event, Shirley Dawson Moses, a daughter of Mrs. Lula Dawson. Following that are additional details and (rhetorical?) questions supplied by her son, Fred, as a result of further discussions about the matter.

EXERPT FROM SHIRLEY MOSES' TRANSCRIPT:

1) Shirley's husband was coming to Haggar headquarters for a semi-annual four day sales meeting, "sequestered from Friday evening through Monday afternoon."

2 "I would not see nor talk to him until Monday afternoon." The teller at the window (of the neighborhood bank) involved a bank officer when Mrs. Dawson tried to close her savings account. He said he was "concerned for her carrying around that much money" and convinced her to take a certified check.

3) When Mrs. Dawson arrived back home with the earnest money (certified check), "Ruby was sitting on the front porch swing."

4) When the sisters searched for evidence of the certified check, "we found a copy of it in her cedar chest tucked in a purse."

5) Monday morning Detective Dickenhorse was introduced to Mr. Dawson's daughters, and was updated on events involving Ruby and her initial contact and discussions with "mother" up to that point. The detective stationed himself in the front bedroom where he would have a full view of the street, front yard and entrance to the front door. "He advised us to stay quiet and out of sight. He suggested for Mother to watch the news or whatever she watched on TV at this time of the morning while waiting on Ruby to arrive."

"I don't recall how long it was before Ruby came calling, although it seemed forever."

6) "Detective Dickenhorse saw the police unit pull up and block the suspect's car (out front) and his partner questioning the driver, then handcuffing and placing him in their car." He then emerged from the front bedroom, placed Ruby under arrest. "He handcuffed her and tied her to a chair," then left. "Shortly, the detective returned to retrieve Ruby. He untied her, leaving her handcuffed, and secured Mother's certified check before escorting Ruby to the waiting patrol car where they rushed away to a downtown jail facility." Dickenhorse "placed the women in an unmarked car and headed downtown." "Back then, in the 50's, if a lady was on the streets of downtown Dallas, she would be wearing a dress, high heels, hat, and gloves." They weren't. "On the drive downtown, Dickenhorse instructed us on things we should be aware of, including "anyone approaching Mother; anything that looked suspicious." "If we did witness any of these things, he would be across the street and we were to signal him." "Once Detective Dickenhorse was in position across Elm Street, Mother was to exit the car and begin walking toward the bank."

EXCERPT FROM FREDDY'S NOTES:

I have been told that the certified check for $4,600 mother gave Ruby, in today's market would be the equivalent of just short of $40,000. I am now 89 and the only surviving family member or anyone who would have any knowledge of the events of this pigeon drop. This is the first time I have ever put this story in writing or recall ever discussing it in the past thirty plus years, therefore I certainly do not recall every detail. I did talk to my son while writing this story and he was able to question and talk to me about the events which helped me remember certain facts I would not have recalled. I have not exaggerated this writing in any way that would magnify the substance of this pigeon drop.

There are several questions, that if could be answered, would be enlightening to know:

#1-As you may remember, Ruby made a call from mother's saying "Everything is fine here. We will be leaving soon." Also, mother was walking to the bank alone. It would seem that Ruby's accomplice who approached mother must have suspected something was bad wrong when Ruby was a no-show. His greed must have overridden his common sense.

One would also have to surmise he was about to introduce himself as the lawyer Ruby had confided in concerning the package of money. He then would hopefully coax mother into cashing the check and placing the money into a bag containing what mother believed to be a very large some of money. Once outside the bank, he would jump into the waiting car leaving mother on the street never to be seen again.

#2-How did Ruby's partner know who mother was? At some time before or during the scam, Ruby's partner must have pulled surveillance on mother so he would know what she looked like should their plan not go perfect. I am sure he regretted ever knowing what she looked like.

#3-As hard as it may be to believe, I have no knowledge of whatever happened to the pigeon drop crew. All I know is that Ruby and three of her partners were arrested and booked in the Dallas jail. Of course at the time, I lived in Monroe, Louisiana where I still reside. As far as I know, no one in the family was ever called to testify. If the case ever went to court, to my knowledge, no family members were ever informed. Back then crimes were treated differently than now. Today, it seems like criminals have more rights than the victims the crimes are committed against. Maybe before we

6

EDITOR'S NOTE:

As in most cases of this kind, witness reports differ in the details, and this event is no exception. But, the main facts are true, and quite rare. Con men (and women) are hard to catch. They have a sixth sense to know exactly when to leave town. I, have had several encounters with them, while working for Dun & Bradstreet, and missed catching them by—minutes. Hats off to the Dawson clan for making this catch

RGR

Appendix 2: Delbert Demosthenes

EDITOR'S NOTE: Wayne came to stay the weekend at our house in Oak Cliff when we were twelve. He was born in December, I in September. I had a Dallas Times Herald paper route, so we took off on my bike to throw the route. Wayne was riding on the back fender. As luck would have it, I was pulled over by a policeman and given a ticket for overloading the bike. I received a court summons, but Wayne conveniently couldn't come from Ft. Worth to Dallas for my "trial." Full of trepidation I went alone. Fortunately, Eagle Scouts were standing in for court personnel, so I didn't have to face the dreaded judge. I paid a small fine and was released without parole. Our parents were never told.

Delbert sitting on car fender with Sister beside him

Delbert and Bea sitting on wall

Delbert in Navy uniform

Appendix 3: Sylvia Emma

EDITOR'S NOTE—One day when I was about thirteen, living in University Housing, Richmond California,
I answered a knock on the door, as neither parent was home. To my surprise, there stood my Uncle Cecil Kersey from back east. He didn't have much time to spend before his train left, so he invited me to a nearby drug store, where he bought me a banana split and we talked. Uncle Cecil left from there to catch his train. I reported his visit to my folks. He was always number one in my book, because it was my very first banana split. That's right up there with your first girlfriend (later in life.)

Portrait of Sylvia

Sylvia (3ʳᵈ left)and girls friends in line up

Cecil and Sylvia Kersey

Cecil Kersey in Office

Appendix 4:   Thomas Glenmore

Author's note: Commentary on changes now and then—Of all those in my class in high school, all graduated, none dropped out. During the time I lived in Cooper, the most sensational crime that ever happened in the area involved a man who had been released from the insane asylum at Terrell. He lived with his mother in Cooper and began breaking into people's homes and stealing things. He was caught on the third try. Nothing much else happened in the 10 years that I remember.

TGR and Cousin

Graduate LaVerne Dawson

LaVerne and son John

Appendix 5: Homer Ray

EDITOR'S NOTE–1

My first memory of Uncle Homer Ray, he was a hero cut from the same cloth as Superman or Captain Marvel. Our family was visiting his; Jimmy and I were outside playing when a bright idea hit me and we climbed inside our 1937 Packard parked on the street in front of the house. Well, we were "driving" merrily, along, three on the floor, when I noticed the car was rolling and picking up speed. We must have started yelling, because Uncle Homer Ray came flying out of the screen door and caught up with us lickity-split and saved the day. After that, my Uncle Homer Ray was always the hero to me.

EDITOR'S NOTE–2

During college I came to Dallas for a holiday, staying at my Grandma Dawson's house. I borrowed her car and decided to pay Homer Ray and his family a visit. Uncle Homer Ray and Bobby were the only ones home. Bobby was very excited at my arrival and was especially eager to command attention by showing off their new German Shepherd dog. He swung his leg over the sitting dog's back, as if to ride a horse. The dog was having none of that, and just sat there. Wishing to show off some action, Bobbie leaned forward and yelled in the dog's ear. Quicker than a flash, dog spun around, bit Bobbie in the face and gave one slash of his paw. Bobby screamed, blood flew, and Uncle Homer Ray came bolting out the kitchen door. We hurried to the hospital and Bobby was admitted into Emergency. Once in the operating room the nurses deftly wrapped the patient in a long sheet, pinning his arms to the side of his body and holding his legs tightly immobile. One nurse held his toes; one held his ears, and he couldn't move a muscle. Of course, Bobby was screaming for all he was worth – it sounded more like a death rattle, than a scream. His eyelid had been sliced open, so the doctor proceeded to suture it up. Homer Ray and I had been allowed to stand at the back and observe. All of a sudden, my uncle slumped straight down onto his shoes—out cold. To tell the truth, I wasn't doing much better. We retired to the waiting room for the duration.

Homer Ray

HR & Family

HR, Flo, and Leslie

Appendix 6: Dorothy Marie

Marie

Marie and Ridjell Lee

Appendix 7: Robb Family

EDITORS NOTE: My Grandpa T.J. Robb, was not an overly tall man, but he was a giant of a man to me. Even tempered, respected by all. When we were little, what he said, quietly, we DID without question. He was never scary, we just jumped to be pleasing in his sight When I got older he kept track of what I was doing in my life, and gave me help when I needed it. We talked a lot. His values and ethics guide me today. When I walk alone and I feel his presence in my memory, I am proud that he is there. I am proud to bear his name.

TJR on knees with young Children

Delbert, Glen and Family

TJR Family Reunion

TJR Family Get Together

Delbert, Glen and Sylvia

TJR100[th] Birthday Party

Vintage family portrait

Delbert, Sylvia & Glen

Rillie, Delbert and Glen

Paris house

Glen, Sylvia & HR